THE LATTER DAY SAINTS

A Study of the Mormons in the Light of Economic Conditions

RUTH KAUFFMAN AND
REGINALD WRIGHT KAUFFMAN

INTRODUCTION BY
John S. McCormick and John R. Sillito

University of Illinois Press
Urbana and Chicago

Frontispiece: Photograph of Ruth Kauffman and Reginald Wright Kauffman, *The Bookman: A Magazine of Literature and Life* 37 (April 1913): 121.

Manufactured in the United States of America
P 5 4 3 2 1

This book is printed on acid-free paper.

Library of Congress Cataloging-in-Publication Data

Kauffman, Ruth, 1883–1952.
The Latter Day Saints : a study of the Mormons in the light of economic conditions / Ruth Kauffman and Reginald Wright Kauffman : introduction by John S. McCormick and John R. Sillito.
p. cm.
Originally published: London : Williams and Northgate, 1912.
Includes bibliographical references (p.) and index.
ISBN 0-252-06423-2 (alk. paper)
1. Mormon Church. 2. Church of Jesus Christ of Latter-Day Saints. I. Kauffman, Reginald Wright, 1877–1959. II. Title.
BX8635.K3 1994
289.3—dc20 94-6260
CIP

CONTENTS

Ruth Kauffman and Reginald Wright Kauffman

INTRODUCTION

John S. McCormick and John R. Sillito

The Latter Day Saints: A Study of the Mormons in the Light of Economic Conditions was published in England in 1912 during a period of intense anti-Mormon agitation that lasted from about 1910 until 1914.[1] It was written by two well-known American journalists and writers, Ruth Kauffman and her husband, Reginald Wright Kauffman. They intended to summarize for a British audience the voluminous literature about the Mormons, largely negative, that the American periodical press had published during the previous dozen or so years, and they brought a particular outlook to the task: they were Marxian socialists who took it as a given that economic forces were primary in society and that capitalism was an unethical system of compulsion and domination. That perspective had not previously been brought to bear on the Mormon church, and it yielded important insights. As an unsigned review in the *New York Times* noted, "The authors of 'The Latter Day Saints' are Socialists—And whether or not their read-

1. See Malcolm R. Thorpe, "'The Mormon Peril': The Crusade against the Saints in Britain, 1910–1914," *Journal of Mormon History* 2 (Summer 1975): 69–88.

ers agree with them, a study of Mormonism from the standpoint of socialist belief is absorbingly interesting."[2]

Long out of print and difficult to find, *The Latter Day Saints* is valuable in a number of ways: as a historical document that anyone interested in the history of anti-Mormonism should read; as a radical analysis of a religious phenomenon that could easily be dismissed as merely exotic, or as a personality-driven perversion; because it has much to tell us about the confrontation of a collectivist ethos with capitalist and monopolistic practices that ended in the triumph of the latter at the expense of the former; because it makes the study of Mormon history something more than an isolated episode of interest only to the specialist; and because it raises a number of important questions about the nature of American society in the early twentieth century.

Founded in 1830, the Mormon church long occupied a precarious position in American life. In its first fifteen years, church members were driven successively from New York, Ohio, Missouri, and Illinois, and in 1844 a mob killed the church founder, Joseph Smith. Even after the Latter-Day Saints settled in Utah, where they sought isolation and the freedom to establish their "Zion," violence did not cease, and in 1857–58 the senseless, and in some ways comic, Utah War was fought between Mormons and federal troops. By the 1860s, violence had ended for the most part, but the antagonistic attitude of millions of Americans had not. Mormonism remained a suspect religion into the twentieth century, and denunciations of it in books, pamphlets, and magazines constitute almost a separate genre of American literature. As Marvin S. Hill and James B. Allen say,

2. 12 January 1913, 12.

"During most of the nineteenth and the first generation of the twentieth century, the Mormons attracted attention in the popular press and also among many scholars as a useful counterimage, a glaring example of what America was not and should not be. They were considered so different in their fundamental institutions—theocratic government, plural marriage, and communitarianism—that joining them seemed to constitute an un-American activity."[3]

An important episode in the history of anti-Mormonism in the United States, and the last major outburst of anti-Mormon sentiment in this country until the 1960s, occurred in the opening decade of the twentieth century when the American popular press, including so-called muckraking magazines—low-priced, mass-circulation journals that specialized in the exposure of social and political problems—published scores of articles denouncing the Mormon church as one of the evils plaguing American society and threatening to destroy democratic institutions.[4] Much of this literature was careless, exaggerated, and sensationalized, but some of it was of lasting and considerable value.

3. Marvin S. Hill and James B. Allen, eds., *Mormonism and American Culture* (New York: Harper and Row, 1972), 1. See also Gary L. Bunker and Davis Bitton, *The Mormon Graphic Image, 1834–1914: Cartoons, Caricatures, and Illustrations* (Salt Lake City: University of Utah Press, 1983).

4. Examples include Alfred Henry Lewis, "The Viper on the Hearth," "The Trail of the Viper," and "The Viper's Trail of Gold," *Cosmopolitan,* March, April, and May 1911; Burton Hendrick, "The Mormon Revival of Polygamy," *McClure's Magazine,* January and February 1911; Richard Barry, "The Political Menace of the Mormon Church," *Pearson's Magazine,* September 1910, 319–30; and Barry, "The Mormon Method in Business," *Pearson's Magazine,* October 1910, 571–78.

The Smoot Trial (1904–7) provided much of the stimulus for the press's attention to the Mormon church in the early twentieth century. In 1903 Reed Smoot, a member of the church's Council of the Twelve Apostles, was elected United States Senator from Utah. A three-year congressional investigation followed his seating, at the end of which the Senate Committee on Privileges and Elections recommended his expulsion. Only with the active support of President Theodore Roosevelt and other powerful Republicans did the full Senate vote to allow Smoot to retain his seat, which he held for thirty years. A number of issues were raised during the hearings: the compatibility of Mormon communitarianism with American society; the attitude of the Mormon church toward the federal government; the nature of Mormon marriage customs; and the loyalties of elected Mormon officials. Those substantive issues, together with such lurid aspects of Mormonism as the doctrine of blood atonement, suggested to the nation's press the suitability of the Mormon church as a subject of exposure and furnished it with an abundance of material. In *The Latter Day Saints* the Kauffmans intended to summarize and synthesize this literature and provide, from their point of view, a needed perspective on it. The book's publication brought to a close the campaign against the Mormon church, though the church did not begin to receive extensive favorable comment in the nation's press until World War I, which the Mormons supported enthusiastically as part of their conscious effort to remove remaining doubts about their patriotism and adherence to American values.[5]

5. On the Mormon church and World War I, see Leonard J. Arrington and Davis Bitton, *The Mormon Experience: A History of the Latter-day Saints* (New York: Knopf, 1979; 2d ed., Urbana: Univer-

For some writers Mormonism was mainly a religious problem. Shortly after the turn of the century, John Nutting expressed a common view in saying that "the fundamental question is whether Christian truth can overmatch Mormon error. Hence the real solution of the problem must be a religious one."[6] Mormons must become Christians, he said, and when they did the Mormon church would no longer be troubling for American society. The Kauffmans, in contrast, were not much interested in Mormon theology, which they dismissed as at best curious and at worst absurd, and in *The Latter Day Saints* sought to provide an overview of Mormonism, with particular emphasis on its socioeconomic aspects. This approach had its drawbacks, of course, in that it may have led them to underestimate the appeal of the church's spiritual message, but it also served as a needed corrective to a narrow interpretation of Mormonism and resulted in a number of valuable insights.

The Latter Day Saints dealt with a variety of subjects, including the origin and founding of Mormonism; the theory and practice of polygamy; the church's political activities; and various aspects of Mormon history, in particular the Utah War and the Mountain Meadows Massacre. Written within the tradition of the Mormon exposé, much of it simply repeated old charges that were sensational and exaggerated—for example, the extent

---

sity of Illinois Press, 1992), 252; Leonard J. Arrington, "Crisis in Identity: Mormon Responses in the Nineteenth and Twentieth Centuries," in *Mormonism and American Culture,* ed. Hill and Allen, 173; and Ronald W. Walker, "Sheaves, Bucklers, and the State: Mormon Leaders Respond to the Dilemmas of War," *Sunstone* 7 (July/August 1982): 43–56.

6. John D. Nutting, "A Study of the Present Mormon Problem," *The Independent,* 17 April 1902, 929.

of Mormon political influence beyond Utah—but it also had much to say that was both new and insightful. The Kauffmans' voice was unique. They realized, as Jan Shipps observed in her discussion of Utah politics,[7] that the Mormon church in the early twentieth century continued to dominate the social, political, and economic life of its people and that such a conclusion did not necessarily proceed from faulty logic or deliberate exaggeration. The Kauffmans saw a number of similarities between conditions in Utah and those in the United States as a whole. They knew that antagonism toward the Mormon church in the late nineteenth century was not simply a case of the persecution of a defenseless minority by an overzealous federal government and that more than just polygamy was at issue. Friction was caused in large part by differing economic, political, and social orders and was, therefore, inevitable.[8] Most important, they understood that in many ways the history of the Mormon church was the story, as Dale Morgan put it, of the transformation of the Kingdom of God into another among the kingdoms of the world.[9] That evolution began in the 1890s, and the period from then until about 1920 became a crucial one in the history of the Mormon church. As Robert Gottlieb and Peter Wiley have observed, those years were the period of "The Great Accommodation," when "Mormonism's most distinctive fea-

7. Jan Shipps, "Utah Comes of Age Politically: A Study of the State's Politics in the Early Years of the Twentieth Century," *Utah Historical Quarterly* 35 (Spring 1967): 91–111.

8. For an insightful discussion of this point, see Henry J. Wolfinger, "An Irrepressible Conflict," *Dialogue: A Journal of Mormon Thought* 6 (Fall 1971): 124–31.

9. Dale Morgan, "Salt Lake City, City of the Saints," in *Rocky Mountain Cities,* ed. Ray B. West (New York: Norton, 1949), 197.

tures gradually faded into the past and became the stuff of history. Henceforth, the Saints would . . . identify more and more with the America of Main Street and the Model T."[10] The Kauffmans were among the first to recognize this all-important transformation from a communitarian experiment to a modern church, and to deal with it at any length, and they drew out and explored its implications in perceptive and suggestive ways.

Though largely unknown today, both of the Kauffmans were prolific writers. Ruth Hammitt Kauffman was born in New York City on 5 December 1883. After graduating from Bryn Mawr College, she worked for several years as an investigative reporter examining working conditions for women as domestic workers; she worked in department stores and insurance offices and then taught French, English, and Latin at a private school for girls in New York City. A struggling poet and writer when she married Reginald Wright Kauffman in 1909, she joined him after their marriage in investigating "white slavery" in the United States and England, pursuing their researches "in a living medium," he later recalled, by living in a tenement on New York's East Side and interviewing and getting to know prostitutes and their clients.[11] Their work led to his publication of two novels, *The House of Bondage* in 1910, the same year that their joint novel, *Mr. Desmond's Divorces,* appeared, and *The Girl That Goes Wrong* in 1911. In 1914, two years after the publication of *The Latter Day Saints,* she published her first novel, *High Stakes.* Her poetry also regularly appeared in such journals as *Harper's* and

10. Robert Gottlieb and Peter Wiley, *America's Saints: The Rise of Mormon Power* (New York: Putnam, 1984), 51.

11. Reginald Wright Kauffman, "Introduction," *The Girl That Goes Wrong* (New York: Moffat, Yard, 1911), 1–12.

the *American Magazine.* Briefly a nurse in England at the beginning of World War I, she then worked for the *New York Tribune* as one of the first American female war correspondents. Near the end of the war she organized the publicity department for the Woman's Auxiliary Army Corps. In addition to *The Latter Day Saints,* by the time of her death in Phippsburg, Maine, on 13 August 1952, Ruth Hammitt Kauffman had written a dozen novels and plays, children's books, works of nonfiction, and a large body of poetry.

Reginald Wright Kauffman was born in Columbia, Pennsylvania, on 8 September 1877. After graduating from Harvard in 1900, he studied law briefly but soon turned to journalism, working first as a reporter and editorial writer for the *Philadelphia Press* and then as associate editor of the *Saturday Evening Post,* which Frank Luther Mott described as one of the popular magazines of the "ambitious young men of the great middle-class American public."[12] As Laura Hapke points out, the *Post* featured adventure stories, sentimental romances, and articles praising the virtue and success of the millionaire and suggesting the promise of democracy for the American worker.[13] While there, Kauffman was also the writer of most of the epigrams published under the title "Poor Richard, Jr.'s Philosophy." In 1907, after three years at the *Post,* he was briefly drama critic for the *Philadelphia North American,* and he then became associate editor of the *Delineator,* whose new

12. Frank Luther Mott, *A History of American Magazines, 1885–1905* (Cambridge, Mass.: Belknap Press of Harvard University Press, 1957), 688.

13. Laura Hapke, *Girls Who Went Wrong: Prostitutes in American Fiction, 1885–1917* (Bowling Green, Ohio: Bowling Green University Popular Press, 1991), 120.

editor was Theodore Dreiser. Kauffman and Dreiser had known each other since the late 1890s, when Kauffman had been a founder and the editor of *Ainslee's Magazine,* which published Dreiser's poetry and articles and for which he acted as an unofficial consulting editor. The two remained longtime friends. Under Dreiser's direction the *Delineator,* while mainly a women's fashion magazine, began to question traditional ideas of American womanhood and featured articles on divorce and woman suffrage, as well as on living conditions in city slums. During this period Kauffman also regularly published a wide range of poetry, from the sentimental "April in Paris,"[14] "Farm Wife,"[15] and "Abe Lincoln"[16] to the social commentary of "The Outcast," which explored the desperate living and working conditions of American workers,[17] and he continued to write poetry throughout his life.

In 1909 Reginald Wright Kauffman became managing editor of a leading muckraking journal, *Hampton's Magazine,* which Dreiser had edited before moving to the *Delineator.* Its articles attacked corporate abuses and the growing concentration of economic and political power. According to Laura Hapke, "*Hampton's* contributor Charles Edward Russell, who argued that it was not governmental but a combination of important

14. *Lippincott's Magazine,* April 1905, 460.

15. Ibid., December 1909, 720.

16. *Harper's Weekly,* 1 May 1909, 29.

17. *International Socialist Review,* 13 December 1912, 471. Kauffman's poem was reprinted in *The Survey,* 15 March 1913, 842. In reprinting the poem, the magazine commented that events like the Lawrence strike had produced "an outpouring of verse in the radical press. . . . Many have been crude; some have been of the sort not easily to be tossed aside." The editors included "The Outcast" in the latter category.

business interests that controlled America, helped shape Kauffman's thinking," and the subjects that Russell wrote about,[18] including crime, the slums, and corrupt railroad franchises, were issues that Kauffman addressed in his novels *The House of Bondage, The Sentence of Silence* (1912), and *The Spider's Web* (1913). After a year at *Hampton's,* and now the author of five books, Kauffman resigned to devote full time to writing. He remained interested in women's issues, as did his wife, and in 1912 was the United States representative in London at the First Congress of Men's Societies for Women's Suffrage. During World War I he joined his wife as a war correspondent in Europe.

For most of the decade after the war, the Kauffmans lived in Europe and traveled extensively there and in Africa. Sometime during that period they left the Socialist party, though exactly why and when is not clear. It may have been over the issue of American involvement in World War I, which deeply divided and weakened the party. Both of the Kauffmans were close to John Spargo and Charles Edward Russell, leading prowar socialists who left the party soon after it formally opposed World War I and participation in it. Reginald Kauffman's poem "The March of the Hungry Men" was reprinted in the 15 July 1920 issue of the *Socialist World,* but in 1925 Kauffman reported that "I have long since ceased reforming a world that refuses to remain reformed. . . . I no longer believe in what its believers call Pro-gress; more than conservative or medieval, I am Byzantine. True, I vote the Republican ticket, but I also belong to the Eastern Orthodox (Greco-Russian) Church. . . . [M]y stories now

18. A well-known socialist writer and intellectual, Russell was coeditor of the socialist periodical *The Coming Nation* and was the vice-presidential candidate on the Socialist ticket in 1916.

are the sort that your children think it would be safe for you to read."[19] In the late 1920s, when the Kauffmans were the parents of two small children, he returned to journalism. He headed the League of Nations Bureau of the *New York Herald Tribune* in Geneva, Switzerland, until 1933 and was then a writer and editorial columnist for the *Washington Post,* editor-in-chief of the *Financial Observer,* and an editorial writer for the *Boston Transcript.* Kauffman ended his journalistic career as editor of the *Bangor* (Maine) *Daily News* from 1941 until his retirement in 1947. He continued to write throughout his life, and by the time of his death in Roanoke, Virginia, on 25 April 1959, his published works included fifty books, thirty of them novels, several volumes of poetry, a number of children's books, scores of short stories, and some screenplays.

Between 1910 and 1913 Reginald Wright Kauffman published six books. The first was an exploration of socialist theory and history entitled *What Is Socialism?* which he dedicated to John D. Rockefeller and Eugene V. Debs. The *New York Times* called it "enlightening," saying he clearly distinguished "between the various kinds of socialism and makes clear the main tendency today is evolutionary socialism."[20] Kauffman in the Introduction noted that he had first encountered socialism one autumn afternoon in 1893 when, in the days not too long after the Haymarket Riot (of 1886), "Socialism and Socialists were as vague in my mind as they were awful." He heard a college professor define social-

19. "The March of the Hungry Men" first appeared in *International Socialist Review,* 14 May 1914, 651; Kauffman's remarks of 1925 were contained in *Harvard College—Class of 1900; Records of the Class* (N.p., n.d.), 419.

20. 14 May 1910, 271.

ism as "masked anarchy" and assert that "it has no more chance of succeeding than if it dropped the mask." According to Kauffman, "I do not censure the professor, except perhaps because he spoke professorily; but I do say that he was wrong. Whether Socialism is to succeed or fail remains, of course, to be seen; yet, succeeding or failing it is no more anarchism than it is any of the half-dozen other things that it is popularly believed to be, and, even if it were all of these and more beside, it is recognized by every keen visioned student of politics and economics as the next great problem that will confront the voters of America" (2). The other five books—four novels and *The Latter Day Saints*—were intended as extended studies in capitalism that supplemented and explicated the concepts set forth in *What Is Socialism?* Though their subjects were diverse, all carried the same message: capitalism was not so much a jungle as a prison, and escape for most people and institutions was virtually impossible. In Kauffman's view, the rise of corporations and the trend toward monopoly was the dominant fact of life in the United States in the early twentieth century and perhaps the most serious problem the American people faced. Wealth and power were increasingly concentrated in the hands of a few who thereby dominated the country's industrial, financial, and political life. All institutions were subservient to the interests of capital. Such a situation created class division, facilitated the ascendancy of the strong over the weak, promoted the interests of the wealthy and powerful at the expense of the weak and the poor, and led to the exploitation of the working class, who were condemned to difficult, dehumanizing work and subsistence wages. Under such circumstances, Kauffman said, it was impossible even to speak of freedom. This was demonstrated through a study of prostitution, which was the subject of his best—and best-selling—novel, *The House of Bondage*. This belief was shown through studies of sexual behavior, marriage, and politics, the subjects of his next three novels, *The Sentence of Silence, Running Sands* (1913), and *The Spider's Web,* and it was clearly seen in the history of Mormonism.

A brief discussion of *The House of Bondage* helps in understanding what Kauffman and his wife had to say in *The Latter Day Saints*. "*The* novel of prostitution" of the Progressive Era, according to Walter Rideout,[21] it went through sixteen printings in less than two years and was translated into half a dozen foreign languages. The *New York Times* commended it for "attacking and exposing one of the crying evils of our day,"[22] while Emma Goldman praised it for what she saw as its straightforward and unsentimental explanation of the forces that drove women to prostitution.[23] The plot of the book is simple. Dissatisfied with her harsh life in a small Pennsylvania industrial town, the heroine, Mary Denbigh, goes to New York City with a young man who promises to marry her. Once there, however, she is forced by her lover, who is really a procurer, to become a prostitute in an elegant brothel run by a woman named Rose Legere. Although she eventually escapes from the brothel with the help of a Tammany politician who is one of her customers, Violet, as she is now known, is able to find only menial, low-paying work. Ul-

21. Walter B. Rideout, *The Radical Novel in the United States, 1900–1954: Some Interrelations of Literature and Society* (Cambridge, Mass.: Harvard University Press, 1956), 68.

22. 17 September 1910, 511.

23. Emma Goldman, "The White Slave Traffic," *Mother Earth* 4 (January 1910): 346.

timately, she comes to realize that the department store, the factory, and the tenement are as confining and oppressive as the brothel. Sinking lower and lower, she finally becomes a dirty, diseased streetwalker. The only effective gesture of defiance she is able to make is to deliberately infect with syphilis the man who forced her into prostitution. Finally, in desperation, she returns to her original madam, who refuses to take her back. Nothing is left for her but the street and, eventually, a pauper's grave.

In *The House of Bondage* Kauffman did not criticize the prostitute herself. He did not portray prostitution as a sign of individual moral perversity. His emphasis was not on individual choice and responsibility but rather on social and economic conditions. For Kauffman the prostitute was a victim of circumstances because prostitution was embedded in the oppressive wage slavery and corrupt practices of capitalist society. It was the natural by-product of an economic system whose essential features were low wages, long hours, poor working conditions, and limited opportunities. Hermann Hoffmann, a German Socialist who befriends Mary, makes the point, explaining to her—after a Marxian survey of the economic and political framework of prostitution—that there is only one solution to the problem: "Von vay—und only von. For de single time badness makes poverty, ninety-nine times poverty it makes badness. Do avay vith poverty. Reorganize de whole of de industrial system; gif effery man und woman a chance to vork; gif effery man und voman effery penny dey earns. So only you do avay with poverty, so only you do avay with unhappy und discontented homes und unhappy und discontented people, und so only you do avay with badness" (260). Kauffman's message was that the real house of bondage was capitalism, and prostitution was simply one form of slavery under it. The last line of the book serves as his essential indictment of the capitalistic system, and as an epitaph for all victims of competitive society. When Mary Denbigh, diseased and worn out, returns to Rose Legere's house in a last effort to stay alive, Rose refuses to take her in, saying: "It wouldn't be good business. You see, the life's got you, Violet: you're all in" (466).

Following the publication of *The House of Bondage,* and *The Girl That Goes Wrong* the next year, the Kauffmans turned their attention to Mormonism, though it is not clear how they came to this topic. Perhaps their interest originated during his days at *Hampton's Magazine.* The magazine devoted some attention to organized religion, and while he was editor he published "The Mormon Church and the Sugar Trust," an article by his friend and colleague Judson Welliver.[24] By this time, also, the muckraking press, which at first had emphasized political corruption and business malpractice and the connection between the two, had begun to explore a wider range of subjects, including organized religion, charging that the nation's churches were too conservative and often allied with other institutions that were corrupting the nation and its people. The Kauffmans may also have been acquainted with Murray Schick, a Utah socialist and journalist, and they knew his article "Mormons and Mammon," published in the socialist journal *The Coming Nation.*[25] Whatever the origin of their interest, however, their intent was to use Mormonism as an aid to understanding the larger soci-

24. *Hampton's Magazine,* January 1910, 82–93.
25. *The Coming Nation,* 14 October 1911, 6–7.

ety of which it was a part, just as in *The House of Bondage* Reginald Kauffman had used prostitution as a lens to focus on and illuminate the economic inequities of American life and the exploitation of the American worker. *The Latter Days Saints* is both a story of the Mormon church and a portrayal of the society whose values and practices shaped it.

In this regard the Kauffmans found two fundamental points: by the beginning of the twentieth century the Mormon church was a conservative, even a reactionary, institution, supporting some of the worst aspects of American life; and, more significant, it was a victim, entrapped in the corrupt and oppressive operations of capitalist society. A study of how it came to that position clearly demonstrated that the United States was a giant prison, a system of compulsion that enslaved people, forced them to do what they had to do in order to survive, and thus undercut the very basis of morality. In *The Latter Day Saints,* in other words, the Kauffmans indicted capitalism, not on an economic basis but on moral grounds; they contended not that it was inadequate, failing to provide a sufficient standard of living for most people, but that it was coercive and unjust. The Kauffmans pointed out that the Mormon church, originally theocratic, polygamous, and communitarian, had changed dramatically since its founding. It had once posed a challenge to America and offered a critique of American society and culture, but near the end of the nineteenth century it increasingly conformed to American values and practices. Its members came to embrace what they had once opposed, and the church began a process of integration into American society.

For the Kauffmans the Mormon church was not primarily a spiritual organization but first and foremost a capitalistic one. The Mormon hierarchy was made up of businessmen who operated at least as much from a business point of view as from a spiritual one, and the church itself was an increasingly large business, owning and operating, or having an interest in, street railways, electric light and power plants, saltworks, sugar factories, mercantile establishments, insurance companies, publishing houses, newspapers, theaters, resorts, farms, and ranches. These facts were widely known, but their implications were not often appreciated, the Kauffmans contended, and it was important to explore them. In their view, since the church's interests were the same as those of other large businesses, it acted much as they did. Concerned with making a profit, it opposed labor unions, acted as a strikebreaker, sought to restrain competition, and actively supported the contemporary trend in the United States toward monopoly and the evils associated with the rise of corporate capitalism, a development most clearly seen in the church's relationship with the sugar and railroad industries.

In 1903 the Mormon church sold the controlling interest in its church-owned beet-sugar companies to Henry O. Havemeyer's American Sugar Refining Company, which had a virtual monopoly of the sugar industry in the United States. The sale benefited the church financially, the Kauffmans said, but it also had other effects. At the turn of the century, the emergence of a new source of supply—sugar beets—threatened the American Sugar Refining Company's share of the national market. The company consequently sought a controlling interest in beet-sugar companies and by 1907 had succeeded in the effort, processing 70 percent of the country's beet sugar. Its success was due, in part at least, the Kauffmans argued, to the Mormon church. By selling its sugar beet companies, the LDS hierarchy had assisted the corporate leadership of American Sugar in maintaining and reinforcing its control over the domestic sugar industry. The church, in short, had actively supported the continuation of monopoly in the sugar industry and the abuses that went along with monopoly: effective control over sugar processing throughout the United States; restriction of competition; and the adjustment of supply to demand in many markets simultaneously. More than that, in selling to American Sugar, the Mormon church had created a situation in which its interests were inextricably linked with those of the corporation, and after the sale the church continued to support the interests of the Sugar Trust, since those interests were its own. The trust, in turn, defended and protected the Mormon church when the necessity arose. For the Kauffmans this was most clearly seen in the case of Reed Smoot. In their view the Mormon church saw to it that men attuned to the interests of the Sugar Trust were elected to public office, as when it arranged the election of Smoot, who had negotiated the sale of the Utah Sugar Company, to the United States Senate in 1903. Once in office, Smoot quickly became a forceful and dedicated advocate of a high tariff on a variety of goods, including sugar. Since the tariff was a major factor in determining how secure the market position of the Sugar Trust would be, the American Sugar Refining Company was interested in ensuring that Smoot remained in office, and when his right to his Senate seat was challenged, the company—along with other corporate and government interests—leaped to his defense.

The kind of relationship that existed between the Mormon church and the Sugar Trust was essentially duplicated, the Kauffmans asserted, in the church's alliance with the railroad industry. In 1906, three years after the sale of its sugar company to the Sugar Trust, the church sold the Utah Light and Railroad Company to Edward H. Harriman. Within a year of the sale Harriman controlled 20 percent of the railroad system of the United States and had a virtual monopoly over railroads west of the Mississippi. The effect of the sale was the same as in the earlier sugar sale: The Mormon church contributed in a small way to the consolidation of economic power in the hands of one individual; it became a party to rate fixing, discriminatory freight rates, the use of rebates, and a variety of other arbitrary and unfair practices that Harriman engaged in; and its interests became intertwined with his. Harriman and the Mormon church were in partnership, just as Havemeyer and the church were, and both parties benefited from that partnership.

The Kauffmans argued that by the end of the first decade of the twentieth century the Mormon church had become an appendage of the capitalistic system. It was not involved in efforts to limit corporate abuses of economic and political power. Rather than opposing the concentration of power, which they saw as one of the most serious problems confronting early twentieth-century America, and instead of denouncing the corrupt alliance that often existed between business and government, it supported those things. Subservient to the needs of capital, the Mormon church, they argued, provided one more example of "the present wrong and the future impotence of churches and laws, of politics, government and property."[26] As necessary as it was to un-

26. *The Spider's Web* (New York: Moffat, Yard, 1913), 399.

derstand that fact, they said, it was equally important to understand why the church had acted as it did. In their view it was a victim of economic forces, acting out of necessity, not out of choice. It had begun a process of rapprochement with America, giving up the things that made it different and adopting many of the ways of the larger society as a matter of survival after generations of hostility from the American people, its government, and the corporate community.

The Mormon church had encountered hostility almost from the moment of its founding, the Kauffmans reminded their readers, and conflict was a constant of Mormon history until the beginning of the twentieth century. The issue was not a moral one. Polygamy was not the cause. "Hatred of polygamy—and polygamy itself had been at its height employed for economic reasons—was not the origin of the attack upon Mormonism," they asserted in *The Latter Day Saints.* "The origin of that attack was economic" (105). Mormon communitarianism, not Mormon marriage customs, was under assault. Religious and moral objections to Mormonism were mere smoke screens thrown up by disgruntled groups disturbed by Mormon solutions of their economic problems thorough cooperation, which dried up income for speculative interests. The expansion of capitalism through the elimination of the Mormon church's self-sufficient, cooperative, and egalitarian enterprises, which interfered with the spread of capitalism, not the elimination of polygamy, was the real target for concern. This helped explain the intense hatred the church had long encountered. It also accounted for the extreme pressure the federal government brought to bear on the Mormon church, beginning with the Utah War of 1857–

58 and culminating in the 1880s with the passage of two pieces of legislation, the Edmunds Act of 1882 and the Edmunds-Tucker Act of 1887. These laws not only brought hardship to individual Mormons but threatened the church's very existence. In the face of such pressure the church embarked on what it hoped would be the road to prosperity and security: cooperation with the nation's dominant political and economic forces. It reluctantly gave up the practice of polygamy, disbanded its political party, and began a process of participation in and accommodation to the national economy. When this happened, pressure from the federal government and its corporate allies abated.

The Kauffmans believed that the history of the Mormon church was—as Perry Miller said of the New England Puritans—the history of the failure of a dream, but it was not weakness in the Mormon people that led to their failure. Rather it was the nature of the society in which they lived that made the success of their communitarian experiment difficult, if not impossible. In the Kauffmans' view, victims abounded in a capitalist society. The Mormon church was one such victim. The Kauffmans recognized, in other words, a central fact. According to the historian Christopher Lasch, it "may well be the most important fact" of Mormon history:[27] as long as Mormons were different they would not, and could not, be tolerated by an expanding capitalistic system. Only when they gave up their chief distinguishing features would antagonism toward them cease. Elabo-

27. *New York Review of Books* 8 (26 January 1967): 15. Reprinted as "The Mormon Utopia," in Lasch, *The World of Nations: Reflections on American History, Culture, and Politics* (New York: Knopf, 1973), 56.

ration of that point is the Kauffmans' most valuable contribution and the most important reason their book is still worth reading more than eighty years after its publication.

THE LATTER DAY SAINTS

I

THE FORERUNNERS OF MORMONISM

THE historian of Mormonism has one advantage over the historian of most other revealed religions: he can at least begin by giving a precise date as that on which his religion was revealed. Since this date is of the few Mormon dates concerning which there is no difference of opinion among authorities, it is well to mention it forthwith.

On the morning of the 22nd of September 1827 the Angel of the Lord delivered to Joseph Smith a series of records of the aboriginal inhabitants of North America. These records, graven on plates that had the appearance of gold, declared that the American Indians were the Lost Ten Tribes of Israel, and from these records and the accompanying instructions of the Angel, Smith received orders for the founding of his faith and prophecies concerning the future of things in general. In accordance with the instructions thus received, Smith organized the Church of Jesus Christ of Latter Day Saints, now commonly called the Mormon Church, on the 6th of April 1830, the formal organization being effected near the scene of the

Angel's visit, in the town of Manchester, Wayne County (then Ontario County), state of New York, U.S.A.[1]

So much is relatively simple. To understand, however, how it became possible for a Church to be founded upon the mere statement of Joseph Smith that he had received these records, and that previous to their receipt he had been visited by many celestial visions, one must briefly consider both the economic and religious conditions of the United States of America between the years 1790 and 1830—between, in other words, the moment of the earliest rush of pioneers westward from the thicker settlements of the thirteen original states and the beginning of the "Reign of Jackson," so-called.

The states were then but loosely bound together. They were so loosely bound that threats of secession were constant, and not until 1830, when Jackson summarily informed South Carolina that her proposal to secede from the Union would be met with armed resistance, did the various commonwealths feel the grip of solidarity. Except that they were ready to unite against a common enemy, that they had a national legislative body devised to make laws for concerns of the Union only, and a purely executive president elected for one or two terms of four years, they were to all intents and purposes so many separate countries. The interests of Massachusetts and Virginia were as different as those of France and Russia, and their laws and customs differed accordingly.

There were, to be sure, large tracts of public lands held by the central government, but even these would eventually divide themselves into various self-govern-

[1] *History of the Latter Day Saints*, by Joseph Smith.

ing and self-legislating states. Much of these tracts was, moreover, uninhabited save for scattered and nomad tribes of Indians; and the pioneers, venturing into that wilderness, where, with their own hands, they were compelled to build their own houses, provide their own food and clothing, found themselves cut off from contact with the towns and from direct communication with each other. Merchandise travelled by lumbering vans over trails that were for months impassable; newspapers were almost unknown; the post was infrequent and unreliable. Each family shifted for itself; each family struggled for itself and fought its own war with the forest. In the United States life was then in that halcyon day so loved of the modern reactionary when the family was indeed the unit of society. As a natural consequence, the pioneer was not disposed to concern himself overmuch with written rules from Washington.

West of the narrow eastern strip of civilization there was, therefore, little chance for culture. The world worked hard to keep alive. Children were necessarily brought up in comparative ignorance, and the few existing free schools were hopelessly inadequate, frequented only during the mid-winter months when they were governed by school-masters whose sole qualifications consisted, usually, of no more than "The Three R's: readin', 'ritin', an' 'rithmetic." The parents presented the picture of peasants, but peasants of only one generation: they were bound to no tradition; they were free to explore mentally and morally as well as physically. It was a time and place of chaotic communities and individual restlessness. The reaching out for new lands to conquer, the ceaseless necessity of satisfying new requirements by new agricultural appliances, by better methods of travel, by the natural desire for comradeship and, as the years at last eased them, by more comfortable conditions, as well as the slowly increasing mingling of people whose religious opinions were dissimilar, caused a general readiness for what was novel in theology as well as for what was novel in the other departments of life. The pioneer reached for something new to suit his religious cravings just as he reached for new land and new methods to suit his material desires.

In the cities along the Atlantic Coast, this time was also a time of stress. It was the period of the decline of commerce and the rise of manufacture, which has found its ablest expositor in Mr A. M. Simons, and the transition from commerce to manufacture, especially in the introduction of the factory system, was made with far greater speed than characterised the same process in England. In the elder country, industry progressed toward the factory "from the 'household' stage, in which each family produced for its own consumption, to the 'domestic' stage, when the family was still the productive unit and the home the only factory, but where production was for the market"; whereas, in the newer land, the progress "was almost direct from the 'household' to the factory system."[1] In England, again, in the cotton trade, for example, while machines did the spinning, the weaving was still done in the cottage, whereas in the United States Francis C. Lowell set up an establishment, the first of its kind, for the entire manufacture of cotton-cloth at Waltham, Massachusetts, as early as 1814.[2] The

[1] See A. M. Simons's admirable *Social Forces in American History*, to which we are indebted for much of the data immediately following.

[2] *Industrial Evolution in the United States*, by C. D. Wright.

almost immediate result was a full-blown factory system in those northern cities that were to be a part of Smith's recruiting-ground.

It was, as Simons ably demonstrates, a system "based upon the existence of a body of propertyless wage-workers" not only in the cotton trade, but in most other industries. Though less known, the sufferings of the American proletariat in this period of social evolution correspond closely to those of their English brothers. In the new country as in the old, "the cradle and the home were robbed to secure victims for the natal sacrifice of newborn capitalism." On the floor of Congress in 1816, only two years after the building of Lowell's mill, it was declared that, thanks to Arkwright's invention, the manufacture of cotton was so revolutionized that "five or six men are sufficient for . . . a factory of 2000 spindles," the other hands being mere children.[1] In the same year a Government report estimated that nine-tenths of the 100,000 workers in the cloth-mills were women, boys, and girls. Wages were at their lowest ebb, and work in some cases began at 4.30 a.m. and continued until night had fallen. President Monroe officially rejoiced in this "fall in the price of labour, apparently so favourable to the success of domestic manufactures"!

Nor was that all. Direct voting scarcely existed. The state legislatures, not the people, commonly elected the state governors; the presidential candidates, themselves chosen not by the people, but by Congressional caucuses, were elected by presidential electors also fixed upon by the state legislatures; and a property qualification determined the voters for candidates to the legislature.

1 Benton's *Abridgments of the Debates of Congress.*

Thus practically unrepresented among the law-makers, the labourer was indeed lost. He had no lien on his product, and was therefore often robbed of such small wages as were promised him. His creditors, for no matter how small a debt, could strip him of everything, and, if that everything did not satisfy the indebtedness, could, and often did, send him to prisons where the State furnished no fuel, food, or clothing; where the debtor could earn no money, yet where he must remain until the debt was paid. Frequently he remained for years, sometimes for life. In 1829 the Prison Discipline Society reported that 75,000 persons were annually imprisoned for debt in the United States and that in more than half the cases the debt was under four pounds.

The Government supplied more prisons than schools. According to Simons, who quotes from the best authorities,[1] "the educational facilities of the United States were at their very lowest ebb in the years from 1814 to 1828. The old social order had lost its strength; the new one had not had time to develop educational expression. The most efficient schools were the private academies of New England. The public schools, the only ones accessible to the wageworkers, were less efficient than at any period before or since. The management of the schools had been subdivided in response to the individualistic, competitive, separatist spirit of early capitalism until the little school districts were almost autonomous. Religious education had declined with the overthrow of the theocracy, and the multitude of seceding sects had not yet built up educa-

History of Education in the United States, by Frank T. Carlton; and the same author's *Economic Influences upon Educational Progress in the United States*, the latter a Bulletin of the University of Wisconsin.

tional institutions. Massachusetts, then, as throughout American history, at the head in educational matters, was expending but two dollars and seventy-five cents per pupil annually in education."

Finally, says Simons, "the religious reflex of the decline of commerce and the rise of manufacture was so like the religious movement that accompanied the rise of capitalism in Europe that it has been designated as 'The New England Reformation.' The orthodox clergy that had so long actively participated in the rulership of society were disturbed by the rise of new sects. In the very stronghold of Puritanism the old orthodoxy was attacked and overthrown by the most liberal of creeds—Unitarianism. The Congregational clergy, long a part of the ruling hierarchy, was split into warring sects. . . . By the time the lines were clearly drawn it was discovered that the new religious forces had captured Harvard College. There was also a division of a similar character in the ranks of the Quakers, and numerous peculiar and separatist sects rose throughout the West."[1]

Especially was this true of those agricultural regions that were familiar enough with the hand of man not to present the same difficulties that were presented by their near neighbours to the pioneer, yet were still outlying districts with no broad interests and no close connection with the cities of the sea-coast. Here books were luxuries. The Bible was the only volume to be found in most households, and that, as a consequence, was thoroughly read. Many a man that could not read was at least able to quote more or less accurately whole chapters of Scripture, his teachers, people of a narrow

[1] See also *The Development of American Literature from* 1815 *to* 1833, by W. B. Cairns, to which Simons refers.

faith, not having scrupled to sacrifice his educational to his spiritual welfare. Thus, with the world of politics shut from them, without literature, with their economic interests simple and few, these people, living in an atmosphere impregnated by a calm acceptance of the charms and sorceries of the Old Testament, occupied not a little of their leisure with inquiries into the health of their own souls and unriddling of whatever was not immediately clear to their simple intelligences in the book that they considered the Word of God. Some of them became religious hypochondriacs, and many tortured the text of the King James Version into amazing meanings.

The necessarily suppressed emotions of these people were in part met and in part stimulated by those religious sects, especially the Presbyterians and Methodists, which at this time started waves of evangelistic meetings called "revivals" and of open-air "camp-meetings" held in the smallest villages and hamlets throughout the entire country. Many thousands of persons were greatly affected by these meetings, so much so that they yielded their spirits everywhere to conversion; and, as converts, they would often again alter their views at the breaking of the next wave of meetings over their town, changing their beliefs within a few years, or even a few months. Their form of worship was as variable as are some men's politics; there was not one tide, but many, in the faiths of men.

From 1800 until 1835 new sects were plentiful in the United States. There were the Zoarites, a secession from the Lutheran Church. There were the "Come-outers," a term applied to a large body that had seceded from various denominations in the northern and eastern parts of the country, men that disagreed, rather than agreed, in common, but united in their denunciation of chattel-slavery and of all forms of war. Then, too, was organized by John Winebrenner, in Harrisburg, Pennsylvania, a sect that still endures; that then joined with the "Come-outers" in the declaration against chattel-slavery; that ascribed to their Church the attributes of Visibility, Unity, Sanctity, Universality, and Perpetuity; and that chose and retained the modest title of The Church of God.

The Bible Christians were another significant expression of their times. They rested on the faith that whenever there is wrong, God will send a servant to right it. Abuses in the Church brought their own reformer. Noah, they said, Abraham, and Jesus were sent; when the Christian Church was ill a Luther, a Calvin, or a Melanchthon appeared to cure it.[1] Founded in England by the Rev. William Cowherd, formerly a clergyman of the Established Church, and once attached to Christ Church, Salford, this sect taught abstinence from animal flesh and alcoholic liquors, and in 1817 sent a large number of its members to Philadelphia, Pennsylvania. Some went farther west to preach their doctrines; others remained in Philadelphia, where they finally purchased a building and advertised in the newspapers that "the members of the Bible-Christian Church assembled every Sabbath Day, giving such Exposition of the revealed Word of God as they might be graciously vouchsafed by the goodness of God." They would begin their work in a city by commenting on the first chapter of Genesis in the morning and the first chapter of St Matthew in the evening, and thus, by a sort of stubborn dead-reckoning, work their expository course through the entire Scriptures.

The German element among the immigrants in the

[1] *History of the Bible Christians,* by Rev. William Metcalfe.

United States supplied, as was to be expected, its full share to this confusion of spiritual tongues which explains the beginnings of Mormonism. The Teutonic division of the list is long, but our present purpose will be served by two examples: the Separatists, and the German Baptists, or River Brethren.

The former received their name in Germany, where they originated early in the eighteenth century.[1] George Rapp, their founder, came to the United States in 1803, and about a hundred and twenty-five families of his disciples followed him. They built their church upon the rock provided by the thirty-fourth and thirty-fifth verses of the fourth chapter of the Acts of the Apostles:

"Neither was there any among them that lacked: for as many as were possessors of lands or houses sold them, and brought the prices of the things that were sold,

"And laid them down at the apostles' feet: and distribution was made unto every man according as he had need."

In a word, the Separatists were Primitive Communists, but they carried the principles of primitive communism to such a point that they denied private property even in the matter of one's own body. They built the town of Economy in Beaver County, Pennsylvania, and went at last the way that must inevitably be gone by a small body of passive-resistance communists completely surrounded by competitive capitalism.

The German Baptists were one of the divisions of the Baptist Church that was, at just this time, torn by bitter contentions. They were distinguished from their religious cousins by their manner of administering baptism, for, in the most convenient stream, they placed the candidate in a kneeling posture and then pushed

[1] *Handwörterbuch von Ehrenfried,* article "Separatisten."

him, head first, under the water—a custom that gained them, from their adversaries, the derisive title of "*tunkers*" or "tumblers." Besides these River Brethren there was the Free Will Baptists, who organized an independent General Conference in 1827; and the Seventh Day Baptists, who adopted the Jewish Sabbath, and some of whom emigrated, as early as 1824, from New Jersey and Virginia, to Ohio. When they had gone, they left to quarrel on the Atlantic Coast the Baptists pure and simple, the Six-Principle or General Baptists, the Free Communion Baptists, and the Old School Baptists.

In this mere glance at the more or less peculiar sects that made smooth the way for Mormonism in the public mind, it would be interesting to include many denominations, some of which still linger, but most of which have long since passed away. It would be interesting to tell at length of the Albrights, later known as the Evangelical Association, organized in the United States about the first year of the nineteenth century, and of the Universal Restorationists, who began their universal labours in the town of Mendon, Massachusetts, in the year 1831. But to show the length to which popular credulity would in those days go, it is necessary here to add only the Millerites and the Wilkinsonians.

The same decade that produced Joseph Smith and the Mormon Church produced also William Miller and his followers, who called themselves Adventists and whom the profane called Millerites.[1] Miller was born in Pittsfield, Massachusetts, in 1781. He was poorly educated, but, at an early age, began to study the Bible through the medium of his own unassisted intelligence. His study brought him to a conclusion not unlike that

1 *History of the Adventists,* by Josiah Litch.

held in times past by men of considerably more scholarship, and not unlike that held in general by the Early Christians themselves. He compared the various prophecies; he studied the conditions surrounding the fulfilment of such prophecies as had already been fulfilled, and he decided, from what he thus observed, that the second coming of Christ was an imminent event. He said that this coming was pre-millennial, and he fixed its date at about 1843. He preached his faith for years, and his words produced a tremendous effect. It was indeed the voice of one crying in the wilderness, but the wilderness gave startled ear and began to prepare the way of the Lord. He bade his people make ready, even to the clothes they wore, and many a family slept at night with their "resurrection-robes" ready for donning. His followers came to believe "the coming of the Lord to be at the door," and hundreds, on the dates when He was expected, placed themselves on housetops to wait. The files of some of the English newspapers of that period gave descriptions of these preparations which are not so much exaggerated as are, unhappily, some of the more recent pictures of American life presented by a certain portion of the British press. Several wrong guesses on Miller's part did not materially weaken the faith of his followers. Land was sold for a song, and personal property given to the poor. In 1843 there were said to be 50,000 persons converted to Miller's views, and only the slow passage of uneventful time disillusioned them.

The Wilkinsonians are equally to the present point. They lived, for the most part, not more than twenty-five miles from Manchester, New York, the town in which Mormonism was first preached; and, small as their numbers were in comparison with the Adventists, they very likely influenced the surrounding countryside and assuredly serve well to indicate the character of its people.

Jemima Wilkinson, the founder of this sect,[1] was known throughout that portion of New York. In October 1776, recovering from an illness, during which she had "fallen into a syncope, so that she was apparently dead," she declared that she had, in truth, been raised from the dead and had been divinely appointed to teach mankind. With many followers she at last sought "a new land" where she might lay the cornerstone of her earthly kingdom, selecting for that purpose a place in Yates County not far from the line of the county in which Manchester was situated. She called her town New Jerusalem, and there she taught her followers poverty, it is said. As for herself, she lived on the fatness of the land, and owned most of the property, which she had the forethought to purchase in another's name.

One of her declarations was that commonest to all founders of religions: she could perform miracles. Should the people wish to test her, she had, she averred, such faith that she could walk on water. In fact, all the necessary preparations, at least all the apparently necessary preparations, for her doing this were made at Lake Seneca. A multitude gathered. Wilkinson drove up in her carriage, descended, and announced to the crowd that she was about to walk across the lake and upon its surface. On a path of white handkerchiefs strewn for her by her followers, she walked to the water's very edge. Then she paused and turned to her spectators. She inquired of the

1 *History of all the Religious Denominations in the United States,* edited by John Winebrenner.

crowd if they had faith that she could reach the other shore, for if they did not share her faith the feat could not be accomplished. The crowd gave loud assurance that it possessed the requisite credulity, whereupon Wilkinson returned to her carriage, since it was self-evident that if the crowd really believed in her power, the demonstration would be merely superorogatory. It was a decision of logic equalled only by the Moslem conqueror's declaration concerning the Alexandrine Library, yet it had no worse effect upon the Wilkinsonians' belief in Jemima's powers to cure physical ills, to foretell the future, and to work miracles, than the destruction of the library had upon the faith in the Koran.

It is plain, then, that the economic conditions of the day were ready for Joseph Smith, that the economic conditions of the day, indeed, produced him. "The enormous credulity of the Mormonites in their capacity of followers," said an English writer,[1] "is all a trait of human nature as old as the hills. . . . Sensuality in connection with religion, presumption, the prophetic element, the pseudo Old Testament, the expectation of an earthly paradise or millennium—all separately old and well-known manifestations—had only to combine and adopt in addition, and as the crowning trait, the modern and nineteenth-century impulse for emigration, and we have the whole of Mormonism before us." Southey was also among the prophets:[2] "Were there another Mahommed to arise, there is no part of the world where he would find more scope or fairer opportunity than in that part of the Anglo-American union into which the elder states continually discharge the restless part of their population."

[1] In the London *Times* of 5th January 1858.

[2] *Colloquy X.*, part ii.

II

BEGINNINGS

On his father's side, Joseph Smith was descended from a family in which the wander-lust seems always to have been strong and into which a love of the occult made its way long before the appearance of the founder of Mormonism. That the information is confusing and that various authorities provide various ancestors is not, perhaps, surprising, since the early days of America were not days in which vital statistics were always well kept, and since, at any rate, a certain genealogical confusion is not uncommon in the traditions surrounding the originators of most religions. What is surprising, because it is generally so rare, is the manner in which, in the case of Joseph Smith, even the accounts of the faithful show their first prophet to have been a logical product of his sires.

Of these the first in America was Robert Smith, who left England for the New World either in 1638 or 1640. From what part of England he came, nobody appears to know; but he settled in the village of Rowley, near Newberryport, in Massachussetts. His son Samuel is said to have been the father of Robert Smith, a soldier in the American Revolution, whom some historians name as the grandfather of the first Mormon, while others declare that the grandfather was named Asael

Smith and assert that Asael's house was, until recently, standing in the town of Topsfield, Mass. In either case, Joseph Smith, senior, the father of the founder, was born in Royalston, Vermont, whither his parents had then removed.

The elder Joseph was by inclination a wanderer and by trade a seeker of buried treasure. For the greater part of his life he followed both inclination and trade, though the latter seems to have been the less successful. Nevertheless, it was a not unusual occupation. In those days many a superstitious man would go about the country with his "divining-rod," partly believing that, held loosely in his hands, it would miraculously bend when it passed above soil that concealed golden deposit, and partly accepted by the rural population, who conceded to the rod the same power for the discovery of hidden water and employed the diviner to discover needed springs. The practice still survives in certain portions of America and is still to be found, under the name of "dowsing," in odd corners of England. By such means the father of the prophet earned a more or less irregular livelihood, which, since neither he nor his wife possessed a reputation for over-scrupulousness, and since both owned what were described as babbling tongues, was from time to time relieved by a long series of petty law-suits. The trade, the wander-lust, or the law-suits at last drove the family into the state of New York, where, for some years, they lived much as they had lived in New England.

For Joseph the elder had married. While, by some chance, the owner of a farm on the Merrimack River in New Hampshire,[1] he had married Lucy Mack, who, in

[1] *History of Philip and Gorham's Purchase*, Turner.

spite of her neurasthenic temperament, seems to have been of sturdier stuff than her husband.

According to her own account,[1] written for the most part before the prophet's death and under his personal supervision, her father was Solomon Mack, born in New London County, Connecticut, in 1735. Because his father, Ebenezer Mack, had fallen upon evil days and lost property of considerable value, Solomon was brought up by a neighbour's family, which he left to enlist as a soldier at the age of twenty-one. That was the beginning of a life of adventure in which his wife, Lydia Gates, a school-mistress of East Haddon, Connecticut, and their four children played many parts. They never prospered, and, when it finally occurred to them that ill-doing was sometimes the cause of ill-luck, they proceeded to pursue religion as devoutly as they had formerly pursued the rainbow. Even the children —there were three girls and a boy well named Jason— were taught to read and study and puzzle over the Bible, and when a daughter suddenly recovered from a desperate illness and declared her healing due to a miracle, her word was accepted by the surrounding country-folk, and she began to have visions.

Lucy Mack, the mother of Joseph Smith, was born in New Hampshire in July 1776. She was never a healthy child, and at one time was convinced that life was not worth the living. At length, however, she made up her mind to have a "change of heart." Studiously she set herself to reading the Bible and to praying, and the more she read and prayed the more bewildered she became by the differences between the denominations that waged spiritual war in the town about her. She tells us that her difficulty was to find

[1] *History of Joseph Smith, Junior*, by Mrs Lucy Smith.

in any of these sects a resemblance to the "Church of Christ" as the early Christians knew it, and she adds that she had no taste for what seemed to her the tortured misinterpretations that the existing Churches dragged from the Scriptures.[1] She was still in this mental mist when she met and married the elder Joseph Smith.

There are few stronger forces than a familiar type of indecision. Mrs Smith's indecision was so strong that it appears at once to have impressed itself upon the weak will of her husband, who began to worry about his own soul. As is usually the case in such unions, the joint efforts of the pair effected not a cure, but an intensification. They probed and argued. They experimented with the Universalist faith, and, finding no soul-satisfaction therein, joined the Methodist. In this sort of religious coquetry they passed six years.

During these six years Lucy's two sisters, including the one formerly cured by a miracle, had died of tuberculosis of the lungs. Her husband, at the end of that time, let his farm and invested all his money in a cross-roads "store," where odds and ends, from vinegar and molasses to tobacco, hardware and clothing, were to be bought, and where, of evenings, the village gossips would gather, discussing the affairs of the neighbourhood and those metaphysical problems that, as we have seen, occupied so much of the minds of their class.

Then Mrs Smith became ill. She sought physicians, one of whom told her husband that she was suffering from the same disease that had slain her sisters and that she too must die. The elder Joseph indiscreetly communicated this diagnosis to his wife, who, greatly agitated, passed a night in prayer. She was, according

[1] *History of Joseph Smith, Junior,* by Mrs Lucy Smith.

to her own written words, immediately "healed of her sickness."[1]

But though her health was fixed, her religious sentiments remained unsettled. She must, she tells us, be instructed in the way of salvation, and no one could help her. Nowhere on earth, she concluded, was there an adequate denomination. For several more years she studied the Bible until many of its words were as familiar to her as were her neighbours' daily words of greeting; and then, forced to some definite action, she had herself baptized at a spiritual venture, thus, as she reasoned, saving her soul and at the same time leaving herself free to choose a sect at her leisure.

Meantime, her husband had material worries to add to his worries spiritual. His store did not pay him the profits that he had expected. He therefore invested all his money in ginseng root, in the belief that the root, when crystallized, was a panacea and especially efficacious in the treatment of ills then rampant in the village. Perhaps from his wife's dead sister he had contracted an interest in the cure of disease.

So, no doubt, had Mrs Smith's brother, Jason Mack. He now reappeared, after several years' unaccounted absence, and went about performing miracles, not hesitating, he confessed, to raise the dead. He was having a wonderful success and everywhere held "revivals" crowded by followers.

It was but natural that the Smiths should be sensibly affected by the gospel of Jason. It is not recorded that he attempted any of his powers for resurrection upon his dead sisters; but there was plenty of ocular evidence on his part that occultism was a better in-

[1] *History of Joseph Smith, Junior,* by Mrs Lucy Smith.

vestment than shop-keeping or ginseng-crystallization. At any rate, Mrs Smith's visions, acute until now, straightway became chronic. She was restless in her sleep and dreamed always. These dreams of the night she would ponder by day and then endeavour to interpret. Even Joseph senior was not exempt. He contracted the contagion, and began to have visions of his own. Still unable conscientiously to adhere to any of the existing sects, he urged his wife forward in her search for a religion with none of the present complexities, a religion that would comply literally with the interpretation of the Scriptures. He even achieved a point whereat he declared that those who professed the accepted religions were as ignorant of superhuman matters as those who did not.

The benefits of vision are uncertain. At first nothing came of Smith's save that business decline which is inevitably experienced by the man who, serving God and Mammon, does not devote himself entirely to his faith. Smith lost money. He slipped back into his old trade of money-finder, but found little. Then, one night in 1811, having again changed his place of residence, he awoke, we are told,[1] "clapping his hands together for joy." The cause of his rapture we are not informed of, but concerning its effect we are left in no perplexity : for some years thereafter the family prospered, and the children were sent to school.

Misfortune, however, had not yet done with the parents of the prophet. It was necessary that they should be driven to that portion of the country where *The Book of Mormon* was lying in the earth, awaiting its predestined discoverer. Hardly, therefore, had prosperity substantially obtained than there came an

[1] *History of Joseph Smith, Junior,* by Mrs Lucy Smith.

epidemic of typhus fever against which both medicine and charms were for a time powerless. The children fell ill, and, when they had recovered, financial disaster again overtook their father, who then gathered together his few belongings and went to the state of New York.

Arriving destitute at Manchester, N.Y., the family secured in Stafford Street, near the Palmyra line, a small clearing enclosed in underbrush. Here they built themselves a rude house of logs, and here, scorned by the more successful inhabitants of the two nearest towns, they lived for four years, when they again moved, this time to a similar place, six miles away, near Manchester.

There were now a number of children in the Smith establishment. Joseph, the second son, the prophet-to-be, had been born in the town of Sharon, Vermont, on the 23rd of December 1805;[1] but his appearance was not, as one might have expected, heralded by any mystic portents, and his earlier childhood was, even in his mother's eyes, in no wise remarkable. Indeed, Mrs Smith had never expressed the opinion that her son "Joe," as he was called, would be the founder of the faith of which she dreamed. Her visions had brought her to no such conclusion. They had, nevertheless, impelled her to the belief that a new prophet should appear, and, assuming a more or less personal application for her revelations, after the manner of seers, she gave out hints that Alvah, her eldest son, was the divinely-appointed. But Alvah, according to unkind gossip, was a greedy boy, and, one day eating

1 This according to Joseph himself. Richard F. Burton, in his *City of the Saints,* differs. He gives Whittingham, Vermont, as Joseph Smith's birthplace, and 1st June 1801 as the date of his arrival there. It is possible that Burton has confused Joseph with his brother Alvah.

too many green turnips, died. Thus did the mantle descend upon Joseph.

Perhaps the first definitely noticeable inclination of Providence in the direction of Joseph occurred during the typhus fever epidemic before referred to. The disease left the lad, then about ten years old, suffering from abscesses. One leg was especially troublesome, so much so that a surgeon decided to amputate; but the mother, declaring—later—that she had been providentially inspired, begged the surgeon once more to try the remedy that had until then failed, and the leg was made well.

In Manchester the dreams and visions continued, mostly to Mrs Smith, until the children came to regard them as an everyday matter. They were all prepared to receive similar visitations, and, while their minds were thus made fertile, they were living in the midst of general religious excitement. All the evangelical denominations about them were floating upon a high tide of "revivalism." In Palmyra and Manchester, after the advent of camp-meetings in the woods on the Vienna road and animated congregational services in the towns proper, contentions arose among the sects, and the rural brain was plunged into a fog of metaphysical discussion in which it wandered hopelessly mazed. The younger Smiths were at an age when the effect of all this was a foregone conclusion. Joseph was "converted," and "held forth," although but a boy, both in debates in the school-house, where he had found a friend in the young school-master, Oliver Cowdery, and in other meetings, until as an extemporaneous speaker he had acquired ease of manner and power of voice.

Mrs Smith was moved. She prayed. She asked

God to direct her toward the sect that was right. She was told, she says, to join no sect that then existed: none represented the will of God.

While the family continued its shiftless existence, Joseph the younger reached the age of fifteen. He is described[1] as being at this time an awkward, unpopular lad, who would go, too often for his own good, among the gossips that gathered at the nearest grocery-shop. A well-known figure, he was even then six feet tall, lank, and often to be seen laden with "jags of wood," which he bore from the paternal cabin to the town, there to exchange them for other commodities. Except that he could exhort well and was of a sociable disposition, he was not liked. The young people of the town considered him not quite full-witted and, with the cruelty of youth, made him the butt for their practical jokes.

The boy gauged correctly the esteem in which he was held. He could not well fail to do so. The jests were not of the kindest, and the inking of his face when he visited the printing-office to secure the weekly newspaper was not conducive to his contentment with surrounding conditions. It is, then, not to be wondered at if, derided, he should wish to make himself respected; if, joked, he should want to retaliate by a joke upon the community that joked him; if, in short, he should begin as a mere hoax, or a mere vain bid for decent treatment in a rough and ignorant community, what—if it was so begun and was not the partial self-delusion of an ill-balanced lad in an environment of superstition—was at any rate to have consequences that even a visionary could scarcely foresee.

Stooping a little as he walked, with high shoulders, a narrow forehead and scanty brows over calm eyes,

[1] Turner's *History of Philip and Gorham's Purchase.*

Joseph went his way about the countryside. He seems to have had small opportunity for social intercourse, and he certainly must not have been liked by the neighbourhood girls; yet, at just about the time of his great discovery, he successfully courted one of them. He married Emma Hale.

And now the time for the discovery had come. In Joseph Smith's own words, this is the story of the formation of the Mormon Church:—[1]

"The Church of Jesus Christ of Latter Day Saints, was founded upon direct revelation, as the true Church of God has ever been, according to the Scriptures (Amos iii. 7, and Acts i. 2).[2] And through the will and blessings of God, I have been an instrument in his hands, thus far, to move forward the cause of Zion. . . .

"My father was a farmer, and taught me the art of husbandry. When about fourteen years of age, I began to reflect upon the importance of being prepared for a future state; and upon inquiring the place of salvation, I found that there was a great clash in religious sentiment; if I went to one society they referred me to one place, and another to another; each one pointing to his own particular creed as the *summum bonum* of perfection. Considering that all could not be right, and that God could not be the author of so much confusion, I determined to investigate the subject more fully,

[1] *History of the Latter Day Saints*, by Joseph Smith, published in 1848, by John Winebrenner, Harrisburg, Pennyslvania, in a *History of all the Religious Denominations in the United States.*

[2] "Surely the Lord God will do nothing, but he revealeth his secret unto his servants the prophets" (Amos iii. 7).

"Until the day in which he was taken up, after that he through the Holy Ghost had given commandments unto the apostles whom he had chosen" (Acts i. 2).

believing that if God had a Church, it would not be split up into factions, and that if he taught one society to worship one way, and administer in one set of ordinances, he would not teach another principles which were diametrically opposed. Believing the word of God, I had confidence in the declaration of James, 'If any man lack wisdom, let him ask of God, who giveth to all men liberally, and upbraideth not, and it shall be given him.'

"I retired to a secret place in a grove, and began to call upon the Lord. While fervently engaged in supplication, my mind was taken away from the objects with which I was surrounded, and I was enrapt in a heavenly vision, and saw two glorious personages, who exactly resembled each other in features and likeness, surrounded with a brilliant light, which eclipsed the sun at noonday. They told me that all the religious denominations were believing in incorrect doctrines,[1] and that none of them was acknowledged of God as his Church and Kingdom. And I was expressly commanded to 'go not after them,' at the same time receiving a promise that the fulness of the gospel should at some future time be made known to me.

"On the evening of the 21st September, A.D. 1823, while I was praying unto God and endeavouring to exercise faith in the precious promises of Scripture, on a sudden a light like that of day, only of a far purer and more glorious appearance and brightness, burst into the room; indeed, the first sight was as though the house was filled with consuming fire. The appearance produced a shock that affected the whole body. In a moment a personage stood before me

1 Compare his mother's visions, both those received about the same time and those received before.

surrounded with a glory yet greater than that with which I was already surrounded. This messenger proclaimed himself to be an angel of God, sent to bring the joyful tidings that the covenant which God made with ancient Israel was at hand to be fulfilled; that the preparatory work for the second coming of the Messiah was speedily to commence; that the time was at hand for the gospel in all its fulness to be preached in power, unto all nations, that a people might be prepared for the millennial reign.

"I was informed that I was chosen to be an instrument in the hands of God to bring about some of his purposes in this glorious dispensation.

"I was informed also concerning the aboriginal inhabitants of this country, and shown who they were, and from whence they came;—a brief sketch of their origin, progress, civilization, laws, governments, of their righteousness and iniquity, and the blessings of God being finally withdrawn from them as a people, was made known unto me. I was also told where there were deposited some plates, on which was engraven an abridgment of the records of the ancient prophets that had existed on this continent. The angel appeared to me three times the same night and unfolded the same things. After having received many visits from the angels of God, unfolding the majesty and glory of the events that should transpire in the last days, on the morning of the 22nd September, A.D. 1827, the angel of the Lord delivered the records into my hands.

"These records were engraven on plates which had the appearance of gold; each plate was six inches wide and eight inches long, and not quite so thick as common tin. They were filled with engravings in Egyptian characters, and bound together in a volume, as the leaves of a book, with three rings running through the whole. The volume was something near six inches in thickness, a part of which was sealed. The characters on the unsealed part were small and beautifully engraved. The whole book exhibited many marks of antiquity in its construction, and much skill in the art of engraving. With the records was found a curious instrument which the ancients called 'Urim and Thummim,'[1] which consisted of two transparent stones set in the rim on a bow fastened to a breastplate.

"Through the medium of the Urim and Thummim I translated the record, by the gift and power of God.

"In this important and interesting book the history of ancient America is unfolded, from its first settlement by a colony that came from the tower of Babel, at the confusion of languages, to the beginning of the fifth century of the Christian era.

"We are informed by these records that America, in ancient times, has been inhabited by two distinct races of people. The first came directly from the city of Jerusalem, about six hundred years before

[1] Urim and Thummim: according to the Hebrews, the literal significance of these words is (Exodus xxviii. 30) light and perfection, or the shining and the perfect; according to St Jerome, doctrine and judgment; at all events, they seem to refer to the stones in the breastplate of the high priest. "It may suffice us to know that this was a singular piece of divine workmanship, which the high priest was obliged to wear on solemn occasions, as one of the conditions upon which God engaged to give him answers" (Cruden's *Concordance*).

"And thou shalt put in the breastplate of judgment the Urim and the Thummim; and they shall be upon Aaron's heart when he goeth in before the Lord" (Exodus xxviii. 30).

It is interesting to note that Alfred Henry Lewis, the apologist of Diaz, calls the Urim and Thummim angels.

Christ. They were principally Israelities, of the descendants of Joseph. The Jaredites were destroyed about the time that the Israelites came from Jerusalem, who succeeded them in the inheritance of the country. The principal nation of the second race fell in battle towards the close of the fourth century. This book also tells us that our Saviour made his appearance upon this continent after his resurrection; that he planted the gospel here in all its fulness, and richness, and power, and blessing; that they had apostles, prophets, pastors, teachers, and evangelists; the ordinances, gifts, powers, and blessing, as was enjoyed on the eastern continent; that the people were cut off in consequence of their transgressions; that the last of their prophets who existed among them were commanded to write an abridgment of their prophecies, history, etc., etc., and to hide it up in the earth, and that it should come forth and be united with the Bible, for the accomplishment of the purposes of God, in the last days. For a more particular account, I would refer to *The Book of Mormon*, which can be purchased at Nauvoo, or from any of our travelling elders.

"As soon as the news of this discovery was made known, false reports, misrepresentation, and slander flew as on the wings of the wind, in every direction; my house was frequently beset by mobs, and evil-designing persons; several times I was shot at, and very narrowly escaped, and every device was made use of to get the plates away from me; but the power and blessing of God attended me, and several began to believe my testimony.

"On the 6th April 1830 the 'Church of Jesus Christ of Latter Day Saints' was first organized. . . ."

That is Smith's own story. When comparing its

earlier portion with the known facts of Smith's younger days, as already set forth in these pages, the reader may notice certain discrepancies, certain glossings-over. How far the concluding portion is to be judged by these discrepancies may be left to the discretion of their discoverer. There remains another story to tell—another story of the finding of *The Book of Mormon.*

Solomon Spalding[1] was a retired minister in New England, a Presbyterian by latest avowal and practice. He had not succeeded in the ministry, and finally abandoned that vocation for a trade. Then, his manual ability not sufficiently compensating him for his efforts, he decided to write a book. This was in 1809, eighteen years before Joseph Smith met the Angel of the Lord on Cumorrah Hill. Afterwards, Mrs Spalding pathetically explained that her husband "thought he had a literary taste, and thought to redeem his fortunes by the composition of an historical romance."

The resulting volume was entitled *The Manuscript Found,* and, in five thousand dull octavo pages of fine print and bad grammar, fancifully accounted for the American Indians. Spalding used anew the already old idea that these Indians were the descendants of the Lost Ten Tribes of Israel, traced the fates of the wanderers for the space of a thousand years, from the time of the reign of that king of Judah whose name

[1] *Exposé of Mormonism,* by John Bennett. The case of Spalding, or Spaulding, is well known in the United States, though there are not lacking non-Mormon critics who declare that the similarity between Spalding's book and Smith's does not justify the accusations of plagiarism. Thus David Utter: "No one who ever carefully read *The Book of Mormon* could fail to see that it never in any part was written for a romance. . . . Now, at last, the Spalding manuscript has been found, and it rests secure in the library of Oberlin College."

was changed to Zedekiah, who did "that which was evil in the sight of the Lord," to the fifth century A.D. The son of one Nephi, Mormon, the fictitious final compiler of the thousand years' records, was credited with having buried the entire manuscript before his death.

The book was painstakingly completed in 1812, fifteen years before Smith's discovery, and a copy then given for publication to a printer or bookseller in Pittsburg, Pennsylvania, a man named Patterson. Here the story created no favourable impression, but was allowed to gather dust for several years. The author died without seeing his romance in print, and Patterson, on an occasion, lent the manuscript to a compositor in his employ, Sidney Rigdon, who was also a preacher of chameleon faith. Then, in 1825, Patterson died. Rigdon next came into view as the right-hand man of Joseph Smith at the start of the Mormon Church.

In 1839 the widow of Spalding published a statement in a Boston, Massachusetts, newspaper, which led to a public meeting. At this meeting the manuscripts of *The Manuscript Found* and *The Book of Mormon* were compared, and it was established beyond question that the similarity of the two could not be disregarded. The names of the different characters were exactly the same, and whole pages were word for word alike. Moreover, since Spalding had not been an educated man, traces of illiteracy were observable in his work, and these errors were repeated in *The Book of Mormon*. The only rebuttal offered at the time was that issued by Rigdon, whose reply was not worthy of the name of argument, and whose coarseness did small good to the Mormon cause.

III

THE BLOOD OF THE MARTYRS

SMITH's statement to the contrary notwithstanding, the first news of his discovery of the golden records of the American Indians was received in Manchester with general derision, and, in spite of the assistance of Rigdon, who had turned up in the town, the effort to find a publisher was met with many difficulties. Not a few neighbours declared that the statements of the Smith family regarding the discovery did not agree.

A slight difference does, in fact, appear to have been at one time noticeable. The elder Smith was known, because of his trade as a searcher for buried treasure, to have spent many hours in nocturnal digging in the hills about the countryside, and Joseph had early imitated his parent. Some of their excavations had been made at Cumorrah Hill, since called Mormon Hill, or Joe Smith's Gold Hill, where the plates, according to the younger Joseph, were eventually found. But all the family differences were soon patched up, and in the mother's account a fairly consistent story is told. Her case is this :—

When the younger Joseph was eighteen years old, in 1823, his first vision appeared in the shape of Nephi, who came to him saying that there was a book written on gold plates, which gave an account of the former inhabitants of North America. Nephi, the angel, informed Joseph that in this book the fulness of the Everlasting Gospel was contained; that there were also two stones set in silver bows, fastened to a breastplate, and named Urim and Thummim. The seers of old times, Joseph was assured, were so constituted because they possessed, through divine gift, these stones and used them; now, in the modern days, God had so prepared the stones that they would, when worn like spectacles, translate, from its exalted characters into English, the precious book. If, however, the new prophet should ever show to any person the Urim and Thummim, he should be destroyed. Upon parting from him, the angel bade him tell his father of the vision.

Joseph was working in the vineyard on the following day, with his father. Suddenly he became pale and weak, and, seeking the shelter of a tree, he saw again the angel Nephi.

"Why," asked the angel, "did you not tell your father?"

Joseph explained that he feared disbelief; but Nephi bade him repeat every word, which would be believed.

And it was, so it is alleged, as the angel said. Joseph Smith, senior, was much impressed by his son's vision, and charged the boy to be obedient to the heavenly man.

Joseph went to the hill where he had so often dug. He found, not far from the crest, a stone "of considerable size, thick and rounding in the middle, on the upper side, and thinner toward the edges, so that the middle part of it was visible above the ground, but the edges all round were covered with earth." He lifted the stone with a lever, and saw beneath it the plates of *The Book of Mormon* together with the stones called the Urim and Thummim, which gave the appearance of an immense pair of spectacles. But hardly had he seen these things when his friend, the angel, again appeared and warned him not yet to touch them. Every year at the same time he was to come to the same place, and finally the things should be his. Meanwhile he was to prepare his soul.

So Joseph spent his life in meditations. He worked not more than he had to work, but each evening he would tell his family, attentively listening to his every word, stories of the aboriginal inhabitants of America, anecdotes, tales of their cities, their buildings, their different religions, and their warfares. It was not, however, until three years after Smith's first sight of the plates that Nephi, the angel, allowed Joseph to take them away.

Joseph Smith and his friend, the schoolmaster, Oliver Cowdery, translated the plates. Since the Prophet was to show the Urim and Thummim to no one, he arranged a screen and sat behind that while Cowdery, on the other side, wrote, at dictation, what was read. Cowdery made an affidavit to the effect that he had seen the plates of gold. A vision appeared to Smith, which told him that Cowdery and he were to baptize each other by immersion, after which they were to be ordained to the Aaronic priesthood. This they did.

Then came the troubles of having the extensive manuscript published. No one would attempt the work without remuneration.

There lived, in the environs of Palmyra, in the little town of Macedon, Martin Harris, a good, honest farmer. He owned his farm, and, by being thrifty, took good care of his family. It was to him that Joseph Smith early went to seek a convert, by telling the farmer of a convenient "revelation." Smith declared that he had received a vision in which it was revealed to him that Martin Harris was "a chosen instrument to aid in the great work." Harris hesitated, but yielded. His wife opposed him at every step. But in March 1830, when Smith repeated his latest revelation—"I command thee that thou shalt not covet thine own property, but impart it freely to the printing of *The Book of Mormon*,"—although neighbours and wife warned him, Harris mortgaged his farm and gave up £600 for the payment of the printing of 5000 copies of the book.

In 1858, Thurlow Weed, formerly a printer, then a politician well known in both the United States and England, spoke of this incident as follows:[1]

"Within our recollection, Mormonism was a speck no bigger than a man's hand. The original impostor, Joe Smith, came to the writer of this article only thirty-two years ago, with the manuscript of his Mormon Bible to be printed. He then had but one follower (a respectable and wealthy farmer of the town of Macedon), who offered himself as security for the printing. But after reading a few chapters, it seemed such a jumble of unintelligible absurdities that we refused the work, advising Harris not to mortgage his farm and beggar his family. But Joe crossed over the way to our neighbour, Elihu A. Marshall, and got his 'Mormon Bible' printed."

The Book of Mormon, therefore, "an account written by the hand of Mormon, upon plates taken from the plates of Nephi, by Joseph Smith, Author and Proprietor," was published; and Joseph's brothers, himself, and Cowdery peddled the book throughout the surrounding country. Even Don Carlos Smith, Mrs Smith's youngest son, only fourteen years old, was

[1] *The Albany Journal*, 1858.

ordained a minister of the Church, and went about playing the double rôle of preacher and book-agent, approaching his possible customers by asking them if they desired an accurate history of the Indians. Moreover, Joseph secured a prefatory certificate, signed by Martin Harris and nine other witnesses, to the effect that: "We declare with words of soberness, that an angel of God came down from Heaven, and brought and laid before our eyes [*sic*] that we beheld and saw the plates and the engravings thereon." This because, before the book had been printed—indeed, in the very act of its translation from the original plates—attempts, said Smith, had been made to rob him of his treasure, so that he was first obliged to hide it from profane eyes, and so that at last, the translation being complete, the heavenly messenger declared that the plates had accomplished their purpose, and forthwith took them away for safe-keeping.

The missionaries were jeered and hooted, but persecution only goaded them forward. Smith was several times tarred and feathered, and many of his early converts were imprisoned on charges that, it must be confessed, seem to have originated rather in the ill-will of their enemies than in the acts of the accused. And all the while the young Joseph continued his control over all such as gave their faith to him.[1]

[1] These three revelations received by Joseph Smith indicate the extent of his early power; they are quoted verbatim from *The Doctrines and Covenants of the Latter Day Saints*:—

"In temporal labours thou shalt not have strength, for that is not thy calling."

"It is meet that my servant, Joseph Smith, junior, should have a house built in which to live and translate."

"If ye desire the mysteries of my kingdom, provide for him (*i.e.* Joseph Smith) food and raiment, and whatsoever thing he needeth."

Among the first openly to embrace the new creed was, of course, Sidney Rigdon. The whole Smith family followed him, Oliver Cowdery, the schoolmaster, who had acted as "scribe," and Martin Harris, the farmer, also belonging to the original congregation. Altogether, the Church started with about thirty members; and in an upper room where Joseph Smith lived there was held what was called "The School of the Prophets," where was instituted the sacrament of foot-washing and where the prophets "spake and prophesied." When, in June 1830, the first regular meeting of the Mormon Church was held, not only did the believers appear, but also large crowds of the curious, and Smith showed a spirit that won him new adherents. A dam was arranged in a stream for the immersion of candidates; the crowd broke it down, turned on Smith, threatened him, and accused him of having led a life not strictly in keeping with the conventional morality. To the amazement of all present, the Prophet calmly and humbly admitted the charge. "But that," he added quietly, "was before my conversion." He drew the crowd from derision to attention, and, after holding them for some time by his sermon, led them in prayer.[1]

In the meantime, people were consequently curious about the mysterious golden plates from which Smith, under the divine instruction, had been able to translate a book that, in print, made a volume eight inches long by six wide and six inches thick. It was a very dull and turgid book, but the rustics that read it did not consider the qualities of suspense and sprightliness as characteristic of inspired utterance. Its literary qualities were, in fact, favourable to the acceptance of its theological pre-

[1] *The Mormons Unmasked,* by C. Sheridan Jones.

tensions; but the story of its origin was one that, even in that place and time, challenged proof.

Smith repeated his original story, with sundry amplifications; but in vain. He said that the language on the plates was "Reformed Egyptian," but his critics asked him what "Reformed Egyptian" might be. He said that it was true that he was no master of this rediscovered tongue, and that he had made his translation while in a trance—spiritualistic trances were then just becoming popular—dictating to his amanuensis from behind a screen; but the doubters refused both this and the affirmation of those who declared that they had seen the plates. At last, therefore, perhaps in that faith which the successful charlatan always has in himself, perhaps in the hope that the characters, being meaningless, would at anyrate puzzle a linguist, the prophet, apparently recovering certain of the plates that the angel had taken from him "for safe-keeping," agreed to submit an example of the lost language to Dr Charles Anthon, an American classical scholar of standing, and the best philologist in the country at that time.

Harris was the messenger from Smith to Anthon. He went away confident and returned triumphant. He said that Professor Anthon, although believed to be familiar with the characters of every known language, had been forced to admit that the submitted "Reformed Egyptian" was something new to him. Obviously, therefore, said Smith, the angel had not lied: the plates were what they had been represented to be. The neighbourhood was satisfied; since the plates could not be deciphered by the scholar, they were accepted as divine.

Dr Anthon himself has, however, given a different

view of the matter. In a letter to a Mr Howe, dated 17th February 1834, he said:—

"They (*i.e.* the characters) were evidently prepared by someone who had before him a book containing various alphabets, Greek and Hebrew letters, etc.; the whole ending in a rude delineation of a circle decked with strange marks, and evidently copied from the Mexican Calendar given by Humboldt."

Some time later the Mormons declared that Anthon had admitted to Harris that the characters were affiliated with the Egyptian. Anthon, in reply, issued a public statement to the effect that the paper shown him by Harris was a singular scroll, filled with crooked characters in columns: Greek and Hebrew letters crossed and with flourishes, Roman letters inverted and placed sidewise, and strange marks evidently copied from reproductions of Aztec inscriptions. He added that he had advised Harris not to be deceived by this hodge-podge, a warning that Harris later heeded, but heeded too late.

Of the doctrines of Mormonism as then preached and later developed, there will be full treatment in a later chapter. It is here enough to say that Smith, basing his declarations on the words of *The Book of Mormon*, on direct inspiration and on heavenly visions that continued to be vouchsafed from time to time when needed, declared that it was the mission of the new faith, the only true Church of God, to reclaim the Lost Ten Tribes, to build the New Jerusalem, to convert the world to a literal acceptance of the Bible, and thus to be ready for the second coming of Christ, which could not occur until the Saints had prepared for Him.

But, though the faith grew by leaps and bounds, it suffered from those dissensions that beset the early days of every creed. Its enemies say that Rigdon used his knowledge of the Spalding manuscript to coerce Smith and have himself made a prophet with powers equal to Joseph's, and certain it is that Smith received a revelation to that effect. Harris, also, recanted, after his family had been beggared, and was denounced by Smith, in a paper that the Church had founded, as a lackey and a "white-skinned negro." Then a young woman convert contracted the visionary habit and prophesied that the Church's founder would be supplanted in his leadership. Smith lost no time in denouncing the woman as a false prophet, but soon saw the approach of danger and was "warned by the Spirit" that the time had come for the Saints to leave the disrupting influences of civilization and seek out the site of the New Jerusalem.

A temporary asylum was selected at Kirtland, Ohio, where the new comers were regarded with that distrust which is always given to new comers, and where the elder inhabitants charged the immigrants with strange practices among themselves and with raids upon their neighbours' live stock. Thereupon, with Rigdon, Smith made a tour of inspection through a part of the west and selected a locality that promised richness of soil and abundance of water. Another revelation announced that this place, later known as Independence, and situated in Jackson County, Missouri, was the site designed by the Lord, where Christ would come for His thousand years' reign of temporal power. Smith directed the Saints to sell all their eastern holdings and move to Independence, and at least twelve hundred of the faithful obeyed the call.[1]

Smith spent much time in Independence, but retained a residence for himself and his own family in

[1] *Doctrines and Covenants of Latter Day Saints,* Nauvoo, 1846.

Kirtland, awaiting the proper settlement of Independence before risking there the well-being of the Church's founder; and this was well, since trouble followed the Saints even to the chosen place of God. Smith ruled that, as the Saints were building a city for the reception of divinity, none that was profane must reside within the limits of the town. All unbelievers were banned; the boast became frequent that the Mormons, whether by settlement or force, would soon possess the entire surrounding country; inside the city the Church's hierarchy ruled unquestioned and supreme, in matters ecclesiastical, moral, legal, and financial. The result was inevitable. The inhabitants of the neighbouring strips of land became indignant at the pretensions of the elect and envious of the prosperity gained for the elect by their system of combination. There was soon begun something very like open war.

The angry older inhabitants held meetings. They passed resolutions. Then they formed them—resolutions that culminated in a determination to burn the building from which the official Mormon newspaper, *The Star*, was published. The Mormons protected their property. The neighbours sent them orders to "move on." The Church organized a militia and fought dismissal with firearms.[1]

For the time, Smith himself was safe. In the midst of the threats of storm, an angel had warned him to maintain his residence in Kirtland, with his family, where he would, as Prophet, be protected; but he made occasional visits to Independence, kept a tight hand upon the government of that town, and directed his

[1] Mackay notes that Lieutenant-Governor Boggs, of Missouri, was at this time nearly a victim of assassination, at unknown hands, and tried to lay the assault at the Mormons' door.

hard-working and resolute followers through a series of manifestos. But this could not long continue. At that time the chief requirement of all Mormons was the payment of tithes to the Church. The sums thus conscientiously handed over were held by Smith and Rigdon in a stewardship from which no accounting could be exacted. They were used by the heads of the Church for anything that the Church's heads chose to use them for. The end was a bank-failure and the escape of the two Prophets from Kirtland with the sheriff almost at their heels.

The guerilla war of the Saints meanwhile continued. Now they would be almost driven out of Missouri, and again they would re-establish themselves there. The country was then a wild one and torn by the struggles of the slavery and anti-slavery factions; but at last the governor of the state found space to deal with the disciples of Smith. Declaring that the Mormon disturbances were a menace to the peace of the commonwealth, he ordered out the state militia to quell disturbances and maintain order. The militia took the hint, as the militia always does, and, in accord with militia traditions, proceeded to maintain order by exerting violence. The soldiery conquered their enemy and commanded the vanquished:

1. To deliver up their leaders for trial.
2. To lay down their arms.
3. To sign over their properties as an indemnity for the expense of the "war."
4. To leave the state forthwith.

The Mormons, now several thousand strong, accepted these terms because they were forced to accept them. Smith was given up to the authorities, but later escaped and fled to the state of Illinois, where he for a time evaded justice. His disciples, in the utmost misery, made their way across the prairies, submitting to tempestuous weather, to sickness, to death. Some went into Mississippi, others into the neighbouring state, where Smith had found a refuge, and there, again through a storm of persecution, established themselves and increased their numbers until, in 1837, they were said to total 15,000. In the same year missionaries were sent to England and made 10,000 converts there.

Smith joined the Illinois flock of his sheep. He reported to them that the Deity had changed his mind, and that not Independence, but a town still to be built in Illinois, was destined for the capital of Christ's earthly kingdom. A site was selected, a charter by some means secured from the state, and the building of the new city, which they named Nauvoo, at once begun, the temple alone costing nearly £200,000.

Something had been learned from the mistakes made in Ohio and Missouri. Smith pushed to their limit the rules of industrial combination, and the community grew rich. He permitted, because he had to, the fiction of a representative form of government within the limits of Nauvoo; but he saw to it that none save those whom he could implicitly trust were elected to office, and he remained an absolute dictator.[1] He was of course elected mayor, was chosen "General" of the militia that he immediately established and severely drilled, and was even put forward by his disciples as a candidate for the Presidency of the United States.

[1] Dixon, in his *New America*, says that Smith was thirty-nine times brought before a court without being once condemned, and the historian suggests that the Prophet "contrived to have himself falsely accused" for the sake of the effect that acquittal would have upon his followers and upon possible converts.

This militia has been the subject of much controversy. Adverse critics of the Mormons accept the stories of surrounding non-Mormon and poorer farmers, who could not successfully compete against the trust methods employed by the followers of Smith, and declare that the Prophet maintained a band of "Danites" or "Destroying Angels," who were bound to utter silence and implicit obedience and were in reality nothing more than organized assassins hired to execute the vengeance of the Church and to pay the personal grudges of its leaders. That, in later times, some such organization existed there is more evidence, although even in later times the crimes laid at its door are not all proven; but to the less prejudiced observer it seems that, at Nauvoo, the militia was in a reality a militia. If it was composed for the protection of the faith, it was so composed because persecution made that necessary for the faith's maintenance: if it owned allegiance to Smith rather than to the state, it was at anyrate little more dangerous than the average militia that is obedient to the commands of a capitalistic government; and if its formation was contrary to law, its action was no more illegal than the general action of militia in times of economic war.

Yet even Smith's precautions were unavailing. The Prophet's end was near, and it is significant that his death was concerned with the earliest charges of polygamy brought against his Church. The story is one that has been told, though not without some slight, but probably unguessed, exaggeration, by John Hay, the biographer of Lincoln.[1]

"No fact is more notorious," says Mr Hay, "than

1 "The Mormon Prophet's Tragedy," *The Atlantic Monthly*, December 1869.

that Smith's daily life had established polygamy in Nauvoo long before Rigdon had invented his jargon of 'spiritual wives'[1] or Hiram[2] received his revelation to justify it. The elders of the Church, Brigham[3] and others, clamoured rebelliously against the Prophet's exclusive licence, and together they began cautiously to lay the foundation of a new doctrine, which, properly arranged, should prove a strength instead of a weakness to the Church. . . . In the great hierarchy of Nauvoo there were no fanatics; the flocks were sheep, but the keepers were wolves. The doctrine of spiritual wives was the result, not the cause, of the lewd lives of Smith, Young, and their fellow-blackguards, and was invented to justify the immorality which the ignorance and credulity of their female worshippers rendered so easy, to serve in the future as a bait for the rascal few, and to blind the eyes of the honest and stupid mass.

"In the year 1844 the attempt was made to graft this abomination upon the creed of the Church. . . . In the spring . . . in Nauvoo, the Prophet saw the wife of Dr Foster, admired her, and, led by his evil genius, marched to conquest, and found defeat. . . . Her husband, the doctor, found that something must be done. He talked the thing over with Mr Law, whose *placens uxor* had received and declined the same saintly overtures, and they came to the eminently American conclusion that the light should be turned upon such an iniquity. They bought press and types, and appealed

[1] The subject of polygamy and "spiritual sealing" is treated of in a later chapter.

[2] Hiram Smith, the brother of Joseph, and his associate in the early days of the Church.

[3] Brigham Young, of whom more anon.

to that court of final resort for all Anglo-Saxon blood—printer's ink.[1] . . . The first and last number of the Nauvoo *Expositor*[2] was published on the 7th of June.

"*The Expositor* girds on its armour and gives a half-dozen dreadful columns to the preamble, resolutions, and affidavits of the seceders from the Church at Nauvoo. . . . There are only two things worth noting in it—one, the bold and distinct allegations of the open and cynical licentiousness of Smith and his apostles, the other, the earnestness with which, even amidst the wreck of their personal illusions, the seceders still hold to their faith in the original imposture.[3] . . .

"The affidavits of William Law and his wife, and of Annie Cowles . . . established the fact that Hiram Smith had read to them a pretended revelation of the dogma of 'a plurality of wives, and of the sealing up of persons to eternal life against all sin, except the shedding of innocent blood'—the innocent blood meaning the blood of Mormons. In the case of Sister Law, the revelation was strengthened by assurances of damnation to any woman who objected to her husband embracing the new doctrine."

Smith was frightened by the publicity thus given to his secret acts. He denounced the offenders and cut them off from the Church and the Church's benefits, but, says Mr Hay, "he never denied the authenticity of the

1 As a matter of fact, they caused a schism, for which the prosperity of the Church as a body and the hard lives of its members had made sufficient preparation. This schism was the origin of a non-polygamous branch of the Mormon Church that continues to this day.

2 The name given to Foster and Law's paper.

3 These affidavits were chiefly those of sixteen women, who declared that Smith, Rigdon, Young, and others in authority had "invited them to enter into a secret and illicit connection, under the title of spiritual marriage."

revelation. On the contrary, during one of those singular trials in his own municipal court,[1] he stated squarely, 'Brother Hiram is a prophet of the Lord; and when the Lord speaks let the earth tremble.' In all Smith's curious history there is no fact more clearly established than this effort to legalize and consecrate his immoral life. It formed the first link of that chain of circumstances which within a few days dragged him to his doom."

But the trouble was not confined to Nauvoo. The people of the surrounding country were only too ready to believe evil of their peculiar neighbours, and they seized upon the charges published in *The Expositor*. Smith's fright changed to anger. "To resort to violence might lead to bloody reprisals. But his rowdy instincts decided the question. He procured from his corrupt and servile municipal court an order declaring the new journal a public nuisance. A party of the myrmidons destroyed the press and *pied* the offending types. That was his death-warrant. Thereafter the mob could say to the Prophet, 'The villainy you teach me I will execute.'"[2]

Smith's official paper, *The Neighbor*, justified the outrage and pleaded, what other slave-holders everywhere have always pleaded: "We want nothing but to be left alone." Nevertheless, the disaffected procured from without warrants against Joseph and Hiram Smith and sixteen other of the rioters; but the form of arrest being gone through with, the hearing before Smith's municipal court was a farce, and acquittal was of amazing promptness.

[1] As mayor of the town, Smith could sit as a magistrate and administer the law.

[2] "The Mormon Prophet's Tragedy."

Then the outside world acted. Incensed not only by the riot, but also by Smith's audacity in announcing himself in his paper as a Presidential candidate and in suggesting for the Vice-presidency a creature of his named Bennet, the citizens of the county brought pressure to bear upon the sheriff, who again summoned the offenders; and after repeated violation of promises of surrender, the Smiths rode into Carthage, the county seat, attended by their Common Council, had a hearing before a justice of the peace, gave bonds for appearance at court, and were promptly discharged; whereupon they were immediately rearrested on a charge that they had not expected to have to meet, the charge of treason —levying war against the government of the state— and, this not being a bailable offence, they were committed to the county jail.[1]

Governor Ford of Illinois, a weakling, feared violence, ordered out the militia, vacillated, disbanded his forces. The "broken men," who had come out for blood, were dissatisfied: from organized militia, they became an armed mob, marched to the jail, where there was scarcely a show of defence, and slaughtered the obnoxious prophets. By a curious carelessness, or lenity, these prisoners were armed, and put up a plucky fight. It appears that Joseph Smith died bravely: "he stood by the jamb of the door and fired four shots, bringing his man down every time."[2]

1 *The Death of a False Prophet,* by Samuel Wright.

2 "The Mormon Prophet's Tragedy." One of Smith's fellow Mormon prisoners, a Mr M'Bride, "with feeble frame and tottering steps, unable to run, had cried in vain: 'Spare my life; I am a Revolutionary soldier. I fought for liberty. Would you murder me? What is my offence? I believe in God and revelation!' 'Take that, you G—d d—d Mormon,' was the reply of the Missourian, as with

The governmental investigation into this mob-murder ended as most investigations into mob-law end in the United States. There was a trial at which it was found impossible to identify the accused as the leaders of the mob, and the jury returned a verdict of "Not guilty," to the entire satisfaction of the community. Even the followers of Smith did not greatly protest, were already quarrelling over the succession, were afraid of bringing down upon themselves the same fury that had ended the career of Joseph.

But the great work had been done, and not even internal dissension was to be able to undo it. From the 27th of June 1844 the death of their first Prophet became one of the best tools in the hands of the Mormon propagandists. In 1830 Smith had but a handful of followers. In 1837 his missionaries had appeared in England; in 1840 in Australia; in 1841 in Palestine; in 1843 in the Pacific Islands. But in 1849 they redoubled their efforts in all the countries that they had formerly visited, spread to France, Germany, Switzerland, and Italy; proceeded a year later into Sweden, Norway, and Denmark; appeared in 1852 in Siam and Ceylon; and by 1853 had spread their nets to Gibraltar, Malta, the West Indies, Hindustan, China, South Africa, and British Guiana. The blood of the martyrs had once more become the seed of a Church.

the butt of his gun he dashed out his brains." (*Utah and Its People*). In his diary, Josiah Quincy denies the early charges of murder made against the Mormons.

IV

THE MARCH OF THE CONVERTS

UPON the death of its founder, nearly every religion has experienced an unseemly struggle for leadership among that founder's more ambitious survivors. Mormonism, as has just been noted, was not exempt. Says Mr Hay:[1]

"The Prophet's brother William was an aspirant (to the succession). But he was a weak, indolent, good-natured sensualist, and was readily bought off and suppressed. He carried on for some time a flourishing trade in 'patriarchal blessings.' He had probably never heard of Tetzel, and yet the old Dominican himself could scarcely have systematized his traffic better. He advertises in *The Neighbor*:

> Common Blessings, 50 cents;
> Extraordinary Blessings, $1.00;
> Children, half-price;
> Women, gratis.

"Rigdon made a desperate stand for the Prophet's mantle. But he was defeated also, and, being recalcitrant, was solemnly 'given over to be buffeted of the Evil One for a thousand years.' The coolest and most

1 "The Mormon Prophet's Tragedy."

unbelieving of them all succeeded to the autocracy. Brigham Young, whether guided by instinct or reason I do not know, avoided the fatal mistake of Smith, who turned back from Missouri to Illinois, and the crazy fantasy of Rigdon, who would have gone from Illinois to Pennsylvania. Tribes and religions cannot travel against the sun. Young, during the troubled year that followed, exerted himself to gather all the reins of (Mormon) government into his own hands; and there was not in all the slavish East a despot more absolute than he when at last he started, with his wives and his servants and his cattle, into the vast tolerant wilderness."

Of how this new migration was begun, and of the man that conceived and ordered it, mention will be made later. Now our attention must be turned for a moment overseas.

For, as we saw at the end of the last chapter, while the Mother-church was in difficulties at home, its missionaries, deluded and deluding, had been busy abroad, and had made especial progress in England. That they sought that island in particular was due, in part, to the fact that they were uneducated men, and at the start no linguists, who had no tongue save that to which they had been born—a tongue at least intelligible in England; their success in the island was due almost entirely to economic reasons.

From about 1820, in the reign of George IV., there had been general and well-founded discontent among the English working-class. The country still suffered from the greatest revolution that the world has ever seen: the decline of the handicrafts upon the introduction of machinery. This is a matter already sufficiently familiar, and sufficiently familiar should be the fact that the discontent thus aroused found, and continued long to find, expression in a hundred ways. In 1820 occurred the Cato Street conspiracy, with the destruction of the entire Ministry for its end. Thistlewood, with his thirty-odd comrades, plotted to blow up the Ministers met at Lord Harrowley's dinner. Riots, so-called, became so common in Ireland that the timid authorities suspended the Habeas Corpus Act and renewed the Insurrection Act. Brazil and other Spanish-American states declaring their independence in 1823, added to the still potent influence towards republicanism spread by the example of France. Two years later the King's speech to Parliament so warmly congratulated the country on its general prosperity that there swept over the country an epidemic of speculation, which, added to the appearance of a flood of paper money and general over-production under competitive capitalistic methods, ended, as it was bound to end, in a commercial panic.

To relieve this panic, which followed within a twelvemonth, there was devised an elaborate system of emigration, and that system, once adopted, was hard to end. The rapid issuing of one-pound and two-pound notes only increased the evil. In 1826 a law was passed forbidding the issue of any notes under the denomination of fifty-one, after a period of three years, and providing, within that period, for a gradual decrease of the present issue. Corn, too, was to be imported at a specific duty; bonded corn was to be admitted at ten shillings per quarter. The emigration continued.

In the reign of William IV. the first railway was constructed in England. It ran between Liverpool and Manchester, and its success led, as everyone now knows, to more wild speculation and consequent distress. Lord Russell presented his Reform Bill for the disenfranchisement of sixty "rotten boroughs," and passed it at the end of 1831 only after an appeal to remedies that many critics considered desperate, and only after so much disturbance among the incensed people that at Derby a jail was sacked and the prisoners freed. More than a hundred persons were killed or wounded in Bristol by the stupid military, and public buildings were destroyed. The castle of the Duke of Newcastle was razed. Ireland was in a state of turmoil. And, as a climax, the Asiatic cholera appeared, in October, to terrorize and kill.

The final passage of the Reform Bill did not help the sister island, and matters there grew steadily worse. On 15th February 1833 Lord Grey introduced the Irish Coercion Bill, granting the Lord-Lieutenant the right to prevent any public meetings and, when he thought the case required it, to proclaim military law. Those Irishmen were few who would not have been glad of a chance to get away.

Poverty had its hand upon the entire United Kingdom; there had come the natural reaction against the over-exertion of competitive capitalism. Lord Althorp's new Poor Law did little; other legislation, dealing with symptoms and neglecting the disease, did less. In 1836 Lord Russell's Bill for the Commutation of Tithes passed, and the rent-charge was consequently calculated on the average price of corn for seven years; but there was no relief.

Followed, in 1838, the Chartists, who represented one of the most democratic impulses that had yet appeared in England. Their six principles—universal suffrage, annual parliaments, vote by ballot, salaries for members of Parliament, the division of the country into electoral districts, and the abolition of the property qualification for a seat in Parliament—need surely not here be gone into. It is sufficient to remind the reader how Chartism spread from one end of the country to the other; how a frightened Government, on December 12th, issued its tyrannical proclamation "Against Illegal Chartist Assemblies"; how, in retaliation, the famous petition, signed by 1,280,000 persons, was presented to the Commons; how a motion to consider this petition was lost, and how, as a matter of course, protesting disturbances occurred everywhere. The Chartists divided themselves into two parties, the practically non-resisting Chartists and the "Physical Force Chartists"; the latter expressed their sentiments in what was called an "attack" on Newport in 1839, and the leaders, Frost, Williams, and Jones,[1] were sentenced to transportation for life.

Even though separated by seas, men placed in the same economic situation will react upon that situation in like manner. The conditions in England at this time were much the same as those conditions in the United States which produced, in the religious field, the Wilkinsonians, the Come-outers, the Mormons. Thus, however distant the United States might be—and

[1] "Ernest Jones, the Chartist—I never knew him personally, but my husband was a personal friend of his. My husband used to feel that Ernest Jones was his inspirer in the part he took in public affairs later on. That man—a man who had great expectations of wealth, a man of great learning, a man who might have risen to the highest position in his profession—chose to give it all up, chose to relinquish all opportunity of advancement in his profession, because his conscience made him espouse an unpopular cause." — Mrs Pankhurst, in her address to the jury at her trial at the Old Bailey, 21st May 1912.

it was then, of course, much farther away from England than it is in these days of ocean liners, the cable, and the wireless telegraph—it was to be expected that there would be in England much such a religious expression as there was in the United States. And that is precisely what there was.

Religious inquietude followed, as it always does, economic unrest. In May 1838 a madman named Thom, who called himself Sir William Courtenay, announced himself as the Saviour of the world, succeeded in securing many disciples from among the ignorant and oppressed round about Canterbury, and was suppressed only by those ancient theological controversialists, the military. Similar aberrations were frequent, and most of them are familiar to all Englishmen.

Meanwhile, in the less extreme creeds, dissent thrived and evangelicalism flourished. In 1834 it was determined by the Wesleyans to establish theological institutions for the training of ministerial candidates, and there was immediate trouble among the members of this body because of strenuous objections to anything with the supposedly Popish tendency to distinguish between the clergy and the laity. By the agreement of the trustees, and with the consent of the Conference, an organ was in 1828 installed in Brunswick Chapel, Leeds, and a violent agitation resulted in the congregation, the prejudice against such music rising to an extreme pitch throughout the entire West Riding of Yorkshire. In 1836 the practice adopted of ordination by the imposition of hands added to the organization's difficulties, and, though the dissenting sects increased in membership, they also increased in variety. One body of seceding Wesleyans designated itself the

"Protestant Methodists," and a second, the "Wesleyan Methodist Association," was later merged into "The Methodist Free Churches."[1]

Emigration, encouraged during the panic of 1825, continued, and the desire to go to a country where conditions were erroneously reported to be easier fired village after village, town after town. From 1820 to 1830, statistics show that 82,000 emigrants entered the United States from Great Britain; from 1830 to 1840 there were 283,000; and in the following decade over a million. In each of these series of years, moreover, more persons entered the United States from Great Britain than from all other countries put together.

Just when thousands of Englishmen were in the throes of the economic troubles sketched above, just when they were by thousands seeking after new religions, and just when emigration was becoming popular, Joseph Smith was sending to them from his American Zion missionaries that would promise their converts a land flowing with milk and honey and a Heaven that would assure salvation. Smith knew that his Church, like most Churches, was dependent for its endurance upon increasing membership. He knew that a war would have to be waged against the forest, and he must have guessed that a war might sooner or later have to be fought against hostile neighbours or a hostile government. Polygamy would increase the number of the faithful, but immediate increase was necessary. Smith could not wait upon Nature; he evolved his doctrine that a Mormon's duty was largely propagandist, and he sent forth his missionaries with promises of reward both here and hereafter.

[1] *Methodism*, by the Rev. J. H. Rigg, D.D.

Two elders of the faith, O. Hyde and H. C. Kimball, were the first to be sent. Others followed fast, and an energetic band was soon scouring the United Kingdom.

That these men believed the teachings of their Church in most particulars there is small doubt. But there is also small doubt that when, under accusation, they swore that their people were monogamous, they committed perjury. Certainly some such oaths were sworn after polygamy was openly established among the Saints in America, and certainly these missionaries must have known it. Certainly, too, some of these evangels had themselves left more than a wife apiece at home, and certainly, in spite of this, they courted girls in England.

John Taylor, one of the missionaries thus accused, made this answer to the charge brought against him:[1]

"We are accused here of actions the most indelicate and disgusting, such as none but a corrupt and depraved heart could have conceived. These actions are too outrageous to admit of belief. . . ."

As proof of his innocence, and especially of the innocence of his sect, Taylor proceeded to quote from what he declared was the official Mormon *Book of Doctrine and Covenants*, selecting, among other passages, the following:

"Marriage is ordained by God unto man; wherefore it is lawful that a man should have *one wife*, and they twain should be one flesh. . . .

"Thou shalt love thy *wife* with all thy heart, and shalt cleave unto her, *and none else*."

Yet Mrs Stenhouse, who was in a position to discover

[1] *The Tyranny of Mormonism*, Fanny Stenhouse.

the truth,[1] affirms that, at the time this statement was made by "Brother Taylor," he had five wives living in Salt Lake City, where the authorities of the Church, in absolute power there, and many of them living in open polygamy themselves, must have known and approved his actions. She adds that, at this meeting, which was publicly called in Boulogne-sur-Mer to refute the charge of polygamy, Taylor was supported by one Mormon missionary that had two wives and another that was married to a mother and a daughter.

The protests of the missionaries seem, however, to have been generally believed. At anyrate, in England economic pressure continued to urge the working-class toward a frame of mind that would readily accept promises of earthly ease in a new land and eternal salvation to come, and some men were no doubt attracted by the possibility that polygamy would be secretly allowed them in Utah. Converts were everywhere made. Dr Charles Mackay estimates that, during the six years from 1837 to 1843, 10,000 conversions were accomplished in England, mostly in the cities where manufactures were rapidly replacing hand-work—Manchester, Birmingham, Leeds, Liverpool; and in Scotland, Glasgow—although not a few converts came from the south of Wales and others from the Sussex coast.[2]

1 Mrs Fanny Stenhouse was herself a Mormon, and, though it must be remembered that she left the Church after receiving what seems to have been great suffering at its hands, no sound evidence has been produced to contradict her utterances as above referred to.

2 Dr Mackay had become interested in the question of emigration from England, and wrote a number of articles on this subject for *The Morning Chronicle.* In the course of his investigations he found that among the emigrants a large number, steadily increasing, were converts to Mormonism, and expected, after reaching America, to

The forces that made for emigration when the Mormon missionaries appeared continued to grow in strength. The Corn Law Bills, made, altered, and ultimately practically repealed, did not cease to create disturbances that were sufficient to drive Englishmen from home. In the year 1847 there was an abnormal rainfall and consequent heavy loss in harvesting. That same year a potato disease severely injured the English crop and destroyed the Irish. In 1849 the Irish potato crop was again destroyed, and the peasantry died by the hundreds from famine and famine-bred diseases, with the result that the Irish exodus grew until, in 1850, over 1,200,000 Irishmen sailed for America. Meanwhile a similar service had been done for England by the commercial panic of 1847, more or less definitely the consequence of continued railway speculation.

So alarming did emigration finally become that England found it necessary to examine the matter and contrive some means of limiting it. *The Times* of 24th September 1851 speaks at length of the extraordinary emigration of the past five years, and concludes that it "threatens to permanently (*sic*) drain Great Britain." At the port of New York alone, within the first eight months of 1851, immigrants numbered 192,836, and most of them were British. "The Irish emigration," says *The Times*, "is unparalleled in history. . . . Not only the labouring class . . . (but) many of the higher class, bearing not merely

make their way to Utah. He came upon the fact that the Mormon Church had a regular emigration agency in Liverpool, and that there was a Mormon representative in every English port. He laid at the door of these agents the exodus, in 1849, of 2500 farmers and merchants of what he called "good class," who sailed for New Orleans. He was by these discoveries led to investigate Mormonism itself.

their savings but all the qualities that belong to their position," were taking part in it.

On the Mormon exodus *The Examiner* spoke more specifically in 1863. It appears that not long before, a Wesleyan remarked that there were very few Mormons left in Cardiff; but, according to *The Examiner*, only a few days after that remark was made, "about eighty men and women—the latter nearly all young, good-looking, robust girls—left Cardiff *en route* for Salt Lake. They had been gathered from the surrounding country, and many were respectable in appearance."

The Examiner continues:

"The Mormon agents are ever watchful and active, while the Established Church and Dissent make the fatal mistake of treating them as members of a decaying sect, and as impostors unworthy of regard. . . . In Liverpool, where there are many Welsh, there are also many Mormons. . . . Statistics and census returns do not give the full measure of its (Mormonism's) progress, for the simple reason that as fast as converts are made they are sent off to Utah.[1] *A perpetual emigration fund is in existence for this purpose.* . . . The women, young and old, adopt Mormonism greedily. The case has been mentioned of a woman of sixty, who left her home in Wales to be married in Utah, leaving behind her a husband of seventy."[2]

So energetic were the missionaries that in 1844, after carrying away from the United Kingdom more than 10,000 converts, they sent a copy of *The Book of*

[1] The Church needed its recruits immediately in Utah, and it taught them that their duty, as well as their earthly comfort, directed them to Salt Lake to prepare the City of God.

[2] The subsequent history of this sanguine convert is not given.

Mormon, doubtless with the distant hope of conversion or at least public Royal approval, to Queen Victoria and the Prince Consort; and a Mormon poet, with more religious fervour than lyric power, wrote of the Queen:

> "Oh! would she now her influence lend—
> The influence of Royalty—
> Messiah's kingdom to extend,
> And Zion's Nursing Mother be,
>
> Then with the glory of her name
> Inscribed on Zion's lofty spire,
> She'd win a wreath of endless fame,
> To last when other wreaths expire."

The perpetual emigration fund mentioned by *The Examiner* was indeed a fact. It was established in 1849, ostensibly to enable only indigent converts to immigrate to the promised land. At its start, three and a half tons of gold were laid aside for the fund's beginning, gold gathered in the mining camps of the Rocky Mountains and the Sierras, and equal to about £376,320. That done, donations and taxations kept up the amount, which, from the Mormon point of view, was wisely administered.

How wisely, the Mormons themselves have proudly shown. Before 1844, when Joseph Smith was murdered, there were, say the Saints, thirteen vessels plying between Liverpool and New Orleans and carrying on their voyages out only Mormon converts; their return cargo consisted of Mormon missionaries, proceeding, according to the Scriptural injunction, without money and trusting to Providence and the ravens for their means of existence. In 1857 it was announced by the Church that it had nearly 5000 converts in Wales, over 1000 in Glasgow, and a number approaching 30,000 in the entire United Kingdom. In addition to these, 17,000 are said to have sought the American Zion.

That Zion had now been firmly established in Utah. Seizing the command of the Church, Brigham Young saw that he must lead his flock as far as might be from the contaminating, not to say destroying, influences of the unbelievers. He knew, in a general way, of the vast resources of the Great West, and he certainly dreamed of the opportunity there apparently offered to build an empire. During his residence in Missouri he had probably heard strange tales, from returned explorers, of the wonderful Salt Lake Valley, and had talked of it to St Vrain, Sublette, Jim Bridger, Bent, and other fur-traders and trappers.[1] At all events, he decided to found his kingdom in that valley, then almost a mythical country; so he announced to the faithful that the divine mind had again been changed, that the site of Christ's capital was shifted westward; and westward across the weary, dangerous prairies he led his credulous and indomitable followers.

The sufferings of these pilgrims were the sufferings of all that, in those days, attempted the great overland journey. They were the sufferings of the English converts that followed. But they seem to have been borne with a fortitude that amounted to zeal; and at last, after hideous hardships, the pilgrims reached their destination and built the town that was to be at once the Rome and the Bourse of the world.

Mrs Stenhouse, in her book published in 1888,[2] graphically describes the experiences of one army of

1 "The Viper's Trail of Gold," by Alfred Henry Lewis, *Cosmopolitan Magazine,* 1911.

2 *The Tyranny of Mormonism,* before referred to. This book is now out of print.

English converts seeking Zion, and their experiences appear to have been common to all the pilgrims. As at that time herself a Mormon and a pilgrim, Mrs Stenhouse writes whereof she knows.

"Toward the end of the year 1855," she says, "it was determined that a company of Mormon emigrants, numbering several hundreds, should leave Liverpool *en route* for Salt Lake City; and for that purpose a vessel was chartered early in November. This was not the ordinary season for emigration,[1] but there were then in England numbers of the Saints, anxious to go to Zion, but too poor to pay their passage all the way. It was thought that when they arrived in New York they would have time to earn sufficient to carry them on, and it was then supposed they could join those who came over by the ordinary spring emigration."

The emigrants were forced to shift for themselves. Thus the Stenhouse family made their long sea trip without bedding, because the bedding that they had brought with them had been mislaid. Meals, moreover, were not provided by the steamship company; each family cooked and served its own. Marriages being not uncommon on shipboard, it was difficult for a family to secure the aid of any unattached young woman: the brethren would handicap her usefulness by courtship.

It was a weary journey across the Atlantic. The emigrants had little money: they had been told that they needed little, and, on landing, the few that found work or had places to which to go were fortunate. The rest of this army, about a hundred and fifty men, women, and children, were huddled together in a

[1] The time of year chosen for the voyage probably explains why one of the vessels regularly used by the Saints was not employed.

dilapidated schoolhouse, borrowed by the Mormon authorities. Their only food was what was left from that which they had brought aboard ship at Liverpool. They were unused to the biting cold of New York in winter. Many began to go about the streets begging, and for this a snugly-clothed "Apostle" rebuked them, telling them that it was contrary to "the dignity of the Saints of the Most High."

Somehow these people lived through the winter months, and in the spring were joined by a second shipload of converts, when preparations were made for the journey overland.

Until this year the "Saints" had gone west in ox-carts if they had, individually, the money to pay for them; if not, they had travelled, with little expense to their seducers, on foot. Provisions and luggage were transported by wagon. But this year a revelation of a new method came to Brigham Young. Hand-carts were to be constructed, light enough for even the young girls to draw, and no other help was to be given by the Church itself. This "plan," well advertised, so affected the world that "it was roughly estimated that no fewer than five or six thousand emigrants travelled from Liverpool to Salt Lake City" in that single year.

The hand-carts, however, were not provided in Iowa City, a midway point of the journey, as had been expected. Indeed, nothing was in readiness there for the arriving army of converts. These had to wait idly for three weeks while the hand-carts, wholly inadequate even when completed, were building. Only seventeen pounds of bedding and extra clothing were allowed to each Saint. One cart for every five persons was provided for the five hundred in the Stenhouse party, and then it was found difficult to secure enough able-bodied Saints to do the drawing.

The unmarried women and girls, concerning whom an order from Zion came "not to pick out from the flock the young, fair, and tender lambs," occupied one tent by night. In the other tents slept the families in unorganized proximity. The food allowance was scanty, the money of these converts was "taken care of" by the Church, and there was, therefore, no occasion to purchase provisions by the way.

Finally, several yokes of oxen were provided for the carrying of provisions; and a hundred pounds per ox-cart were added, at Florence on the Missouri River, in order that the winter might be endured. There had arisen a discussion at Florence as to whether a halt had not best be called for the winter, severe on the plains; but the "revelations" of elders prevailed against every suggestion of delay. So the second part of the journey commenced, four hundred and twenty now in the party, with hand-carts, which would retard the travellers by losing their wheels, with old men and tiny children, whose feet wearied, and with the prospect of intense cold on the plains to be crossed. On an average they pushed forward fifteen miles each day. Yet the faith of these people seldom wavered.

On the banks of the Platte River a group of the Apostles passed this struggling mass of converts, and one, Apostle Richards, prophesied. "In the name of the God of Israel," he said, "the Almighty will make a way for you into Zion; and though the snow may fall and the storm rage on the right hand and on the left, not a hair of your heads will be hurt."

However, either Brother Richards was misinformed, or else his god did not keep to his word. It became necessary for the pilgrims to wade through icy rivers, to sleep with insufficient bedding, and worn-out travellers began to die. First one life was ended, and then another. Soon the death-rate started to increase alarmingly, until at nearly every camping-ground a grave must be dug. The old went first, the young followed; yet the fear of mere death did not so much distress the minds of these people marching west through the wilderness as did the fear of being buried by the wayside; they wanted their bodies to rest in Zion.

The story is told of one man who dragged for days his hand-cart, always two of his children above the load. His wife trudged beside him, carrying a baby. Disease at last attacked the husband, but he did not yield. He shivered on, stumbling, his pale face turning to neither side. A day closed, and the camp was pitched. This man halted only when the company halted, sat down then, bowed his head between his hands, and never again moved. Within a few days the man's wife, too, was dead—found in her tent frozen. Another woman, aged, lagged behind and was lost for the night in a snowstorm. The following morning her bones were found, the marks of wolves' teeth still wet upon her skull; and the snow about the bones was red. Not many mornings later five persons were discovered frozen in their tents and were buried in one grave before the rest marched on. A pilgrim has written:

"Many of the unfortunate people lost their fingers and toes, others their ears; one poor woman lost her sight; and I was told of a poor sick man who held on to the wagon-bars to save himself from jolting, and had all his fingers frozen off."[1]

[1] From a letter written by Mary Burton from Salt Lake City.

Seventy-seven out of the four hundred and twenty from Florence were buried during the expedition.

Yet many reached their goal. From each expedition that set out from Liverpool a large proportion travelled, in hardship, to the western Zion; and, as one that suffers most for a cause is least likely to forgo the cause, so these men and women, actually made zealots through their self-sacrifices, poor but industrious, faithful to an ideal created in their minds by energetic missionaries, reached, in joy and full confidence, the city of the Latter Day Saints. Indeed, if they lost faith then, what would it avail them?

Salt Lake City, on its inland sea, surrounded, save at the outlet of the lake, by mountains of snow-peaks, was likewise surrounded by the difficulties of access and egress, both mental and material. The apostate's life is nowhere allowed to be an easy one, and the city of the Saints made no exception to the rule; the runaway would be forced to undergo alone, in the bitterness of a forsworn creed, the hardships of a journey of retreat that he had, as a journey of approach, borne in goodly company and full faith. Even the dissatisfied had to remain and be exploited for the greater glory of the Mormon god.

V

BUILDING THE EMPIRE

In Illinois, Rigdon's schemes to obtain the leadership of the Saints had failed ; his threats to expose the fraud of Mormonism[1] were met with one knows not what threats of counter-exposure, sufficient at anyrate to make him hold his tongue in all matters essential, and his departure for the formation of a rival sect left the Mormons at Nauvoo but slightly reduced in numbers and mostly anxious to follow Rigdon's successful rival, Brigham Young, until then president of the body known as the Twelve Apostles, into the unknown west toward that new Promised Land which God had revealed to him.

Utah, as it is now called—Deseret, the "Land of the Honey Bee," as the Mormons then called it—was, when Brigham's pilgrims first came upon it, and when the English converts of the 'forties joined them there, a barren and unpropitious wilderness. A tremendous table-land, it was separated from the civilization that had proved so inimical to the faithful by an almost uncharted sea of rolling prairies and a wall of mountains that few except wild beasts and wild Indians had ever explored. Yet, so far as it could be said to belong to any established government, it was then, in 1847, the

[1] Mackay.

property not of the United States, which the Mormons had small cause to love, but of distant, uninquiring, and uncolonizing Mexico, with which, in fact, the United States was upon hostile terms. That it contained possibilities of rewarding cultivation greater than those then known of any other soil in the world, that it held mineral deposits of a value beyond specific calculation, may have been guessed by those heads of the Church who were as sagacious as their followers were faithful. That these heads immediately set their followers to work to convert the wilderness into a commercially prosperous garden, and that this enormous task was performed against difficulties that most men would consider invincible, is now matter of history.

The Saints that sought Utah overland from Illinois and Missouri suffered, in many caravans, the same trials that, a little later, beset their brothers and sisters from England. Although the winter of their migration, the winter of 1847, was fortunately mild for that country, extremes of cold assailed them, and, in spite of their making friends with the Indians, whom their religion taught them to respect, disease and death tramped in their weary but indomitable footsteps.

Nevertheless, the expeditions reached, not too greatly reduced, their goal. The first permanent settlement was made, and Young at once divided the entire surrounding territory and began allotting possible farms to his five thousand followers.

One body of the Saints had come by a more pleasant way. At New York, in 1846, they chartered a seaworthy ship, *The Brooklyn*, and in it sailed down the eastern coast of South America, around Cape Horn, and up the western coast, landing on the shores of the Pacific Ocean. Their only overland journey was hard, but briefer than that of their fellow-believers. They marched eastward to Salt Lake across the Sierra Nevada Mountains, found gold on their way, and brought not a little of it along with them.[1]

In Utah itself, trouble did not at once forsake the empire-builders. Before the first spring arrived, the provisions that they had brought with them were almost exhausted, and they were compelled to eat roots and, game being scarce, even the hides of such animals as they could find. Then, with warm weather, came an Egyptian plague of locusts from the Tinpanogo Mountains. Nothing checked the devourers, and the growing crops seemed about to be ruined. The final recourse was prayer—" and lo! the Great Jehovah, or his Prophet, effected a miracle": flock after flock of "white birds with red beaks and legs" appeared from the islands of the Salt Lake and quite did for the locusts what the locusts had nearly done for the crops.[2]

For those Saints who lingered in Nauvoo there was also little peace. The United States was waging its abominable war upon Mexico for the conquest of fresh territory in which to set up and maintain negro chattel-slavery, and, at the suggestion of Colonel Stephen Kearney, there had been made upon the Mormons a call for five hundred men to enlist for one year's service in a contest the object of which was to give to the United States land which included that whereunto five thousand Mormons fled to escape United States persecution. The call, however, was one that had to be complied with, and, sadly as the Church needed its men, it formed "The Mormon Battalion" in three days.

[1] Mackay.

[2] *Bentley's Miscellany,* quoted in Littell's *Living Age,* vol. xlvi. p. 530 *et seq.*

Those left behind were given to understand that, if they started soon to join their brethren in the west, they would be permitted to make their preparations for departure unmolested. But persecutions increased. It was charged, and, considering the golden promises held out by the Mormons to all that would devoutly join in the western pilgrimage, it was probably justly charged, that not a few fugitives from the law entered the ranks of the Saints. Mobs raided the Mormon houses and destroyed them. On the evening of 19th November 1848 the enemy fell upon Nauvoo and burned the costly Mormon temple to the ground.

On almost the same date another blow descended upon the Zion of Salt Lake. The Mexican War came to an end, and, together with California, Nevada, Arizona, and New Mexico, Utah came into the hands of the United States.

It now behoved the Mormons to exert every effort toward growth. The prairies and the mountains still protected them, but they were already known and hated in one portion of the United States, and the newly conquered land was certain soon to be invaded by fresh colonists. Brigham Young realized that he must have a following large enough to command general caution, and he ordered his missionaries to redouble their efforts. The Irish rising of 1849, with its defeat of the adherents of O'Brien and Mitchell, helped the Mormon cause in Ireland; the offer of farms to emigrating converts helped it in England and in the eastern portion of the United States.

Neither in Utah was any effort spared. Salt Lake City grew to be a thriving town. In the surrounding country, which had once been barren of inhabitants except for some scattered nomad Indian tribes, farms had appeared in plenty. One of the first difficulties encountered was the lack of proper water-courses, and so one of the first duties of the Saints was the digging of ditches for irrigation and the careful preparation of the land for the raising of crops; yet, the irrigation once well begun, the earth gave a response grateful far beyond the average farmer's hopes. The hardships arising from the lack of transportation facilities had to be met. All the clothing, all the food, the very nails for carpentering, the very paper for the journals that would convey to the Saints the news of the colony and the revelations of Heaven, had to be supplied by the Saints themselves; yet supplied they were. Meanwhile, the tithe-revelation of 1834, whereby every member of the Church paid a tax to the Church of one-tenth of his income, was more than ever insisted upon. At first this tax was paid in kind: "The herdsman could pay in cattle, the farmer in hay, the housewife in butter and eggs; tithing-offices became public markets, and the commercial side of the religious establishment expanded."[1] The result was the foundation of the fortune of the Mormon Church.

With so substantial a start, the Mormon hierarchy—which was another way of saying Brigham Young—lost no time, as soon as the United States had secured its land from Mexico, in asking the Government at Washington to admit the Saints' Zion to the standing of a state in the Union, under the Mormon name of Deseret. The reason for this request was simple. By the issue of the Mexican War, Zion had lost its chance of becoming an independent nation, but under the flag of the United States it might be either a "territory,"

[1] "Mormon and Mammon," Murray Schick, *The Coming Nation*, 1911.

that is, a portion of the country in the direct control of the Federal Government, with a governor appointed from Washington, or an autonomous state in which the Mormon majority would elect its own officers, make its own laws, and exist under legalized Mormon rule. Being a man with a mind that, like Cecil Rhodes's, thought in no small units of space, Brigham Young added that he would like the western limit of his state to be the shores of the Pacific Ocean.

While the decision was awaited, Joseph Smith's successor cemented the Mormon power in his own dominions, and, by the stupidity of Congress, was allowed two years in which to do it. During all that time his "hierarchical and independent government" was permitted "to act its own will, with graceless conformity to such Federal laws as did not interfere with the plans of its leaders, exercising authority under the name of the 'State of Deseret,'"[1] a state that had no reality in law.

Washington at last thought it best to compromise. In 1850, during the administration of President Fillmore, it decided that the Mormons, far from being granted dominion to the shores of the Pacific, should be limited to their present enormous table-land. It christened this land Utah, refused statehood, and enrolled it as a territory. And then, as a sop to Cerberus, the President appointed Brigham Young territorial governor, superintendent of Indian affairs, and commander of the militia!

What followed? About what might have been expected to follow.

The government of Brigham Young, Federal

[1] *Illiteracy and Mormonism,* Henry Randall White, Ph.D., Statistician, Tenth U.S. Census.

Governor, became merely a mask for the government of Brigham Young, Mormon Prophet. "We find this illegal government in 1850, under cover of laws formed to suit the plans of men more astute than the members of Congress who blindly enacted them, cunningly overlaid by a 'territorial government,' beneath whose framework, as under the ribs of the wooden horse which decided the fate of Troy, were concealed and brought within the domain of recognized law—in the substance of the abridged code of Deseret—enemies of good government sufficient to account for the present condition of Utah."[1] From then forward, we see "schemes devised and executed with little opposition, by which the choicest acres of the territory are converted into the property of the Church, and held for distribution among, and, prior to this, as inducements for emigration of, converts to the Mormon faith. By evading the provisions of the Government land acts for the above and other purposes, through the perversion of laws relating to incorporated towns in every other way possible, we see the Mormons come into possession of an area vastly beyond the wants of their population, and including, as shrewdly pre-arranged for, so large a part of the arable soil of the territory as to threaten the ultimate closing of the door to an immigration not welcome."[2]

Some there nevertheless seem to have been that detected the advancing danger and tried, although vainly, to check it. The inquiries of the period are thus viewed by a hostile critic:

"We have heard of them (the Mormons) at intervals as claimants for a place within the broad pale of the

[1] *Illiteracy and Mormonism.*

[2] *Ibid.* The doctor's style is foggy, but his facts are clear.

Republican Government, and as the aspirants of the provisional organization which they demanded. . . . Now they reappear, in the report of the United States' judges to the President of the Republic, as indulging in the licence of Oriental manners under the laws of an Anglo-Saxon democracy, as utterly alienated in feeling from the American Government, obedient to a rule of conduct completely inconsistent with its principle, pillaging its public funds, outraging its officers, and cursing the memory of its immortal founder. . . . The Supreme Court of the United States, whose functions always follow and control those of executive authority, despatched judicial officers to Utah who had no original connection with it whatever. . . . It is difficult to see how the Central Government, consistently with its dignity, can avoid inflicting condign punishment on the Mormons. They appropriated to the purposes of their Church a fund which Congress had voted for the erection of public buildings. They arrested an official who was charged with the conveyance of public moneys, in the avowed design of confiscating them. They contemptuously refused to put in execution the enactments of Congress fundamentally applicable to the new territory. They selected the most public and solemn ceremonies as occasions for putting slights upon the judges. They openly disowned the United States Government, and execrated the name of George Washington."[1]

Of the grounds for some of these declarations, more hereafter. It suffices now to say that President Pierce was weakly unfavourable to Young as governor of Utah, and that, just before the American War of the Rebellion, President Buchanan, during one of the rare resolute moments of an irresolute mind, audaciously

[1] *The Morning Chronicle*, 28th January 1852.

appointed a "Gentile"[1] executive for the territory, thus, with this President's characteristic method of doing much to little purpose, officially deposing Young, while leaving intact that ruling body, the Church of which Young was the head.[2]

Before all this, however, the Mormons had found themselves in the course of the great "gold rush" of the middle years of the nineteenth century, had begun by suffering therefrom, and had ended by turning its dangers to their enrichment. Gold was discovered in California, and a stream of prospectors from the east began to cross the prairies, climb the mountains, and flow through Utah on their way to the mining camps of the Pacific Coast. Some of these argonauts might corrupt the faith of the Saints, some of them might seduce the people of Zion to forsake that city of the Lord for the flesh-pots of the gold-country, and some of them might remain and build up an anti-Mormon voting majority in Utah. This might be the first thin trickle of the fatal water through the plates of the holy ship. Young saw, approaching before his empire was fully ready to repel it, the advance of the eastern civilization, and he applied himself to meet it with that industrious genius which characterized his entire career, and was, in large part, founded on his knowledge of human frailties and his willingness to play thereon.

[1] In Mormondom all that are not Mormons are "Gentiles." An aged Jewish lady of the authors' acquaintance having removed to Salt Lake City very late in life, wrote in a letter to some eastern friends: "All my life I have been punctiliously orthodox. It seems, therefore, rather strange to be classed as a 'Gentile' at the age of eighty."

[2] Greig's *United States,* in other respects about the most futile history ever compiled of a country that has had even more futile historians than most.

Those Saints whose faith was so weak as to be in danger of corruption by impious argonauts he organized into militia companies and sent into outlying districts, ostensibly to fight the Indians, who, according to the Mormon's own bible, were a remnant of the Lost Ten Tribes of Israel. Those who, he feared, would be tempted to join in the westward quest of gold he retained by promises of greater riches, easier won, to be had at home. And those travellers who seemed at all likely to remain and thrive like weeds in the garden of the faith he harassed so successfully that few could long remain. Some of the more adventurous and less loyal Mormons slipped away, some of the more hardy and less gold-crazed argonauts remained. But, upon the whole, Brigham achieved, for the time, his purpose.

A war was waged and won with the Utahs and the Digger Indians. A proclamation against emigration was issued, backed by a divine revelation to the effect that "the Lord in His own time will permit the people to seek the metals." The Danites, or "Destroying Angels," pillaged often and sometimes slew the argonauts.[1] And, finally, the Saints were shown the commercial advantage, not of accompanying such travellers as were allowed to pass their way, but of selling to those travellers the provisions and supplies that they imperatively needed, and charging whatever prices the Saints had a mind to require.

So Zion grew. At the first, from the rags of their own clothing and equipment in their pilgrimage, the

[1] "Brigham hated these gold-seekers, fearing what their advent promised. By his order, the Destroying Angels 'got busy' and 'saved' as many gold-questing Gentile travellers as they could without exciting too much eastern interest and resentment."—Alfred Henry Lewis, "The Viper's Trail."

Saints had made paper for the publication of *The Deseret News.* Then from their own sheep they made their own woollen garments. Now cotton-growing was attempted and silk-culture was introduced. At last the wooden pegs that had fastened the first bridge over the Mormons' Jordan could be replaced by iron nails made in Mormon iron-foundries.

Yet the invaders could not for ever be suppressed or turned aside. The gold rush gradually increased transportation facilities, and the industrial supplies of the east, made in greater quantities and with less expense than the Mormon supplies, were carried into Salt Lake City and defied those of local manufacture. The Gentiles that came to sell these imports came as the representatives of great commercial enterprises that would not suffer in silence the "removal" of their agents, and the agents, because they had no tithes to pay, had an added advantage over their Mormon competitors. Tempted by the lure of lower prices, many of the faithful failed to heed their Church's injunction that they should buy only from their co-religionists, and the allegiance of several of the Saints, engaged in competition with the profane, began to waver.

At this period the leading Mormon merchants of Salt Lake were the Walker brothers. This firm, seeing the lower prices charged by their rivals and divining one of the causes, decreased their contributions to the Church to such an extent that awkward questions were asked, and a controversy between them and their masters followed. At its close the members of the firm apostatized, and the usual punishment of social ostracism and the withdrawal of Mormon trade would have accomplished its announced purpose in the economic destruction of the apostates, had not the apostates themselves discovered, by a timely chance, gold upon some of their property. They prospered in spite of Mormon prophecy and opposition, and for a while their prosperity in the face of the Church's open and violent disapproval gave other Mormons the courage to follow in their wake.

A new revelation was obviously indispensable to cope with this new situation, and the revelation was accordingly vouchsafed. Brigham Young's astute mind again triumphed. He told the merchants of the faith to combine in an enterprise to be conducted by the Church, a "trust" which, through combination and consolidation, could successfully meet the low prices of its Gentile rivals. This corporation, Zion's Co-operative Mercantile Institution, the control of the capital stock of which was to be held by officers of the Church, so succeeded that it now carries on a larger retail business than any other shop or store or combination of shops or stores in the state of Utah.

In the days when this institution first became necessary, the Mormons[1] had "spread themselves throughout all that broad region, the heart of which is now the state of Utah,"[2] and in that region the Mormon Church reigned supreme and unquestioned. One needs only to realize that the Church, in its turn, was the slave of the supreme and unquestioned Prophet, to understand the power that was vested in Brigham Young.

"The Saints," said *The Millennial Star*,[3] an official Mormon organ, "will reign on earth as kings and

[1] In 1850 the Mormon population of Utah was about 11,000.—*Illiteracy and Mormonism.*

[2] Alfred Henry Lewis.

[3] *The Millennial Star*, vol. xiv. p. 186.

priests of God": that was an article of their faith. But another article of their faith made them kings under an exacting emperor, for a favourite expression of Brigham Young's was this: "We follow the forms of a republic, but this is a monarchy"—and of that absolute government the at anyrate outspoken Mr Young was the absolute head.

About all this there is no opportunity for dispute. Young held his Church above the State, and he ruled his Church. Addressing his followers, he said:

"There is not a man upon the earth who could magnify even an earthly office without the power and wisdom of God to aid him. When Mr Fillmore[1] appointed me governor of Utah, I *proclaimed openly that my priesthood should govern and control that office. I am of the same mind to-day.* . . . That office (the governorship) shall be sustained and controlled by the power of the eternal priesthood of the Son of God, or *I will walk the office under my feet.* Hear it, both saint and sinner, and send it to the uttermost parts of the earth, that whatever office I hold for any government on this earth shall honour the government of Heaven, or I will not hold it."[2]

And Young's power extended over the property, the liberty, and the life of all the Saints. Again it is the Prophet himself that bears witness. In an address delivered in the Salt Lake Mormon Tabernacle on the 27th of March 1853, Young said:

"I will tell you a dream that I had last night. I dreamed that I was in the midst of a people who were dressed in rags and tatters. They had turbans upon their heads, and they were also hanging in tatters.

[1] *I.e.* President Fillmore.

[2] *Journal of Discourses,* vol. x. p. 42.

The rags were of many colours, and when the people moved they were all in motion. Their object appeared to be to attract attention. Said they to me, 'We are Mormons, Brother Young.' 'No, you are not,' I replied. 'But we have been,' said they; and they began to jump and caper about and dance, and their rags of many colours were all in motion to attract the attention of the people. I said, 'You are no Saints; you are a disgrace to them.' Said they, 'We have been Mormons.' By and by along came some acrobats, and they greeted them with, 'How do you do, sir? I am very sorry to see you.' They kept on that way for an hour. I felt ashamed of them, for they were in my eyes a disgrace to Mormonism. Then I saw two ruffians, whom I knew to be robbers and murderers, and they crept into a bed where one of my wives and children were. I said, 'You that call yourselves brethren, tell me, is this the fashion among you?' They said, 'But they are good. They are gentlemen.' With that I took my large bowie-knife that I used to wear as a bosom-pin at Nauvoo and cut one of their throats from ear to ear, saying, 'Go to hell across lots.' The other one said, 'You dare not serve me so.' I instantly sprang at him, seized him by the hair of the head, bringing him down; I cut his throat and sent him after his comrade. Then told them both if they would behave themselves they should yet live, but if they did not I would unjoint their necks. At this I awoke. I say, rather than apostates should flourish here, I will unsheath my bowie-knife and conquer or die. (Great commotion in the congregation and a simultaneous burst of feeling assenting to the declaration.) Now, you nasty apostates, clear out or judgment will be put to the line and righteousness to the plummet.

(Voices generally, 'Go it; go it!') If you say it is right, raise your hands. (All hands up.) Let us call upon the Lord to assist us in this and every good work."[1]

Young claimed to have derived from on high, as head of the Mormon Church, the power that he thus assumed, and there is sworn testimony that goes to show that the Mormons accepted his claim. In the Federal District Court for the Third Judicial District of Utah, in 1889, one witness, who had been an officer of the Church under Brigham, thus testified. He was James M'Guffie, a former Mormon Bishop, and we quote his words as recorded by the court stenographer:

"Am seventy-five years old . . . came from Liverpool to the United States in 1848, came to Utah in 1850 . . . in the fall of 1850 went with George Smith, John D. Lee, and some other (Mormon) notables . . . and located Parowan and organized Iron County (Utah)—got there in January 1851 and lived there until 1874. . . .

"Q. You knew Brigham Young?

"A. Well acquainted with him, nearly fifty years personally. . . .

"Q. You covenanted that you would obey the laws of the Church and its regulations and ordinances?

"A. The authority of the Church, one thing is a law one day, and another another day, and whatever the authority was—*it is a living priesthood; the man that is placed between God and the people, that is the law*. . . .

"Q. You entertain kindly feelings . . . toward the heads of the Mormon Church generally?

"A. Why, yes, they haven't injured me as individuals.

[1] *Journal of Discourses*, vol. i. p. 81.

I have no fellowship with them. I am not bound to hate them. I don't know as I hate any human being. I feel toward them that they are human beings like myself, and they are under a great delusion, as I was under it too, and I got out of it, and I pity them instead of hating them, and do them a good turn if I could. . . .

"Q. *You say Brigham Young was God on earth?*

"A. *God on earth. Yes.*

"Q. I suppose you know that as you know these other matters?

"A. Well, Heber[1] says, '*Brother Brigham is my God; I got no other God. He is God to this people as Moses was God to the children of Israel.* Moses he spake to the Almighty in Mount Sinai, and because he was there so long the reflection of God was on Moses' countenance, and he had to put a veil on and go and talk to the people, and *Brigham was just the same as Moses was, a God to the people.*'

"Q. *You mean by that a leader to the people, do you?*

"A. *No, he was a God to the people.*

"Q. *He was your God?*

"A. *Yes, everybody's God that lived. . . .*

"Q. *And you think that because he was your God he was everybody's God?*

"A. *He was every Saint's God.*

"Q. Do you mean to say that that was the doctrine of the Church?

"A. *Yes, sir; and I preached it myself, too . . . preached it in Europe and America.*"[2]

[1] Heber C. Kimball.

[2] Testimony taken from the proceedings of the District Court for the Third Judicial District of the Territory of Utah, in the matter of John Moore, *et al.*, to become citizens of the United States, at a

It was because he held this supreme power, and because he feared its ending at the hands of unbelieving invaders, that Brigham Young at last drew his sword upon the tribes of Christian philistines. It was because they believed in this power, and because they saw a threat to the economic advantages which it gave them, that the Mormons obeyed Brigham Young's orders and took up arms against the peaceable citizens of the United States. The result was the Mountain Meadows Massacre and the so-called Mormon War.

hearing commencing 14th November 1889, before the Hon. Thomas J. Anderson, judge; Frank E. M'Gurrin, court stenographer. In this same case we find another witness, former Bishop Cahoon, swearing: "The teachings of the leaders of the people were that the Kingdom of God was set up on earth and that they were bound and pledged to sustain and build it up in conflict with all other powers and governments. The King of that Kingdom that was set up on earth was the head of the Church. Brigham Young proclaimed himself King here in Salt Lake Valley before there was a house built, in 1847."

VI

FIRE AND SWORD—AND RICHES

THE Mormons had trusted too long to the inaccessibility of their dominion. Their treatment of citizens passing through Utah to the Pacific Coast had stirred popular anger in the east, and their flagrant insults to the judges of the Federal courts sent among them to do justice in these matters at last moved even Buchanan to action. Busy as was a portion of the President's Cabinet in strengthening the slave power, and occupied as it was in conspiring with that power to betray to it the national strength in the event of the South's rebellion, Buchanan experienced that moment of resolution heretofore referred to, and sent the Gentile governor to replace Brigham Young as the territorial executive of Utah.

This governor, Mr Cumming, was accompanied by other territorial officers, and a small military force was assigned to escort them to Great Salt Lake City. "At the same time pains were taken to assure the Mormons of the peaceful mission of the troops, and the commander of the force was instructed to avoid any collision with the Mormons, and only to act as a *posse comitatus* in enforcing obedience to the laws, in case he should be called on by the governor for that purpose."[1]

[1] "A Mormon Episode: The War of 1857," *Magazine of Western History*, Feb. 1890.

In order to impress upon the Mormons the peaceable nature of this expedition, as well as to purchase certain stores for the use of the troops on their arrival in Utah, Captain Van Vliet had been sent ahead of the official travellers, the still unconvinced Saints continuing to perpetrate "flagrant acts of rebellion" in the country to which he was going. The captain set out from Fort Leavonworth, in the north-western part of Kansas, and reached Salt Lake City after six months' journeying, going as fast as a half-dozen mule-wagons could go, and meeting many people *en route*, who assured him that he would not be allowed to enter Utah, and that, if he did enter it, he would do so at the risk of his life. These warnings, says Captain Van Vliet, "I treated . . . as idle talk, but they induced me to leave my wagons and escort at Ham's Fork, one hundred and forty-three miles this side of the city, and proceed alone." Nevertheless, the officer met with no molestation, and reached his destination unharmed. Immediately he called on Brigham Young, who treated him, as did all the other Mormon leaders, with hospitality and consideration.

But the Saints were firm. They made it clear to Van Vliet that they were determined to oppose the incursion of the United States troops. Young himself complained—and with reason—that the Church had been persecuted in Missouri and Illinois, and added that it had now in consequence "determined to resist all persecution at the commencement, and that the troops now on the march for Utah should not enter the Great Salt Lake Valley." Such stores as the approaching soldiers would require were to be found in abundance, but the faithful, acting under strict injunctions from the Church, would sell the Government not a pennyworth.

Our captain seems to have matched his hosts in

frankness. He admitted to Young and other Mormon leaders that it might be possible for them to prevent for a time the small force of troops then on its way from entering the narrow mountain passes; but he said that, if the Church showed such opposition, the Government would be sure soon to send out an overwhelming army. "We are aware," was the reply, "that such will be the case; but when those troops arrive they will find Utah a desert; every house will be burned to the ground, every tree cut down, and every field laid waste. We have three years' provisions on hand, which we will 'cache,' and then take to the mountains, and bid defiance to all the powers of the Government."[1] That Young and his people meant this, Van Vliet was assured when he attended a Sunday service of the Mormons and saw four thousand persons raise their hands in affirmative reply to a question asked by Elder Taylor, the preacher, as to whether they would be willing to burn their own houses upon the arrival of the invaders.

The invaders, meanwhile, were put under the command of Colonel Albert Sydney Johnson, who, later, fell on the Confederate side in the battle of Shiloh. Sending a small detachment in advance, Johnson crossed the Platte on 29th September 1857.

On the 9th of October, Colonel E. B. Alexander, at the head of the advance-guard, received, in Utah, some thirty miles north-west of Fort Bridger, letters from Daniel H. Wells, a Mormon that signed himself "Lieutenant-General commanding Nauvoo Legion," and from Brigham Young. Wells announced that he was in the field "*to aid in carrying out the instructions of Governor Young*"; while Young, in his letter,

[1] "A Mormon Episode."

maintained that he was still governor of the territory by virtue of the Act of Congress passed 9th September 1850, organizing the territory of Utah, "no successor having been appointed and qualified as provided by law," and he not having received notice of his removal by the President of the United States. The army of the Government went into winter quarters at Camp Scott, Utah!

Young, however, did not rest. Under the fiction that he had no official notification of his removal from the governorship, and that he was therefore in command of the territory and its militia, and had a right to resist invasion, he had issued a proclamation to his followers.

"We are invaded," he said, "by a hostile force, who are evidently assailing us to accomplish our overthrow and destruction. For the last twenty-five years we have trusted officials of the Federal Government, from constables and justices to judges, governors, and Presidents, only to be scorned, held in derision, insulted, and betrayed. Our houses have been plundered and then burned, our fields laid waste, our principal men butchered while under the pledged faith of the Government for their safety, and our families driven from their homes to find that shelter in the barren wilderness, and that protection among hostile savages, which were denied them in the boasted abodes of Christianity and civilization. . . . The issue which has thus been forced upon us compels us to resort to the great first law of self-preservation, and stand in our own defence: a right guaranteed to us by the genius of the institutions of our country, and upon which the government is based.

"Our duty to ourselves—and to our families—requires us not to tamely submit to be driven and slain without an attempt to preserve ourselves. Our duty to our country—our holy religion—our God—to freedom and liberty—requires that we should not quietly stand still and see those fetters forging around us which are calculated to enslave and bring us in subjection to an unlawful military despotism such as can only emanate, in a country of constitutional law, from usurpation, tyranny, and oppression."[1]

Nor did Brigham Young stop at the point of mere proclamation. On 4th October 1857 the Mormon forces, on Green River, captured and burned three Government supply-trains—seventy-five wagons loaded with tents and provisions for the Federal troops—and they carried away with them several hundred horses and mules. In his report dated 6th December 1858 the Secretary of War said of the Mormons at this time:

"They not only proclaimed martial law in that territory without a pretext, but against every principle of justice, of law, and of the Constitution. They embodied their whole force of effective men and kept them constantly drilled and under arms, hovering about our encampment, seeking a favourable moment, if one should ever offer itself, to cut off and destroy the whole command. They fortified the narrow mountain passes leading towards the town and chief settlements where they reside, and collected from remote neighbourhoods all the deluded people belonging to their sect. Every preparation which indicated a spirit of determined hostility, of rebellion, of treason and war, characterized these people in every action, and nothing but menace and defiance towards the United States authorities ever fell from the lips of their chief impostor or any of his confederates."[2]

[1] *Magazine of Western History*, February 1890.

[2] *Message and Documents*, 1858–1859, part ii.

And immediately after the armed activity of the Mormons had begun, this same Cabinet officer, John B. Floyd, ponderously indignant, had written:

"From the first hour they (the Mormons) fixed themselves in that remote and almost inaccessible region of our territory from which they are now sending defiance to the sovereign power,[1] their whole plan has been to prepare for a successful secession from the authority of the United States and a permanent establishment of their own. They have practised an exclusiveness unlike anything ever before known in a Christian country, and have inculcated a jealous distrust of all whose religious faith differed from their own. . . . This Mormon brotherhood has scarcely preserved the semblance of obedience to the authority of the United States for some years past; nor at all, indeed, except as it might confer some direct benefit upon themselves, or contribute to circulate public money in their community. Whenever it suited their temper or caprice, they have set the United States' authority at defiance. Of late years a well-grounded belief has prevailed that the Mormons were instigating the Indians to hostilities against our citizens and were exciting amongst the Indian tribes a feeling of insubordination and distrust."

The Secretary went on to speak of the neglect of the Government to face the Mormon problem. "This forbearance," he continued, "might still be prolonged, and the evils rife amongst them (the Mormons) be allowed to work out their own cure, if this community occupied any other theatre, isolated and remote from the seats of civilization, than the one they now possess.

[1] The Mormons even defied the law that tried to punish the Mountain Meadows assassins.

But, unfortunately for these views, their settlements lie in the great pathway which leads from our Atlantic states to the new and flourishing communities growing up upon our Pacific seaboard. They stand a lion in the path; not only themselves defying the military and civil authorities of the Government, but encouraging, if not exciting, the nomad savages who roam over the vast unoccupied regions of the continent to the pillage and massacre of peaceful and helpless emigrant families traversing the solitudes of the wilderness. The rapid settlement of our Pacific possessions; the rights in those regions of emigrants unable to afford the heavy expenses of transit by water and isthmus; the facility and safety of military, commercial, political, and social intercommunication between our eastern and western populations and states, all depend upon the prompt, absolute, and thorough removal of a hostile power besetting this path midway of its route, at a point where succour and provisions should always be found, rather than obstruction, privation, and outrage."[1]

Meanwhile—a thing apart from the struggles of the Mormon militia against the Federal troops—in 1857 the supposedly Mormon attacks on civilian non-Mormons desirous of settling in Utah, or even of only passing through that territory to the farther west, reached their climax in the wholesale butchery of an entire caravan.[2] That caravan paused to rest at Mountain Meadows, a lonely spot near Parowan, the chief town of Iron County, Utah, a Mormon settlement. An attack was made by Mormons and Indians, or by Mormons disguised as Indians, and a sort of American St Bartholomew Massacre followed.

1 *Message and Documents,* 1857–1858, part ii.

2 Alfred Henry Lewis.

The Mormons have since protested that the murderers were Indians acting on their own responsibility, or that, if there were any Saints engaged in the affair, those Saints were renegades from the faith and persons of no standing in the Church. The charge of the anti-Mormons, on the contrary, is that the massacre was committed by Mormons, under the direction of the Mormon Danites, or "Destroying Angels," and at the command of responsible officials of the Mormon Church acting for Brigham Young, the Mormon Prophet. What seems most likely is that the Church secretly, but officially, actively, and cold-bloodedly, encouraged such massacres in general as a means of turning back, or at least diverting, the westward-moving stream of dangerous emigration; that certain Mormon officers in this case acted on that general encouragement; that the affair was larger than the Church approved of, because large killings were apt to attract the vengeance of the Federal Government; but that it was nevertheless to all intents and purposes an official Mormon expedition, for which the Mormon Church was responsible; and that, once it was concluded, that Church assumed the responsibility of harbouring its leaders, protecting them as much as it dared from the law, and continuing to them its favours, both ecclesiastical and temporal. To determine this, let us again consult the records of that case in the United States Circuit Court from which we quoted in our last chapter.[1]

The former bishop, James M'Guffie, it will be recalled, testified that he came from England to

[1] Testimony taken from the proceedings in the District Court for the Third Judicial District of the Territory of Utah, in the matter of John Moore, *et al.*, etc. etc.

America and settled with other prominent Mormons in Parowan, Iron County, Utah. He continued:

"Parowan is near the scene of the Mountain Meadows Massacre. I seen them people[1]—the presiding officer, the Bishop of the Mormon Church, wouldn't allow them to go through the town of Parowan,—persons were sent in there to pass them to the north. No, sir, they wouldn't allow that band of emigrants to pass through the settlement where you lived, they had to go past the north wall:—there was a mud wall six feet at the base, twelve feet high. I was superintendent of construction on that wall.

"Q. Who objected to their going through the settlement?

"A. Why, the authorities there,—I mean Wm. H. Dame; he was the Colonel of the Iron Battalion, and I was an officer of that battalion, and there was Bishop Lewis; he was a Bishop over the temporal affairs of them in it, and Wm. H. Dame was what they called spiritual head of the Church—presiding officer. *They were responsible to Brigham Young.*"[2]

The former Bishop went on to show the Church's responsibility for the massacre by telling of the ceremony he previously had gone through at the hands of the Church in Salt Lake City.[3] He said that President[4] Brigham Young, Heber Kimball, and others officiated, and he continued:

[1] *I.e.* the subsequently murdered travellers.

[2] Testimony taken from the proceedings in the District Court for the Third Judicial District of the Territory of Utah, as previously referred to.

[3] This Mormon ceremony, called "Going through the Endowment House," or "Receiving the Endowments," will be treated of more explicitly later.

[4] *I.e.* President of the Mormon Church.

"There was a company came from Parowan and we had a recommend from the Bishop and we had the receipts for our tithing, we were considered in good standing and worthy to receive our endowments, so that we might associate in the circles with the brethren. There might have been twelve or fourteen; they were all married with the exception of Peggy Jane Meeks, and she was a single girl. After we got our washings and anointings they began to instruct us, and they required us to take an oath with uplifted hands to do all in our power, and to teach our children and our children's children to do all in their power to destroy or uproot the American Government, for the reason they hadn't punished the murderers of Joseph and Hyrum Smith.

"Q. What was the substance of the oath that you took by which you agreed to yield obedience to this priesthood?

"A. We took an oath that we would obey the priesthood in all things; we were members of the Kingdom of God; and the Government of the United States—we were to be their enemies on account of them not avenging the blood of Joseph and Hyrum Smith. We were to obey the priests in all things, temporal and spiritual, politically and socially.

"There was three organized bands of murderers in the territory in those days. The leaders of them, Bill Hickman was one, Porter Rockwell was the other, and the other was Lot Huntington. The names of the organizations,—one was 'Blood Atoners,' another was 'Destroying Angels,' and the third was the 'Danites,' and they had the work apportioned out to them by President Young; he was God on earth; he got the word of God and he gave it to the people.

"Q. Now, Mr M'Guffie, you remember the Mountain Meadows Massacre?

"A. Oh, well; I remember it and knew the men that were in that massacre.

"Q. You knew John D. Lee[1] at that time?

"A. Personally acquainted with him.

"Q. You knew W. H. Dame?

"A. Yes, he was my next-door neighbour.

"Q. You knew Brigham Young?

"A. Well acquainted with him, nearly fifty years personally.

"Q. You continued your acquaintance with him after that massacre?

"A. Yes, I left the Church twenty-three years ago last August.

"Q. But your acquaintance with Brigham Young, John D. Lee, and with W. H. Dame continued for some few years after the Mountain Meadows Massacre?

"A. Yes, sir, until 1866.

"Q. Do you know whether or no, after that massacre, John D. Lee continued to be on terms of friendship with President Young?

"A. Oh, yes, and got more wives; had two sealed to him the very year he committed that atrocious murder; as well acquainted with John D. Lee as I could be with any man.

"Q. Was he a member of the legislature?

"A. Yes, sir, and Wm. H. Dame too. . . ."

"Q. What I want to get at is whether you know, of your own knowledge, that after that massacre John D. Lee continued to be on terms of friendship with the President of the Church?

[1] John D. Lee was the Mormon official charged with leading the assassins. Wm. H. Dame was one of his lieutenants.

"A. Oh, yes, and got two more women after that: got two at a lick—an English girl; she died.

"Q. Now, I understand you to say that you took an obligation to obey the priesthood in all matters?

"A. Yes, in all things.

"Q. Was there any penalty attached to your disobedience to the priesthood in that ordeal through which you passed?

"A. There was nothing further than that the throat was to be cut, and the belly to be ripped out; I think that was plenty enough.

"Q. Do you know William Laney?

"A. Yes, I knew him well, he lived about five rods below my house at the time of the Mountain Meadows Massacre.

"Q. Do you know of his having furnished that band of emigrants with supplies?

"A. Yes, Laney recognized in the company a young man named Harris as being the son of a man that had been a great friend to him and treated him kindly when he was on a Mormon mission in Tennessee, and Laney invited the young man to supper at his house,—and invited him to come and get his breakfast, and the young man, after he got his breakfast, saw the onions growing in the dooryard and said he would like to have a few of them, and Laney said: 'Well, take all you want and welcome,' and he took them; and then Dame sent Barney Carter, he was one of the 'Destroying Angels,' there, and he tore a picket out of the fence and hit Laney side of the head, and the man has never been sound in his mind since, just because he let the onions go to the man; it was Laney's only offence.

"Q. What position do you say Dame held in the Church at that time?

"A. He was Colonel of the Iron Battalion, and he was a High Priest of the Mormon Church of the branch of Parowan; that was in 1857. . . .

"Q. How do you know that John D. Lee had three wives that year?

"A. Well, he had been visiting with me and sitting at my table, and was eating as a man would eat at a friend's table, and he cried like a child, and said he would be a scapegoat for this thing, this massacre—was only a tool to accomplish the thing, and the whole country was turned against him; nobody would receive him into the house when he came to Parowan, only me and my wife. I never believed it was on his shoulders. I knew better than that. He was only one among many."

Continuing, the witness said:

"I had a blanket, and three or four of them had dirks or butcher knives, and he told my son Joe to go and tell his father to come out. I had a strong presentiment not to go out. Afterwards Barney Carter said that night they were sent to murder me for talking.

"Q. You knew nothing about it except as it was told you by others?

"A. Barney Carter himself told me.

"Q. Told you what?

"A. He was appointed to murder me, and told me to clear out. He got tired of Mormonism and went to San Bernardino.

"Q. I suppose he is out of the territory?

"A. He is in San Bernardino, or was when I saw him last. I was down there in 1866.

"Q. Did the friendship between Lee and Brigham Young continue after that massacre?

"A. Oh, yes.

"Q. Did the friendship between Lee and Dame continue after the massacre?

"A. Well, no, I couldn't say it did. Dame wasn't there when the massacre was—when the people were murdered, but he came the next day, and when he saw the mountain strewn with over one hundred and twenty human beings, he cried and he said to Isaac Haight, 'I never thought there was so many people as this,' and says he, 'I will have to report it to President Young.' 'Well, now,' says Haight, 'stand up to it like a man,' and says he, 'You were the man that gave us orders to do it.'"

To return, however, to the open war between the Mormon militia and the Federal troops. The condition of affairs in Utah spurred the sluggish Administration of Buchanan to action. Reinforcements were raised, and by the spring of 1858 the little army in Utah included 5608 officers and men.[1]

In its winter quarters at Camp Scott during the preceding months of bitter weather, activity was greatly handicapped by the lack of mules and horses. Many of the draught-mules had died from the cold and exposure, and the horses requisitioned to take their places were largely broken from overwork. The regimental quartermaster, Lieutenant Burns, reported to his chief:

[1] Yet in its issue of 14th January 1858, *The New York Evening Post* asked: "Is not the wisest and most statesmanlike course we can pursue, to withdraw our troops, repeal the Territorial law of Utah, and restore the inhabitants to the unorganized and lawless state from which they were taken by the Territorial Act of 1850? They will then have no laws but of their own choosing, and no enemies but for their own fighting. We shall be released from an expensive war; from the responsibilities of a distant and expensive government of no earthly advantage to us, and for which nobody thanks us."

"The teamsters drove teams for the first time, and were required to break in young and wild mules, which resulted, in many cases, in broken limbs or dead animals. Nearly all of them[1] lacked fitness or interest for the service, experience in its details, regularity and industry in its duties, and honesty in its responsibilities."

In brief, the invasion was a farce. To keep it up, Captain R. B. Marcy, of the Fifth Infantry, had been, on 27th November, despatched with only forty men through the dreadful winter and across dangerous ground, all the way to New Mexico to procure more mules for the use, or companionship, of the invaders. Marcy's men suffered severely. Their route lay directly across the mountains through the Couchetopa Pass, and two hundred miles of it was through deep snow, hard packed, where a way had to be broken. Not until the 1st of January did the expedition reach Taos, its destination, and not until the 11th of June 1858 did it return to Camp Scott, accompanied by an escort requisitioned from the military commander in New Mexico, because the Mormons had threatened to attack the column and stampede its animals.

The Mormons, indeed, had threatened a good deal. In March, Brigham Young had once more declared that the faithful would burn their houses and seek a new resting-place. "If we vacate the ground," he said, "that may satisfy them; but if they undertake to come before we are ready, we will send them to their long home."

Just what his purpose was in all this sort of bragging and threatening is not clear; but it is certain that, if he sought only to delay the approach of the soldiery until he could make some secret bargain with the civil authori-

[1] Mr Burns means the drivers, not the draught-mules.

ties, he at anyrate obtained the desired delay. For the "war" that had begun as a farce ended in opera-bouffe. The Federal military "began preparations for more active service";[1] but President Buchanan's Gentile nominee for territorial governor, Mr Cumming, the man that the military had started out to conduct to Salt Lake, grew tired of waiting for his escort, went into Zion without it, and was received with perfect quiet and courtesy!

The first thing that the gallant Colonel Johnson learned of this event seems to have occurred in April, when he received the news from the new governor himself. The letter was addressed from "The Executive Office, Great Salt Lake City." It announced that the writer had arrived safely, had been on all sides recognized as the governor of Utah, and, instead of violence or even insults, had been "universally greeted with respectful attentions."

Brigham Young, who had at first fled to Antelope Island in the Great Salt Lake,[2] had later, after suing for peace, returned to his capital, called on the usurper, accepted the notification of his own replacement, and offered to assist the new executive to the extent of his power.

By the end of May, Mormon opposition had vanished, and on the 21st of that month Mr Cumming wrote:

"After a careful investigation, I am gratified in being able to inform you that I believe there is at present no organized armed force of its inhabitants in any part of this territory, with the exception of a small party subject to my orders, in or near Echo Cañon."

1 *Magazine of Western History.*

2 Alfred Henry Lewis.

Meanwhile, on the 6th of April, President Buchanan, by proclamation, had offered "a free and full pardon" to all the inhabitants of Utah who should submit to the laws; and so, on the 14th of June, Governor Cumming proclaimed in the name of the President that, "whereas the proffered pardon was accepted, with the prescribed terms of the proclamation," all persons who had submitted to the laws were "freely and fully pardoned for all treasons and seditions heretofore committed."

Two days later, when they were no longer needed, the troops were put in motion for the Salt Lake Valley. The inhabitants feared depredations, and the strongest assurance by Colonel Johnson could not quiet their fears; but on the 26th of June the army—it must have been a rather shamefaced army—arrived at Salt Lake City.

"I found the city abandoned," wrote Colonel Johnson, "except by a few persons engaged in guarding the property and keeping the gardens in good order. I understand that the citizens will return in a few days." The people had, in fact, gone to Provo, about fifty miles south of Salt Lake City, but, upon assurance from Colonel Johnson and the commissioners that had been sent out by the President, they returned to their homes. "It was the intention of the people," the commissioners reported, "if a peaceable adjustment had not been made, to have burned their homes, destroyed the growing crops, and retreated to the mountains on the approach of the enemy. With this view they had removed their women and children and their household and personal property from the city and settlements north of it to the southern part of the territory, and had stored large quantities of grain and provisions in the mountains." The soldiers went into camp at Camp Floyd in Cedar Valley, thirty-six miles south of Salt Lake City. Some of them were detached on other service or discharged, and only the remainder went into permanent quarters here.

That was the end of it. In his next annual message to Congress President Buchanan said: "The present condition of the territory of Utah, when contrasted with what it was one year ago, is a subject for congratulation. It was then in a state of open rebellion, and, cost what it might, the character of the Government required that this rebellion should be suppressed and the Mormons compelled to yield obedience to the Constitution and the laws." Thus did an outraged Government avenge its wrongs.

The rebellion of the Southern States followed close upon the heels of the "Mormon War," and, luckily for Zion, gave the Saints four years in which, since the Government was too much otherwise engaged to think about them, the faithful had leisure to accustom themselves to the new order and to devise ways for its circumvention. The leaders began to consider the possibility of regaining by friendliness what they had lost by force; they recalled their earlier dreams of statehood; they saw how, by acquiring political strength, they could maintain their territory in independence; and they realized that, to control legislation, they must first become industrially and then financially strong. It was at about this time—in 1861, in fact—that sugar-making was first attempted in Utah, the requisite implements being imported from France and carried across the prairies in wagons. Other commercial projects followed, and the plans for them continued to mature, all the while that the rest of the Union's commerce and industry was in the chaos occasioned by the War of the Rebellion. The Saints went steadily and quietly ahead; whatever the issue of the struggle between the North and South, they must be ready to face it.

But four years was too brief a time for maturing plans of such magnitude. Robert E. Lee's mad advance into Pennsylvania failed, Gettysburg was fought, the back of the Confederacy was broken, and, finally, Grant's superior generalship ended the war before the Mormons were ready for its conclusion. Even the throes of the Reconstruction Period did not suffice the Saints. Washington again had its attention called to Utah. There succeeded a squabble between the Mormons and the Federal courts; the execution of John D. Lee as the man directly responsible for the Mountain Meadows Massacre; the legislation against polygamy; the indictment,[1] but ultimate escape, of Brigham Young, charged with the polygamy of which he was openly guilty; the miserable death of Brigham;[2] the advance of John Taylor into the leadership of the Church; and then the passage of the Edmunds law, so called from the United States senator that fathered it, which declared the Mormon institution a menace to the nation, drove Taylor into hiding,[3] reduced his successor, Wilford Woodruff, to temporary helplessness, and confiscated the already vast property of the Church.

[1] 1871.

[2] Alfred Henry Lewis says Young "perished miserably, hiding under a porch, driven mad by what evil ghosts had come to haunt and taunt him" ("The Viper's Trail"); but Mr Lewis is sometimes too picturesque in his conclusions.

[3] *New York Herald*, 4th December 1887.

VII

FROM WAR TO CRAFT

It has been generally supposed that the fundamental causes of the anti-Mormon agitation of 1870–1887 were purely moral, and that the Edmunds law was wholly the legislative expression of a shocked national conscience. Unfortunately for the easy method of history-making, this is incorrect. Hatred of polygamy—and polygamy itself had been at its height employed for economic reasons—was not the origin of the attack upon Mormonism. The man that framed the drastic law and hundreds of good people that insisted on its passage were doubtless sincere in their motives: they wanted Zion robbed of its power because they thought that polygamy was a sin. But the origin of that attack on Mormonism was economic.[1]

[1] Even before 1870 the economic differences between Saint and Gentile had moved the latter to some agitation against polygamy, and as a consequence, on 1st July 1862, Congress passed "An Act to Punish and Prevent the Practice of Polygamy in the Territories of the United States." Lincoln's Utah Governor, Harding, called this Act to Utah's attention in his message, but the Legislature never so much as printed the message. The Mormons raised the cry that the Government was trying to interfere with the Mormon religion. Nothing was, at that time, accomplished by the Act, and when, later, endeavours were made to enforce it, the Saints obstructed it and evaded it in every possible manner.

"Modern Mormonism in Utah," says Murray Schick,[1] "dates from a mining and real-estate boom in the latter part of the 'eighties. At Park City, Utah, the most productive silver mine in the world was developed. Its success gave a great impetus to mining in all parts of the territory. The towns of Brigham and Tintic hummed with life. Sleepy old Mormon communities were stirred into new activity by the spectacle of riches wrung so readily from the ground.

"In the wake of an army of miners, prospectors, engineers, and smeltermen came a camp-following of brokers, speculators, real-estate dealers, merchants, and investors. Over night the little band of pioneer Gentiles in Utah, consisting largely of carpet-baggers, was swelled from a negligible factor to a force capable of aggressive action. The mines, besides bringing re-inforcements, furnished money to finance a Gentile campaign."

For the Gentiles at once felt the necessity of organizing a political opposition to the Mormons. The Mormons were in possession, and could, and did, combine to make the Gentiles' progress as slow as might be; the Gentiles were backed even then by more or less eastern capital, and could, and did, unite to push the Mormons to the wall. It was not Mormonism and orthodox Christianity that were at war: it was a commercial struggle in which the Mormons happened to be united because they were the first on the ground, and were, besides, members of a common organization—any other sort of organization would have served as well; an economic struggle in which the non-Mormons were united because they were thus met by a common enemy, and were, besides,

[1] "Mormon and Mammon," in *The Coming Nation,* 1911.

people from states where Mormons were unfamiliar figures—any eastern states would have done for the purpose. The mass of the Mormons regarded these interlopers in Utah precisely as the fathers of these interlopers had regarded the Mormons' fathers in New York and Illinois. Each side mistrusted the other, as one ignorant stranger always mistrusts another. Each act of opposition led to reprisal, and each reprisal led to more opposition. A quarter of a century before, the matter would have been decided by an appeal to arms; now the economic battle was waged in commerce, and from commerce spread to politics, which commerce controls.

The Mormon Church, diverted from its original purpose of becoming an independent temporal kingdom, had devoted all its attention toward securing that sort of kingdom's equivalent in industrial and financial power. It was in great part a business institution; it imposed as a religious duty upon its members the necessity of patronising exclusively the Mormon tithing-marts and those Mormon stores miscalled "co-operative,"[1] which had amazingly increased in size and number since the apostasy of the Walker brothers brought them into existence; and it possessed a large treasury that was always looking for investment in promising ventures and that was a tower of strength in any competitive war. All this, moreover, gave Zion control in Utah politics. Federal offices were filled by appointment from Washington, but all the places within the gift of the voters, who were chiefly Mormons, were given to the Saints. The only Gentile that was favoured was he that would make an ante-election com-

[1] It was the Mormon Church that profited by these "co-operative" stores, not the Mormon purchaser.

pact with the Mormon hierarchy. These were the Gentiles' complaints.

The Mormon, also, complained against the Gentile's business methods, some of which gave the Gentile an advantage, because the Mormon's religion interfered with his imitation of them. In the face of the new invasion of Gentiles, tithe-paying became more and more a business handicap to the Saint in whatever way he earned his living: the Mormon lawyer, mill-owner, farmer, unskilled labourer, owned one-tenth less of his income than the Gentile unskilled labourer, farmer, mill-owner, or lawyer, and so the Gentile could sell his wares or his work cheaper than his rival. The Mormon Church, because of this, feared desertions from its ranks; it saw a clear threat to its dream of power, and it encouraged its people to fight the invaders and to free the land.

At the start, therefore, polygamy was not an issue, or was, at most, a merely secondary issue. The early Gentiles, among themselves, generally looked upon it as a joke, a rather ridiculous characteristic of a peculiar and therefore inferior race. If it did anything, it kept Utah in the eastern eye, advertised it, nothing more.[1]

But now the Mormon Church suddenly made a move that turned its adversaries' attention to polygamy as a means of exciting anti-Mormon propaganda and securing a Gentile victory in Utah. The elected authorities of the territory, being Mormon, were constantly thwarting the appointive Federal authorities, who were Gentiles, and the Federal authorities were missing no opportunity to thwart the elective, so that the administration of justice was almost hopelessly disorganized. Both sides recognizing this, and the country at large—

[1] "Mormon and Mammon."

now drawn closer by the extension of railway and telegraph—recognizing it, the Mormon Church determined to push its claims to Federal recognition to autonomous statehood, which would mean practically the complete control of Utah by the Mormons and the realization of what had become the Church's fondest hope. To this, of course, the Gentiles in Utah violently objected, for they knew that it would result in an order of things that would place them at a dire disadvantage in their economic struggle against the Saints. If the Federal Government was to interfere at all and would not interfere in their favour, then the Gentiles wanted it to interfere to leave matters as they stood, with at least the Federal offices of the territory in the Utah Gentiles' hands, and with the industrial field a little—because of the tithe system—favourable to the Gentiles. In order, therefore, to excite the rest of the country to their support to such an end, the Utah Gentiles opposed statehood for Utah on the ground that should Congress grant it to the territory, that would, in effect, be giving the sanction of the United States Government to polygamy in at least one sovereign state of the Union.

For only by arousing the country at large against polygamy could the country at large be at all aroused against the Mormons. As Schick well points out,[1] had the Utah Gentiles "appealed for help on the ground that the Mormons would not buy from them, the Methodist merchant in Indiana would have said: 'I have troubles of my own; lots of the Baptists here patronize that Baptist merchant across the street'"; and had they complained that the Mormons would not have elected them to office, the politicians would

[1] "Mormon and Mammon."

have answered: "Well, things aren't much different with us; in certain states certain sects always vote in mass for candidates of their own religion."

But polygamy was a red rag that, properly and persistently shaken, would infuriate the bull of popular indignation. Open polygamy was an anachronism in the United States sufficient to fix the attention, bizarre enough to hold the eye. In our modern civilization, where casual polygamy is the rule, but where it must usually be practised secretly, its secret practitioners are quick to resent what naturally means to them the undeserved good fortune of the man that practises it openly and without annoyance. Polygamy, moreover, so shocked the humanitarian that large employers, who unthinkingly made prostitutes of their women employees by granting them only a starvation wage, could be reduced to tears or roused to rage over the sufferings, actual or fancied, of "plural wives." A crusade on polygamy would give the politician the desired chance of the demagogue; the chance to win votes by an appeal to morals. It was an opportunity for electioneering eloquence and Congressional pose. It was at that time, before the Mormon Church had gained its place among the trusts, a safe crusade, because it not only did not interfere with any vested interests outside of Utah, but diverted popular thought from the spreading power of the great combinations of capital. Although Congress could not enact laws forbidding voluntary tithing, Mormon co-operative stores, or individual freedom of trade, it could forbid polygamy in a territory, and it could be made to do this both for the reasons before given and because—and this is of nearly the chief importance—in the United States the sects that support monogamy as an article of faith are powerful controllers of public opinion and the ballot: no candidate in any state save a Mormon state would dare to ask election on a declaration of principles that those sects as a body and as a common matter of faith opposed.

The country was duly fired. The newspapers and periodicals were filled with exposures of the horrors of Mormon polygamy. Every pulpit thundered; every politician denounced. Although Zion, realizing, as the mass of its opponents did not, that this was an economic war, fought desperately all attempts to legislate against its financial operations, the great anti-Mormon Bill was passed in 1887, and Congress instructed the Attorney-General to begin legal proceedings for dissolving the Church corporation and confiscating all its property in excess of the $50,000, of which, under the Act of 1862, no Church could be robbed.

What Congress enacted, the tribunals of appeal upheld. It was decided that no sect could lawfully hold property for any but charitable and religious purposes. All the cattle, crops, land, stocks and bonds of the Mormon Church were seized by the civil authorities sent from Washington, and were turned into the custody of the United States courts acting as receivers. That is why when in the United States to-day a railway president asks a Socialist what the Socialist's party, once it is in power, will do with the railway president's railway, the Socialist can logically reply: "Only what your parties set the legal precedent for doing in the case of the Mormons—we shall confiscate it."

During the first week of December 1887 the practical work was begun in Salt Lake City. The Tithing House and its grounds, the Gardo House,[1] the His-

[1] Official residence of the President of the Mormon Church.

torian's Office and lot,[1] its books and safes, the wagons, carriages, horses and cattle, the offices and shops known as Temple Block, the Endowment House, even the Tabernacle and the Temple, were all surrendered with a merely formal protest.[2] A Deputy United States marshal took up quarters in the Lion House and Beehive House of Brigham Young; and on the door of Amelia Palace, the ornate house that Brigham had built for Amelia Folsom, his favourite wife, there was hung a sign offering the place for rent and directing those interested to "apply to the receiver, F. H. Dyer, U.S. marshal." The Tabernacle was then leased to the Church for religious services, and the Mormons worshipped in a rented church.

The blow was indeed heavy, for, though the Church as a corporation was rich, its members were, as individuals, in those days by no means wealthy. Few of them, it is true, suffered want, and most of them owned the houses in which they lived, with a bit of land about each; but, save for the very few that had accumulated what were then considered good-sized fortunes, the possessions of the average Mormon would have brought less than £75 in the open market. The Mormons were comfortable because they were industrious and thrifty. They were taught that economy was a virtue and that wastefulness and idleness were sins, whereas the saving of their substance was a means of grace. Half the sermons were exhortations to thrift; the science of making and saving had been reduced to a fine point by the foremost elders from the days of Joseph Smith, until the plain, hard-working New England farmer, Wilford Woodruff, filled Smith's place. Nevertheless,

[1] This was the general office of the Church.

[2] *New York Herald*, 4th December 1887.

the dissolution of the Church as a corporation left the Mormons poor indeed.

Peculiarly enough, the country at large thought that it also left them submissive. *The New York Herald* expressed the general impression when it said:[1]

"The Mormon submission to the authority which they have resisted so long, and with such stubbornness, is so complete that many are disposed to doubt its honesty, and are disposed to regard the seeming compliance as a clever trick, intended to deceive and bamboozle until the leader can gain some point, when they will quickly recover the ground lost. This supposition may be correct, but there is nothing to indicate that such is the case, while there is much to suggest the contrary view of the matter. Whatever may be the ideas and motives or aims of the leaders, the masses are beyond question acting and talking honestly and in sincerity.

"There is no trick with them. Instead, they are heartily glad that the change is taking place.

"It is a remarkable fact that while this change of popular sentiment and deportment has been going on the leading Churchmen have maintained almost complete silence. The two or three times when they have spoken through addresses, or 'epistles,' as they are pleased to call them, in the official newspaper organ of the Church, they have advised to conservatism and peace, counselling the people to do right and place their trust in the Lord. That the 'bosses' are acting in harmony with their own advice and in keeping with the peace sentiment is proven by their ready compliance with the order of the court commanding them to surrender the property of the Church.

[1] 4th December 1887.

"But it matters little, except to themselves individually, what the conduct, the wishes, and the intentions of the Apostles are. The Government has the upper hand in the long contest, and it obtained it when it grasped the source and well-spring of the Church power—its wealth. By the time the suit has been tried and the final judgment rendered there will be no Mormon problem to annoy the nation and worry the long-distressed people of Utah. The peace movement now asserting itself will have eliminated the 'problem' features of the controversy before the courts can adjust financial questions which have been raised."

This fatuous hope was never realized. Mormonism was not beaten. It had, in fact, only begun to fight. And now at least one portion of its fight has been won.

For the heads of the Church were far-seeing men and clever exploiters; they had to be both to become heads of the Church. They perceived the course that modern capitalism was following; they considered the natural resources of their own territory, and saw that those resources would be needed by the growing combinations of capital that would soon control the United States; they recognized that, if they could own the resources, the big combinations would require them as allies and would be willing to offer for their friendship political influence that would give to Utah statehood; and so they set about, not only to regain what the courts had taken from them, but also to increase that, and so first win sovereign power for a Mormon Utah and next, gradually, become so much a growing factor in the capitalistic control of the entire nation that the spread of the Church's dominion would be limited only by the boundaries of credulity upon the one side and, upon the other, by capitalism.[1]

And the first step proved to be beautifully simple. The Church learned it from the great trusts with which the Church intended soon to ally itself. The trusts had found a way of evading the law whereby a corporation that might not own something in one capacity might legally hold that same thing in another capacity. Zion at once played Pooh-Bah. It mustered the pennies of its membership. It demonstrated that, though the Mormon Church could not as a Church own what the escheatment proceedings had taken from it, there was nothing on the statute-books, not even the famous Edmunds law itself, that could prevent the President of the Mormon Church from owning all this and more as an individual. Within an amazingly brief time the President of the Mormon Church did own it all; within an amazingly brief time he proceeded to acquire more. The Church continued to be a dealer in revelations, and became as well a dealer in "railroads, sugar, salt, and salvation."[2] To-day the Mormon Presi-

[1] The alarmists among the critics go even further in their interpretation of the plans of Zion's leaders. Says Alfred Henry Lewis:

"Having had all they would of actual war under Brigham, the Mormons—growing wiser with what tamer souls succeeded him as 'prophets, seers, and revelators'—decided to do by gold and stealth what they dared not forcibly attempt by ways of lead and steel. They would not surrender their original design of dominating the country; only their method of attack was to be changed. They would compact the Church into a political machine, and overcreep the country at the ballot-box; they would invest the Church millions in our 'protected' industries and banks, and overcreep the commerce of the country with their gold. When they had secured victory on fields of politics and trade, they would be the nation's master." ("The Viper's Trail.")

[2] "Mormon and Mammon."

dent is owner of these growing interests as "trustee in trust," and that ownership does not descend from father to son: it descends from a dying President to the President that succeeds him.[1] The great anti-Mormon legislation was as much farce as the great Mormon War.

The nullifying of the action of Congress and the Federal courts had, however, cost some time and much money, and, while the leaders of Zion were busy mending their fences, the unbelievers had increased in Utah in numbers and power. The Church, having just then other uses for its dollars, could not spare money for political purposes; it could not give its attention to politics; so that several political skirmishes were won by the Gentiles. These victories reached a climax in 1889 in Salt Lake City and Ogden. Then Mormonism once more took a hand and resumed the political rulership of Utah with the fixed purpose of attaining statehood and adding to the Union a Mormon state.

Until then there had been in the territory only two political parties of importance. These were not—as throughout the rest of the Union in those days before the rise of the Socialist party—the Republicans and Democrats. They were the Mormon and anti-Mormon.[2] The former wanted statehood, for the reasons already indicated and in order to escape from non-resident government; the latter opposed statehood, for the reasons already indicated and because the terri-

[1] In the Mormon Church the President is President for life.

[2] The anti-Mormon party was called the Liberal. The Mormons called their party the People's Party; but this Utah People's Party is not to be confused with that radical political party of the same name, once powerful in the west of the United States.

torial government gave offices to the Gentiles. Now the Mormon leaders decided upon a master-stroke: they dissolved their party; they told their people to support either the Republican or Democratic party's principles as each individual chose; and the leaders themselves so divided, thus arranging that the Church would have powerful friends in each camp. Then, realizing that, since the nation had once roused itself so much against polygamy, the price of statehood must be the at least official abolition of polygamy, the President of the Church, Wilford Woodruff, pretended to abolish the custom.[1] These two moves left the anti-Mormon party with no platform to stand on; the collapse of the land boom that had helped to bring it into being hastened its end, and the conclusion of the silver-mining boom completed it. Organized opposition ceased. The Mormons asked for statehood, and, Republican and Democratic leaders both wishing Mormon votes, against the protests of Senator Edmunds and a few others statehood was granted in 1894.

From that day to this Zion has gone steadily forward, without any serious interruption, almost without any really serious opposition, along the road that she has chosen. "History," as Dr Waite well said,[2] "affords few examples of the growth, from such humble foundations, of a fabric based on a religious idea, so important and so enduring" as that which has thus been raised upon the fable invented by the illiterate dreamer and trickster of a New York State village less than one hundred years ago.

[1] That this "Woodruff Manifesto," so joyfully received by the sects that preach monogamy, was really a clever evasion will be shown in the chapter on polygamy.

[2] *Illiteracy and Mormonism.*

Politically throughout Utah, "with a power strengthened because used under statutes approved by Congress, we see a government as essentially Mormon as that of the so-called state of Deseret, established and continued to this day in the exercise of supreme executive, legislative, and judicial control."[1] With the end of its economic and political causes, the agitation against polygamy has practically ceased, after turning one Mormon polygamist,[2] a Democrat, from his seat in the national House of Representatives. With the end of those same causes, an agitation that was a by-product of that against polygamy, the agitation against the Mormon Church as a treasonable institution, swearing its members to hatred of the Federal Government, has ceased after an unsuccessful attempt to turn one Mormon Apostle,[3] a Republican, from his seat in the United States Senate. The result is that Mormonism is in absolute political mastery of the state whichever party is in control, and that, whichever party is in control in Washington, Mormonism will be protected from Federal interference and will itself influence Federal legislation, because it has, and will continue to have, Mormons in the national House of Repre-

[1] *Illiteracy and Mormonism.*

[2] Brigham H. Roberts, born at Warrington, Lancashire, England, in 1857, became a member of the Democratic party when the People's (Mormon) Party was disbanded by the Church. Although he had three wives living, the Democrats elected him to Congress 1889. He was unseated in 1900.

[3] Reed Smoot, born at Salt Lake City, 1862, became a Republican after the Mormon Party was dissolved by the Church. The Republicans elected him, and the long inquiry that resulted revealed many secrets of the Endowment House, as hereinafter mentioned; but politics were stronger than patriotism, and Smoot retained his seat, and was even re-elected.

sentatives and at least one Mormon in the Senate of the United States.

Financially and industrially, the Mormon Church, as a great trust, owns Utah, one of the richest states in mineral wealth, agricultural products, and manufacturing resources in the Union, and controls such huge blocks of stock and issues of bonds in the trusts of Wall Street and the east as not only to influence indirectly national politics and national government through them, but also to have its fingers in the entire capitalistic control of American, and thereby international, business and labour. The wilderness of 1846 has been made a golden garden by Mormon energy, and is to all intents and purposes owned by the Mormon Church.[1] Compute, if you can, the sums that this Church has received through its tithing system since Salt Lake City was founded less than a hundred years ago. Allow for the running expenses and the cost of circumventing the now dead and forgotten Federal interference. Remember that every penny that could be spared was invested as soon as it was obtained, and that its profits were "invested and reinvested as fast as they accrued."[2] Reflect that the President of the Church is "trustee in trust" for all these sums, with no account to render, with no one daring to ask an accounting—that he, his two counsellors and his Twelve Apostles, are the only persons that know to what secret uses this immense

1 The resources of Utah are treated in another chapter. Even thirty-two years ago, those once desert regions of the territory were yielding an annual cereal crop of nearly 2,000,000 bushels, and almost £2,000,000 in precious metals. The total value of the assessed population was $25,579,000, or a little more than £5,100,000. See *Illiteracy and Mormonism.*

2 Alfred Henry Lewis.

wealth is put, and that these fifteen men are zealots whose one desire is to enrich and strengthen their Church. "This," says Lewis, "is . . . the basis of the Mormon hope. Every Mormon gives one-tenth of his yearly income to the Church. No one, outside of Prophet Smith[1] and the Holy Twelve, knows the towering sum with which the Mormon tithes pile annually up. Ask a Mormon: he 'guesses' $2,000,000. Ask a Gentile: he 'guesses' $20,000,000 . . . I think it nearer the latter than the former. . . . There is a devout mining and smelting Mormon whose single tithes aggregate an annual $100,000. It would not take many such to heap up $20,000,000. You are to recollect, too—foreign and domestic, in Mexico, Canada, the Sandwich Islands, and America, there are over 800,000 Mormons.[2] All that the world knows is that the investments have been well made, and that to-day the Mormon Church, through its 'trustee in trust' system, owns enormous holdings in transcontinental railways, New York banks, and in the steel, lead, copper, oil, sugar, and tobacco trusts."[3]

And Mormonism grows in numbers as well as in financial strength and political power. The total membership of the Church, as given before, is 800,000. In America its settlements have spread from Utah through surrounding states and territories: Idaho, Wyoming, Colorado, Arizona, and Oregon, to Mexico on the south and to Canada on the north. Through-

[1] Joseph Fielding Smith, the present head of the Church, succeeding on the death of Lorenzo Snow in October 1901. He is the son of Hyrum, the brother of Joseph Smith, the founder of Mormonism.

[2] "The Viper's Trail."

[3] *Ibid.* There are also, it is said, heavy holdings in English securities.

out Europe the missionary campaign continues.[1] In England, where Liverpool has long been the centre of Mormon activity, all the large industrial cities and towns are systematically exploited; there are 82 Mormon churches, 80,000 members[2]—one-tenth of the total membership,—over 1000 missionaries, including 1 apostle, 17 high priests, 67 "seventies," 230 elders, and 856 local missionaries,[3] a force that, in 1910, distributed throughout England 162,222 books and

1 This in spite of such interference as that in Germany when, in July 1910, Herr Dallwitz, Prussian Minister of the Interior, on recommendation of the political police, signed orders for the expulsion of twenty-one Mormon missionaries, mostly Americans and Englishmen under Superintendent M'Kay, whose propaganda headquarters are in Switzerland. Says the *Philadelphia Evening Bulletin* of 22nd July 1910:

"The status of the Mormons in Germany was taken up in exchanges between the Foreign Office and the American Embassy in 1903, when the German Government took the position that the teachings of the missionaries were subversive of morality. It was then arranged with the Mormon superintendent, through the American Embassy, that all Mormon missionaries should withdraw from the country within a month, transferring the Middle European headquarters from Berlin to Switzerland. Subsequently 140 foreign leaders departed, leaving the German societies, with a total membership of 8000, in the care of German pastors. The authorities state that in recent years the Mormons have disregarded the understanding of 1903, and from time to time individual missionaries have been apprehended and expelled. In such instances they have not applied to the American Embassy for relief nor made a protest against their explusion."

In 1904 the Hungarian Minister of the Interior published a decision prohibiting Mormon propaganda within Hungary upon the ground that such a movement is "undesirable from the standpoints of State policy and religion." The effect of this appears, however, to have been but temporary.

2 *The Forum,* June 1911.

3 The "seventies" are propagandists.

5,582,415 tracts, visited 69,139 homes, baptized 936 women, and induced 555 to emigrate to Utah.[1]

And in Utah what do these converts find? The situation has been well summed up by a writer in *M'Clure's Magazine*: "So long as Utah was a territory, the Federal Government could control polygamy; once a sovereign state, however, the people of Utah themselves became supreme. As the state is two-thirds Mormon, this means that the Mormon Church itself controls the law-making and law-enforcing machinery. From 1890 until 1895 the Mormons observed their own manifesto against polygamy, for they were upon their good behaviour; almost immediately after statehood, however, the old polygamous system was revived. The word went through the state, 'Live your religion'; the old polygamists began living openly again with their plural wives, and new plural marriages were once more secretly performed all over Mormondom. . . .

[1] These figures, evidently taken from the missionaries' own reports, were quoted by Hans P. Freece, an expert investigator of Mormonism, who spent last summer looking into the spread of the faith in England, Holland, Sweden, and Denmark. In an interview given to the London *Daily News* correspondent in New York, Mr Freece said:

"I have brought back with me bunches of affidavits by unhappy fathers and mothers whose daughters have sailed to join the Mormons in Utah. You must realize that before these women start they are assured that polygamous marriages no longer exist. The elders and missionaries are young men of good appearance and address, and the women are flattered by their attentions. The women are told that if they go to Utah they will have chances to get good positions and marry well. Their fares are paid to Utah by the Mormon Church. When they get there they find things far different from what was represented. They have no way of getting back. They have no money, and they do not belong to the class of people who can supply funds for the passage. They are obliged to reconcile themselves to their new surroundings."

The 'Mormon Problem' is thus by no means yet solved."[1]

[1] *M'Clure's Magazine*, December 1910. It should further be noted that "the enabling Act under which Utah became a state provided that plural marriages should be for ever prohibited. The new constitution of the state also declares that polygamy shall never be practised. Yet it is said that there is nothing to hinder the repeal of this constitutional provision, and that if this should be done there would be nothing in the way of such legislation by the state as should allow the contraction of plural marriages again according to the revelation of 1843. As a legal opinion this is no doubt correct. The United States would certainly have no precedent in an attempt to revoke the statehood conferred upon Utah, even though the people had clearly violated their agreement. There can be no doubt that many Latter Day Saints look forward to a time when polygamy shall again be practised, under the sanction of the head of the Church. Many outside the Church think that the only safeguard against such a calamity will be a rapid accession of the non-Mormon population. But, unfortunately for such hopes, the increase of the population is quite certain to be pre dominatingly Mormon. More missionaries were (at once upon the granting of statehood) sent out . . . than ever before, and the mission work has been reorganized and put upon a better basis. All parts of the world will be reached, and the proselytizing will go on among all classes. It may be that those converted will be chiefly the poor, the ignorant rather than the educated, and the eccentric rather than the sane and intellectual. If so, they will be all the more surely controlled by the Church leaders, and their votes will count for as much as those of the educated."—David Utter, in *The New World*, March 1897. Mr Utter, however, thinks that the revival of polygamy is unlikely.

VIII

THE OLD MORMON RELIGION

WHAT was the faith that made modern Mormondom? No one familiar with even the outlines of the history of religions is unfamiliar with the fact that a great truth or a high morality is unnecessary for the making of martyrs, or the establishment of vast sects; and it is an evidence of the essentially fine in man that mankind is always ready to die for the sake of an unproven hope. Therefore, though the Mormon faith survived the perils of the wilderness, the persecutions of governments, the trials of both poverty and prosperity, though it is sufficient to build a civilization in a desert, and though it remains to-day a living force with its influence strong in the finances and government of a great nation and its converts increasing among the ignorant over all the world, it is not surprising that Mormonism should have originated in a series of writings that to the sophisticated mind seem almost childish and banal.

Asked the meaning of the word "Mormon," Joseph Smith himself replied with a naïve etymology. "The Bible in its widest sense means Good," he said, "and the Egyptian word for *good* is *mon*; hence, with the addition of the prefix *more*, contracted to *mor*, we have *Mormon*, which *means literally More Good*."[1] And that

[1] Mackay.

this definition was accepted by the Church in general we learn from these words of an officer of the Church, its authorized historian and general recorder, speaking in an official journal:[1] "*Mormon* is the name of an ancient prophet, and signifies *more good. Mormonism*, a new coined word by the enemy, signifies *all truth*, present, past, and future; and the 'Mormon's' creed is the truth, the whole truth, and nothing but the truth. And this creed is what the devil and all his imps are eternally fighting against, and not against the believers of that creed only, so far as the truth influences their actions." Finally, the Latter Day Saints of Jesus Christ so styled themselves because they believed that the discovery of *The Book of Mormon* and their acceptance of that book made a new covenant between God and the earth in which those who had faith were made saints to prepare the second coming of Christ, of which every comet and earthquake, every war and rumour of war, was a sign or portent.[2]

The world had fallen away from its understanding of Christ's covenant, says Parley Pratt,[3] just as once before it fell away from the covenant made at the conclusion of the Deluge; and just as a new dispensation became necessary for salvation at the time of the first coming of Christ, so was a new dispensation now necessary for salvation against his second coming. There was uncertainty and contention concerning the meaning of the Scriptures; there were several disputing forms of faith resulting from these uncertainties and contentions, and there were many differing forms of

1 W. Richards in *The Millennial Star*, 1850.

2 Mackay.

3 *A Voice of Warning; or, Introduction to the Faith and Doctrine of Mormonism.*

ritual growing from these disputing forms of faith. All this was wrong. There should be a unity of faith and ritual, and such a unity could be had only by a literal interpretation of the Scriptures. As for the reconciliation of such an interpretation with modern conditions, that had now been made possible by the renewal, to Smith and his followers, of the ancient system of direct revelation and the ancient gift of prophecy, lost aforetime through man's falling away from the covenants that included these things. The new covenant was made with Joseph Smith, and those to whom he transmitted it were given the power to interpret the new covenant, to explain and amplify the old covenants, to foretell the future, and to receive from time to time still further messages from God.[1]

As the record of this covenant, Smith has left three volumes that, besides the manifestos of his successors and the other official utterances of the Church, form the sacred writings of Mormonism. They are:

(*a*) *The Book of Mormon.*
(*b*) *The Doctrine and Covenants.*
(*c*) *The Pearl of Great Price.*

(*a*) The original manuscript of Smith's dictated "translation" of *The Book of Mormon* was recently said[2] to be in the possession of J. D. Whitmer, of Richmond, Ray County, Missouri, whose father, David Whitmer, had somehow come into possession of it during the Saints' troubled residence in his state.[3]

[1] *A Voice of Warning; or, Introduction to the Faith and Doctrine of Mormonism.*

[2] *St Louis Republic.*

[3] When Whitmer died, 25th January 1888, this manuscript was bequeathed to his son; and to George Schurich, also of Richmond, Missouri, was bequeathed the table used at the time of the translation.

The elder Whitmer, it was declared, had refused for it an offer of £20,000 made to him by Orson Pratt and others, who represented the Mormon Church and would have multiplied that offer by five but for the fact that Whitmer said that the manuscript was not for sale. The first edition of the volume has also acquired a value for bibliophiles.[1] It is one of the rarest products of the early press of interior New York State, an octavo of 590 pages, containing about one-third as much text as does the King James version of the Bible, and printed at Palmyra, New York, in 1830.

Smith's theory of "interpretation," as shown in this production, has all the virtue of simplicity. He sat behind a screen with the sacred golden plates before him. Gazing at those plates through the Urim and Thummim, brought him for that purpose by the angel, he saw the "reformed Egyptian" characters take English form, and dictated the result to Oliver Cowdery, the schoolmaster, acting as amanuensis on the other side of the screen.

The work is, to the lay mind, only mildly heterodox. Contrary to the popular notion, it inculcates neither polytheism nor polygamy, the latter, indeed, being roundly condemned[2] in a fashion diametrically opposed to the subsequent revelation that, after long secrecy, found its way, in 1852, into the supplementary volume of *Doctrine and Covenants.*[3] Baptism, to be sure, must be by immersion only, and is for the remission of sins—a theory held and preached with great success in the neighbourhood of Smith's home by the followers of

[1] *Omaha Bee,* 2nd April 1893.

[2] *The Book of Mormon,* Jacob ii.

[3] *Doctrine and Covenants,* cxxxii.

Alexander Campbell some years previous to the discovery of *The Book of Mormon*;[1] and there is a great deal of denunciation vouchsafed oath-bound secret societies, as represented by a certain band of "Gadianton robbers," who play their part in the narrative, and whose scarifying seems strangely to echo that given the Freemasons in the United States when, in 1826, or three years before Smith began "translating," the alleged but never established kidnapping and murder of John Morgan, in New York State, started an anti-Masonic agitation that became for a time national, and even founded a political party, with a candidate for the Presidency.[2]

And yet, on the whole, the book is rather a narrative than an exposition of doctrine, and provides only the "historical" basis for the doctrines later enunciated. Its general purpose is to supplement the Bible and give an account of God's dealings with the inhabitants of the western hemisphere.

This the book does in a dull manner not beyond the abilities of an ignorant but poetic boy. It has long since been translated into nearly every written language, but its original English, notwithstanding the help, aid, and assistance of Master Cowdery, who must have been a remarkable pedagogue, bristles with faulty grammar. "Ye are like unto they"; "Ye saith unto Him"; "He has fell"; "Our sufferings doth exceed"; "These things had not ought to be"; "All things which is expedient"—these and similar errors abound both in *The Book of Mormon* and its two fellows; and when they are brought home to the Saints, the Saints reply:

[1] Oddly enough, Campbellites joined Baptists and Methodists in a mob that tarred and feathered Smith and Rigdon. (Mackay.)

[2] *The Book of Mormon*, Helamon ii. and Nephi ii.

"True, but neither is the King James version of the Bible always grammatical!"[1]

The story that *The Book of Mormon* tells should delight the lovers of Suetonius, Marco Polo, and Defoe. It is the account of how America was peopled by three expeditions from the eastern hemisphere, and it commences with the departure from Jerusalem, in the first year of the reign of Zedekiah,[2] of Lehi, his wife, four sons, and ten friends, a branch of the house of Israel and the tribe of Joseph.

These early adventurers made their way eastward until they came to the sea—though what sea it is, is not mentioned,—and there they built a ship and sailed for the promised land. When they reached the farther[3] shore, they found there the "horse, the ass, the ox, the goat, and the wild goat,"[4] planted their seed, raised beautiful crops,[5] multiplied and gradually spread northward. The terrible mountains of this district seem to have presented so few difficulties to the wanderers as not to be worthy of record—in fact, mountains do not appear to have been observed; but somehow or other they arrived at the "Isthmus of Panama" and crossed that narrow strip of land which joins "the land northward and the land southward," at last separating into two great divisions, the Nephites and the Lamanites, named for their respective founders. The former were the supporters of Nephi, a younger son of Lehi, whose divine appointment to leadership upon his father's death angered the eldest son Laman and his friends. The

1 Mackay.

2 599 B.C.

3 The name of the port of landing is also lacking. Mormon tradition says that this port was somewhere along the coast of Chili. (Utter.)

4 *The Book of Mormon,* Nephi v.

5 There is no mention of irrigation.

Lamanites rebelled and were cursed by Heaven and condemned to wear the bronze skins that their remaining descendants, the American Indians, wear to-day.[1] There followed a series of wars, tediously narrated, which continued for several centuries.

The descendants of the other two of the three expeditions that had set out from the old world to people the new were encountered by these sons of Lehi on their progress northward. In the "Land of Zarahemla" they found one tribe, whose adventures we are spared, but whose records showed that they had left Jerusalem in 588 B.C. The second, which had, in eight ships, sailed to America upon the occasion of the confusion of tongues at Babel, peopled the land for fifteen hundred years, but, according to the prophet Ether, who wrote their history, were destroyed for wickedness in 600 B.C. They are said by Mormon tradition[2] to have landed on the Californian coast, though, save for its climate and its mountains, Peru would appear to suit better their stay as given in *The Book of Mormon.*[3] The only observably important point about them, however, seems to be their legacy of the honey-bee as a symbol for their spiritual descendants of the nineteenth century.[4]

[1] "Mormons," *Ency. Brit.*, Dr John Fraser, Univ. of Chicago.

[2] Parley Pratt.

[3] Utter.

[4] See *The Book of Ether*, i. The Beehive is the Mormon symbol and the official seal of the state of Utah. On the expedition that the Mormons believe to have landed in California, the brother of Jared, the first comer from the old world, took with him, as if it were by a hint from Noah, his flocks, "fowls of the air, the fish of the waters, the deseret, which is by interpretation the honey-bee." As this emigrant's language was that in use before the confusion of tongues, Brigham Young pointed out that "deseret" was a word from "the original language of mankind."

Meanwhile, the war between the Nephites and Lamanites, of the latter of whom the American Indians are supposed to be a remnant,[1] continued merrily throughout the years. To the former, Christ appeared after his crucifixion in Palestine, at which time the American continent was shaken to its foundations by an earthquake that destroyed cities and created lakes and mountains.[2] The Nephites acknowledged Jesus as the Son of God, but in the third century A.D. they "fell into wickedness"[3] and were practically annihilated at a great battle fought near Manchester, New York State.

These records of the Nephites were largely the work of Mormon, himself a Nephite and a prophet of the Lord. Since he had remained pure in faith, God commanded him to write the chronicle of his own times and compile an abridgment of the history of his forefathers' wanderings. What his death at the hands of his enemies left incomplete his son Maroni continued to about the year 420 A.D., when the plates, because the Lamanites were trying to find and destroy all the sacred writings of the Nephites, were concealed in Cumorah Hill, where the Lord promised Maroni that they should some day be discovered by a Gentile nation.

(*b*) *The Doctrine and Covenants* is a book of occasional revelations strongly reminiscent of the Koran. These revelations concern a variety of matters important and trivial, and were given, in various places and various years, with a grammar that, after the passing of Cowdery, the schoolmaster,

1 See *The Book of Ether*, i.

2 Parley Pratt, *Introduction to Doctrine.*

3 *Ibid.*

became more peculiar than even that of *The Book of Mormon.*

One portion of the volume consists of supplements to the Bible and new "translations" of such Biblical passages as, if taken literally as they appear in the King James version—and the Saints insist on a literal acceptance of all "correctly translated" passages—would conflict with other tenets of the Mormon faith. Thus, for a reason that will be observed later, Smith found it necessary to alter the twenty-sixth verse of the first chapter of Genesis in the following manner:

King James Version.	Joseph Smith's Version.
And God said, Let us make man in our image, after our likeness; and let them have dominion over the fish of the sea, and over the fowl of the air, and over the cattle, and over all the earth, and over every creeping thing that creepeth upon the earth.	And I, God, said unto mine Only Begotten, which was with me from the beginning, "Let us make man in our image, after our likeness"; and it was so. And I, God, said, "Let them have dominion."

That is one example. A little later on, Smith, feeling that there was an undesirable hiatus between the end of the third and the beginning of the fourth chapter of Genesis, received a revelation to fill it thus:

"And they heard the voice of the Lord from the way toward the garden of Eden, speaking unto them, and they saw him not, for they were shut out from his presence; and he gave unto them commandments that they should worship the Lord their God, and should offer the firstlings of their flocks for an offering unto the Lord. And Adam was obedient unto the commandments of the Lord. And after many days an angel of the Lord appeared unto Adam, saying, 'Why dost thou offer sacrifices unto the Lord?' And Adam said unto him, 'I know not, save the Lord commanded me.' And then the angel spake saying, 'This thing is a similitude of the sacrifice of the Only Begotten of the Father, who is full of grace and truth. And thou shalt do all that thou doest in the name of the Son, and thou shalt repent and call upon God in the name of the Son for evermore.' And in that day the Holy Ghost fell upon Adam, which beareth record of the Father and the Son."

The majority of the revelations had, however, to do with matters of doctrine[1] and ritual and the material needs of the growing Church and of Smith himself. Thus, within a year of the fundamental revelation of April 1830, commanding all the Saints to "give heed to all his (Smith's) words and commandments," the god of the Mormons declared:[2] "It is meet that my servant, Joseph Smith, junior, should have a house built in which to live and translate"; and, before the close of the year in which this declaration was made: "If ye desire the mysteries of my kingdom, provide for him (Smith) food and raiment, and *whatsoever thing he needeth*," and "In temporal labours thou (Smith) shalt not have strength, for that is not thy calling." The same god made it clear to Smith that all existing sects save Smith's were in sinful error and that their members were required to seek admission by baptism into Mormondom.

The revelations, which are all dated, extend over the

[1] The most important doctrines of the Church were thus enunciated.

[2] February 1831.

score of years between 1823 and 1843, furnishing the clearest clue to Smith's material and spiritual progress and the material and spiritual progress of the Church. At their start, as Mr Utter has pointed out,[1] "when somebody stole the sheets of *The Book of Mormon* with the intention of having Joseph Smith translate the same matter from the plates again, the seer, more wary than the Psalmanazar, had a special revelation telling him of the perfidy of his pretended friends, and relieving him of the necessity of reproducing what had been stolen."[2] Again, when Martin Harris, the farmer that mortgaged his farm in order to supply funds for the publication of *The Book of Mormon*, is slow in furnishing this money, Smith has the revelation addressed to Harris to the effect that "thou *shalt not covet thine own property*, but impart it freely for the printing of *The Book of Mormon*." Mere underlings that began also to receive revelations are rebuked as false prophets and impious aspirants. The religious and temporal government of the Saints is at least sketched; there are directions concerning almsgiving, temple-building, the earlier migrations, and the tithing system is specifically outlined and enjoined. The business of the bank at Kirtland is treated of on one page and the founding of Zion almost on the next, while close by is a revelation regarding the erection of a boarding-house. Most of the matters of doctrine included in this book are described in the various comments on the Mormon creed in the next chapter. For the rest, there must, in the latter part of Smith's life, have been many revelations unpublished and some even unrecorded, especially certain messages having to do with the

[1] *The New World*, March 1897.

[2] See *Doctrine and Covenants*, x.

Temple ritual, of which non-Mormons are purposely kept in ignorance; but it is important here to note that the volume gives hints concerning baptism for the dead, and that the doctrine of celestial marriage—the doctrine, in other words, of polygamy,[1] which, though received and first inculcated by Smith shortly after his removal from New York State, was kept secret until long after his death—finally found its way into the printed volume in 1852.

(*c*) In *The Pearl of Great Price* the essential portions are, first, "The Vision of Moses" and the "Writings of Moses," and, second, "The Book of Abraham." The former portion supplements the Biblical story of creation by showing that Christ preceded Adam, and then fills a long-felt moral want by accounting for the otherwise gratuitously insulting refusal of Cain's sacrifice on the ground that Cain had previously been told what sacrifice would be acceptable, and so sinned against the light.

The Book of Abraham came to Smith through the help of his god and a travelling showman. The showman, exhibiting some mummies, appeared in Kirtland, Ohio, in 1835, and sold a few of his "specimens" to some of the Saints. When one of the mummies was unwrapped by its inquisitive purchaser, a papyrus was discovered in the coverings; and this, brought to Smith, the Prophet set to work to "translate." It was, he assured his followers, a manuscript in Abraham's own hand, written in Egypt, and in it is now to be found the beginning of Smith's later widely developed polytheism. Evidently the "translator" had at this time first learned that the Hebrew term of divinity, Elohim, is a plural word, so that he now, in debates of the gods

[1] This doctrine will be treated in full in the chapters on Polygamy.

regarding the management of the earth, man, and Satan, explains Genesis accordingly, all amid a geography and astronomy no less astounding than those in the more generally accepted version of the first book in the Bible, and most likely all, together with certain hints from Freemasonry, at once included in the secret ritual of the Temple.

IX

THE NEW MORMON RELIGION

At least at the time of its organization, the chief purpose of the Church of the Latter Day Saints was, like that of early Christianity, to prepare both materially and spiritually for the second coming of Christ. As far as possible, the souls of all mankind were to be made ready, and, specifically, a city was to be built from which the Messiah could suitably reign. This was Smith's version. He saw his army of the Lord marching across the plains to that Utopia which he should found, and which, presumably, he should rule until he resigned its government to God. The early creed of his Church he drew up in the following form:[1]

"Articles of Faith of the
Church of Jesus Christ of Latter Day Saints

"1. We believe in God, the Eternal Father, and in his Son Jesus Christ, and in the Holy Ghost.

"2. We believe that men will be punished for their own sins, and not for Adam's transgression.

"3. We believe that through the atonement of Christ all mankind may be saved by obedience to the laws and ordinances of the Gospel.

"4. We believe that these ordinances are, first, faith

[1] See also *Mormonism Triumphant*, by J. H. Flanigan, elder in the Church of Latter Day Saints, published in Liverpool, 1849.

in the Lord Jesus Christ; second, repentance; third, baptism by immersion for the remission of sins; fourth, laying on of hands for the gift of the Holy Ghost.

"5. We believe that a man must be called of God by 'prophecy and by laying on of hands,' by those who are in authority to preach the Gospel and administer the ordinances thereof.

"6. We believe in the same organization that existed in the primitive Church, viz. apostles, prophets, pastors, teachers, evangelists, etc.

"7. We believe in the gift of tongues, prophecy, revelation, visions, healing, interpretation of tongues, etc.

"8. We believe the Bible to be the word of God, as far as it is translated correctly; we also believe *The Book of Mormon* to be the word of God.

"9. We believe all that God has revealed, all that he does now reveal, and we believe that he will yet reveal many great and important things pertaining to the kingdom of God.

"10. We believe in the literal gathering of Israel and in the restoration of the Ten Tribes; that Zion will be built upon this continent; that Christ will reign personally upon the earth, and that the earth will be renewed and receive its paradise glory.

"11. We claim the privilege of worshipping Almighty God according to the dictates of our conscience, and allow all men the same privilege, let them worship how, where, or what they may.

"12. We believe in being subject to kings, presidents, rulers, and magistrates, in obeying, honouring, and sustaining the law.

"13. We believe in being honest, true, chaste, benevolent, virtuous, and in doing good to *all men*; indeed, we may say that we follow the admonition of Paul.

'We believe all things, we hope all things'; we have endured many things, and hope to be able to endure all things. If there is anything virtuous, lovely, or of good report or praiseworthy, we seek after these things."

All faiths, however, are one thing when they are planted and another when they develop. Any enduring religion is a matter of growth; and there are evidences that Mormonism, if it grew financially and politically upwards, sent down roots that drew their nourishment through the buried dust of absurd creeds long dead and well forgotten. Thus the formal creed just quoted, in spite of the fact that it has often received the Church's official sanction,[1] is in reality, like most formal creeds, an altogether inadequate expression of the living faith of the Church that adopted it. The only manner in which it can be made properly to express that faith is by some such expansion as we shall now attempt.

Article I. We believe in God, the Eternal Father, and in his Son Jesus Christ, and in the Holy Ghost.

This is all very well, but it fails to give the Mormon definition of the word "God," the Mormon idea of the birth of Christ, and the Mormon theory of the procession of the Holy Ghost.

As a matter of truth, the Mormons believe in the existence of many gods,[2] one for each planet in our

[1] The last time was on October 6, 1890, when the General Conference of the Church of Latter Day Saints at Salt Lake City adopted it "as the rule of our faith and conduct."

[2] *The Pearl of Great Price.* On page 13 of the Mormon *Catechism for Children* we read:

"Q. Are there more gods than one?

"A. Yes, many."

"We believe in the plurality of gods." (Roberts's *Mormon Doctrine of Deity*, p. 11.)

solar system, a pantheon of deities of varying degrees of virtue and power; and, though there is a hint that one of these gods is a ruler over the others,[1] upon that matter there is no definite declaration. They hold that God has a material body, a body that can be seen and handled, like the body of a man; in fact, in Joseph Smith's own words: "God is a man like one of yourselves; that is the great secret."[2] The particular god[3] that is the object of the Mormons' worship and of the first article of their creed is that god having charge of the conduct of this earth and the men upon it. He has attained his position through a process of evolution that achieved in him an exalted intelligence;[4] yet he also has a material body: he eats and drinks, can be talked to and joked with; so that the faithful are admonished regarding him: "As man is now, so God has been; as God is now, so man may be."[5] He is of

[1] *Doctrines and Covenants,* cxxi. 32.

[2] *The Passing of the Mormon,* A. L. Mearkle.

[3] Even here the word, as will be seen, might better be plural: the persons of this godhead are distinct.

[4] Utter.

[5] Bishop Orson Whitney.

Also: "We know that both the Father and the Son are in form and stature perfect men; each of them possesses a material body, infinitely pure and perfect, yet a body of flesh and bones." (James F. Talmage, *Articles of Faith.*)

"What are men? They are the offspring of God, the fathers and mothers in Jesus Christ. . . . They are capable of receiving intelligence and exaltation to such a degree as to be raised from the dead with a body like that of Jesus Christ, and to possess immortal flesh and bones, in which they will eat, drink, converse, reason, love, walk, sing, play on musical instruments, go on missions from planet to planet, or from system to system; being gods, or sons of God, endowed with the same powers, attributes, and capacities that their Heavenly Father and Jesus Christ possess." (Parley Pratt in a sermon quoted in Roberts's *Mormon Doctrine of Deity.*)

two persons, the Father and the Son, and cannot be omnipotent save through his Holy Spirit, whom he can send forth as he may desire. He and his Son are one only in that they are in complete harmony and agreement with each other. Since the God of the Bible is continually spoken of as "Our Father," he is identified with Adam, and is considered the literal father of the human race, Adam's celestial intercourse having apparently been with a superior deity that had temporary charge of the creation of this world. This Smith's followers did not appreciate during the lifetime of the first Prophet; but the doctrine as later emphatically extended by Brigham Young seems indeed to have originated with the founder of Mormonism, who further declared that Adam was "Michael, the Ancient of Days,"[1] and this is now unanimously accepted in Mormondom.

The son of this god existed at the earth's beginning,[2] Adam having first begotten him spiritually in the celestial world. In his terrestrial body, as it is definitely held, this son was Jesus Christ, and was "the material offspring of the material Father, by the Virgin Mary,"[3] at least upon the occasion of his earthly birth,[4] the Virgin being actually married to the god in question.

God the Father having, then, been the first man, peopled our earth, which through his Son he later redeemed. It has followed logically to the Mormon mind that "any man can rise by faith and obedience

[1] Utter.

[2] See the quotation hereinbefore given from Smith's amplification of Genesis i. 26. Also the Gospel of St John i. 1–5.

[3] Mearkle.

[4] See the suggestion of a general celestial birth preceding earthly birth later given.

to the position of a deity when he can, like the Creator, form a planet, people and redeem it, and be enthroned as its god for ever."[1]

Lastly, in this connection, the Mormons' simple form of exegesis and their belief in a literal interpretation of the Bible, with Smith's corrections to our translation, led them to a faith in men's spiritual birth, preceding material birth, and pre-terrestrial existence in heaven. It was held that this had happened to Adam. "As God was, so man is": consequently, it had occurred to man; and this belief is thus set forth in a popular Mormon hymn:

"O my Father, thou that dwellest
In the high and glorious place!
When shall I regain thy presence
And again behold thy face?
In thy holy habitation
Did my spirit once reside?
In my first primæval childhood
Was I nurtured near thy side?

For a wise and glorious purpose
Thou hast placed me here on earth,
And withheld the recollection
Of my former friends and birth;
Yet ofttimes a secret something
Whispered, 'You're a stranger here,'
And I felt that I had wandered
From a more exalted sphere.

I had learned to call thee Father
Through thy Spirit from on high;
But until the Key of Knowledge
Was restored, I knew not why.
In the heavens are parents single?
No; the thought makes reason stare!
Truth is reason; truth eternal
Tells me I've a mother there.

[1] Mearkle.

When I leave this frail existence,
  When I lay this mortal by,
Father, mother, may I meet you
  In your royal court on high?
Then at length when I've completed
  All you've sent me forth to do,
With your mutual approbation
  Let me come and dwell with you."

The Father and Son live on a star called Kolob,[1] which, though unknown to astronomy, was familiar to Joseph Smith, who described it as being situated in space "near the throne of God," and who, with a literal regard for the Scriptural statement that with the Lord a thousand years are as one day, said that it revolved upon its axis once in a thousand years. On this star Deity begets the spirits that are later to have an earthly birth. That is their destiny. If on earth they are good Mormons, living the faith and giving every opportunity—as polygamy gives it—for other spirits to come to their period of earthly probation, then they will return to starry kingdoms prepared for them. The sinners will descend into a lake of fire;[2] but those who by good works of this sort have become eligible will return to the spheres that are "the future abode of the gods," there themselves to become gods.[3]

Article II. We believe that men will be punished for their own sins, and not for Adam's transgression.

Why not? The answer is found in the Mormon *Catechism for Children.* There we are ingeniously

[1] It is not on record that Smith read Dante, or was familiar with the theological sources of Dante's great work, but it is worth remembering that an English translation of Dante had a wide vogue in the United States during the Prophet's creative period.

[2] Mearkle.

[3] *Doctrine and Covenants,* cxxxii. 20.

told that Adam and Eve "rejoiced and praised God" because of their sin, because their sin had become, through God's mercy, the means of the final exaltation of themselves and all mankind. The spectacle of a faith that insists on obedience founding an important benefit upon disobedience is not without its amusing phase, but the rationalist that sees injustice in the orthodox theory of the fall of man cannot but applaud Smith's words in *The Pearl of Great Price*:

"In that day Adam blessed God and was filled, and began to prophesy concerning all the families of the earth, saying, 'Blessed be the name of God, for by my transgression in the flesh I shall see God.' And Eve, his wife, heard all these things and was glad, saying, 'Were it not for our transgression, we should not have had seed, and never should have known good and evil, and the joy of our redemption, and the eternal life which God giveth to all the obedient.'"

Article III. We believe that through the atonement of Christ all mankind may be saved by obedience to the laws and ordinances of the Gospel.

There have been Mormons that tried to stretch this article until it agreed with that article which is the cornerstone of the Universalist's faith, but their labours do not appear to be entirely successful. *The Book of Mormon* again and again furnishes plain implications that salvation is not for the wicked, and in one passage [1] we read that "he that endureth not unto the end will be hewn down and cast into the fire from whence (*sic*) they (*sic*) *can no more return*, because of the justice of the Father," due allowance being made for the unen-

[1] Nephi xii.

lightened adult.[1] Nevertheless, the Mormons consider as an insult to God the doctrine of some orthodox Christians regarding the damnation of unbaptized children, and, in later life, Smith qualified his theory of future punishment by explaining that "eternal punishment" and "endless punishment" were so called only because they were inflicted by an eternal and therefore endless god.[2]

Article IV. We believe that these ordinances are, first, faith in the Lord Jesus Christ; second, repentance; third, baptism by immersion for the remission of sins; fourth, laying on of hands for the gift of the Holy Ghost.

To this article Elder Flanigan[3] adds the ordinance of the Lord's Supper, and the article as a whole is thus ably explained by Mr Utter:[4]

"The rigid insistence upon these saving ordinances makes the Mormon faith something very different from Universalism, and allies it closely with the teaching of Alexander Campbell and the Church of the Disciples. Indeed, it has often been surmised that this part of the Mormon doctrine may have been derived, through Sidney Rigdon or otherwise, from the early preaching of these reformers, then called Campbellites. They insisted upon a return to primitive Christian teaching and to the original form of Church organization, and they interpreted the Bible in the same literal way that is characteristic of Latter Day Saints.

1 Mosiah i.

2 *Doctrine and Covenants,* xix. 11–12.

3 *Mormonism Triumphant.*

4 *Mormonism To-Day.*

"That forgiveness of sins is absolutely conditioned upon immersion in water[1] by a properly qualified priest has given rise to some extensions of the doctrine of baptism among this people, namely, baptism for the dead and re-baptism. Baptism for the dead is provided for in *The Book of Doctrine and Covenants*; and the subject seems to have occupied the mind of Joseph Smith during his last troubled days on earth. These proxy baptisms are carried on in the temples, and probably constitute a large proportion of the 'temple work.' All zealous Mormons look up the history of their ancestors for as many generations back as possible, being anxious to secure their salvation by means of this substitutional immersion. There are workers in each of the several temples whose daily employment it is to baptize and be baptized for the dead, one worker often being baptized for hundreds or even thousands of the departed. Salvation has thus been brought within the reach of very many of the heroes and men of mark of recent and ancient times, including not only Washington, Franklin, and Jefferson, and such men, but Richard Cœur de Lion and many farther away from us in space and time. Re-baptism, being indulged in by Brigham Young soon after his arrival in Utah, had quite a vogue for a time, and is yet in use by those who have apostatized, or for a time been unfaithful, and who wish to return to the Church. No limit has been set as to the number of times that remission of sins may be thus obtained; but it is not taught that one may deliberately sin, looking forward to

[1] At a Mormon baptism near Rutherford, North Carolina, the participants—seven women, three men, and four missionaries—were said to have been nude during the ceremony.

baptismal forgiveness, and successfully secure the desired pardon."[1]

Article V. We believe that a man must be called of God by "prophecy and by laying on of hands," by those who are in authority to preach the Gospel and administer the ordinances thereof.

Since "those who are in authority" are the officers of the Mormon Church, this article effectually bars all possible rivals. The Latter Day Saints have their own apostolic succession and are very clear and positive about it. Their authorities, in fact, do not descend from St Peter; they descend from a predecessor of St Peter, from the forerunner of Christ.

Smith, brought up by a mother who had been told in a vision that all the orthodox sects were in error, himself received a revelation confirming his mother's. As things were, therefore, nobody on earth was qualified to administer divine ordinances; and to remedy this deplorable condition, John the Baptist was sent by God in 1829, appeared to Smith and Oliver Cowdery, and conferred on them "the order of the Aaronic priesthood." Cowdery was then authorized to baptize and ordain Smith, and matters were thus restored to a safe basis. By the laying on of hands, the Prophet himself transmitted this authority to his chosen ministers, and the elect of these may still so perpetuate it, none being permitted to preach Mormonism without having received it. Later a higher and more select

[1] It should also be noted that "every Mormon *must* submit to this rite for the benefit of his dead. The practice has about the same object as that of masses *pro defunctis*: fees to priesthood" (*Edinburgh Review,* quoted in Littell's *Living Age*, vol. cxlii. p. 147 *et seq.*). The Chancellor of the University of Deseret declares that "unless this is done for the dead they cannot be redeemed."

order of priesthood, that of Melchizedek, was instituted by revelation and vision, and there was given to the head of the Church the highest authority, which includes that of "sealing in celestial marriage." This right is held by the selected priest alone, and descends from him only to his lawful successor.

Article VI. We believe in the same organization that existed in the primitive Church, viz. apostles, prophets, pastors, teachers, evangelists, etc.

Christianity at large has been long at strife over the original organization of the early Church, but that organization was explained to Smith in a vision. He was commanded to use it for the conduct of the Latter Day Saints, and he did so, producing "a hierarchy hardly excelled by any in existence for unity, division of labour, and due subordination and personal liberty of action."[1]

At the head of the Church, a supreme pontiff of the western world, executive, receiver of revelations from God, and unaccounting "trustee in trust" for the wealth of Mormondom, stands the President or Prophet, whose term is for life and whose heir is the head of the body directly under him. This body is called the "First Presidency." It is composed of two men known as the Prophet's Counsellors, together with the board of Twelve Apostles. The Prophet is *de facto* the head of the First Presidency, and the board of Twelve Apostles elects its own members, thus perpetuating itself. The oldest member of this board is the heir to the veil of the Prophet.[2] Below the Twelve Apostles,

[1] Utter.

[2] The Prophet, his two Counsellors and the Twelve Apostles constitute the "Living Constitution" of the Church. ("The Viper's Trail.")

in the order named, come the High Priests, Seventies, Elders, Bishops, Priests, Teachers, and Deacons. The duties of this hierarchy may thus be roughly described:

The Prophet . . .	Supreme Head of the Church.
Counsellors	Advisers of the Prophet.
Apostles	Preside at religious services, baptize, administer charities, and, under the Prophet, are all-powerful.
High Priests . . .	Preside in the absence of an Apostle, baptize and preach.
Seventies	In charge of propaganda, and assist the High Priests.
Elders	Assist the Seventies.
Bishops	Their duties are largely temporal; they preside over wards,[1] collect tithes, and look after the poor.
Teachers	Preachers only.
Deacons	Have the care of the churches and tabernacles, and serve, even to the extent of wood-chopping, the Bishops in their care of the homeless.
Priests (Melchizedek)	Spiritual workers under the High Priests.
Priests (Levitical) . .	Stand between the Deacons and Bishops in matters temporal.

To these orders might also be added the order of General Missionaries, for every male Mormon, and

[1] See beyond.

nearly every female, must give certain years to missionary work. If one remembers that the greater number of souls that a Mormon saves—or for that matter brings into this world and rears in the faith—the greater will be his rank in heaven, one will the more readily understand why these missionaries at one time received no pay, took up no collection, supported themselves entirely from their own resources, and why, unless they inherited the necessary money, they generally alternated between a year of missionary endeavour and a year of work at wages.[1] Now, however, matters appear to have changed, and it is asserted that there is detailed evidence to the effect that every Mormon missionary is paid by the Church per convert shipped to Utah on a sort of "commission basis," with additional bonus if the convert is a girl and is "placed," that is, secured as a plural wife for a brother in Zion. The alleged rate of payment is:

Man and wife, sixteen shillings.

Girl over sixteen, one pound.

"Placed" girl over sixteen, from eight to twelve pounds.

According to this statement, the missionaries' earnings run all the way from £160 to £500 a year.[2]

Geographically, the Church is divided into stakes and wards. There are from 3000 to 8000 Mormons in each stake, which is composed of several wards of from 300 to 800 Mormons. At the head of each ward there is a Bishop, and at the head of each stake there are a President and two Counsellors assisted by a High

[1] *New York Evening Post*, 9th September 1899.

[2] Mrs Frederick Schoff, Chairman of the National League of Women's Organizations, and President of the National "Congress of Mothers," U.S.A., quoted, 1904, in the Philadelphia *North American*.

Council of twelve. It is one of the chief duties of these councils to keep disputing Mormons out of the civil courts, and thus the Counsellors adjust such differences between laymen as arise in regard to property boundaries and water rights. It is also the duty of the heads of each stake to conduct their stake's tithing-house, an undertaking that amounts to the conduct of a general store.[1]

Article VII. We believe in the gift of tongues, prophecy, revelation, visions, healing, interpretation of tongues, etc.

Founded as it is on faith in direct revelation, and nearer to the time of its revealed foundation than orthodox Christianity, Mormonism has neither fallen away from its belief in the former interposition of the supernatural in earthly affairs nor in that interposition at the present day. There is no Mormon elder that will not tell of miracles attesting his ministry, no layman that does not believe he has seen wonders wrought to confirm faith, to answer prayer, or to benefit individuals especially favoured of God.

Nowadays the gift of tongues is not so frequently conferred by Heaven, among the Mormons, as it was a few years ago, when it was greatly exercised by the devout, especially the devout women.[2] It consisted, of

1 Each stake has its tithe-house. That one in Salt Lake City resembles a country store with shelves for "harness, vegetables, flour, butter, eggs, meats"—and all for sale. "Much is sold for cash, but most . . . for script—a species of money which the Church issues to its pensioners and its poor." (Charles N. Crewdson, *The Other Side of Mormonism.*)

2 Utter.

"Sister Bybee spoke in tongues. President Young declared it to be a proper tongue, and inquired what the nations would do if they were

course, not of an inspired ability on the part of its recipient to speak an alien earthly language and so bear the Mormon gospel into foreign lands; instead, it was a sudden bursting forth into a flow of words that, because they belonged to no earthly tongue, were supposed to be utterances in the language celestial, and in order to be understood, even by the devout, or the very speaker, had to be "translated" by a Saint inspired for that purpose. The custom undoubtedly endangered the hierarchal monopoly of revelation, and as, to the sceptic, it sounded, as the same gift when exercised by the Irvingites sounded to Carlyle, like an idiotic "la-la-ing," it is probable that the Church quietly discouraged it on the ground that, divine as was its origin, its exercise nevertheless brought holy things into ridicule and disrepute among the ungodly. Yet it remains firm in the Mormon faith as a heavenly phenomenon.

Though prophecy, visions, and revelation went so far with the earlier fathers of the Mormon Church as to leave little to be revealed, and though they are therefore now largely confined to occasional Presidential manifestos, the Saints still believe in both the accuracy of those past and the occurrence of such as may be needed in the present and future. Indeed, Parley Pratt extended this article of the creed by declaring that many of the prophecies of the Old and New Testaments had already been literally fulfilled, and that all must some day, before the reign of Christ, be fulfilled to the letter. He insisted that every prophecy

here. He said, if he were to give way to the brethren and sisters, the day of Pentecost would be in the shade in comparison to it." (Report of a conference at Utah, from an article in *The Edinburgh Review* quoted in Littell's *Living Age*, vol. xlii. p. 147.)

delivered by a true prophet be taken at its face value, and he inveighed against the school of theologians of whom, said Pratt, if Noah were one of them to-day and were warned of the Flood and the way to escape it, he would interpret the message of a Deluge as meaning a spiritual deluge and the Ark as being a spiritual ark.[1] Of course, it is just possible that human errors may creep into such utterances because they come through a human medium, but revelation is literal, direct, and continuous, and the head of the Church remains God's mouthpiece in addressing his people.[2]

Finally, in the matter of healing, the Mormons preceded Mrs Eddy and the "Christian Scientists" in the United States by a great many years. There are no doubters in Mormondom. "If God made the world," they demand, "can He not cure the sick?" Until recent times physicians were rarely sought, and to-day, though science is admitted by the less uneducated to be of assistance to prayer, there is still a wide prejudice against such as "seek not unto the Lord, but to the physicians."

1 *Introduction to Doctrine.*

2 Although revelation affecting the Church or the world beyond one's self is jealously confined to the hierarchy, "besides these revelations given in public, and for public purposes, through the seer or revelator, each individual is privileged, according to the purity of his life, to receive revelations, for his own comfort, instruction, or benefit. One thing, it seems, is personally received by each one, and that is the faith to say, 'I know that Mormonism is true.' This is said, as a rule, by every speaker who opens his mouth in any religious meeting; and the meaning of it is, not that the individual has investigated the history of the faith, and learned of its truth through processes that convinced him intellectually, but that he has an inward faith or feeling that came to him as a direct divine revelation." (Utter.)

Article VIII. We believe the Bible to be the word of God, as far as it is translated correctly; we also believe The Book of Mormon to be the word of God.

What "translated correctly" means we have already seen. We have also already seen how Smith "corrected" the Bible and amplified it to suit the needs of himself and his Church, and how his people, with this reservation in mind, insist upon a literal interpretation. The Mormon theologian Flanigan added to this article the words, "And in all other good books,"[1] thus including, as all Mormons do, *The Doctrine and Covenants* and *The Pearl of Great Price*, which none can read and doubt their being the work of the same man that composed *The Book of Mormon*.

Article IX. We believe all that God has revealed, all that he does now reveal, and we believe that he will yet reveal many great and important things pertaining to the kingdom of God.[2]

This article in part covers the question of a literal interpretation of the Bible, already covered, and is in part a provision for the finding of more of the golden plates from some of which Smith "translated" *The Book of Mormon*. At the time of that discovery Smith insisted that certain plates had not yet been unearthed, and that others were "sealed" against the arrival of a more propitious season. That more plates will be "found" is, of course, unlikely, and this for the excellent reason that the other articles of the Mormon faith

[1] *Mormonism Triumphant.*

[2] Flanigan adds: "And the Messiah's second coming" (*Mormonism Triumphant*).

sufficiently provide for all the revelations likely to be necessary; but the article is also helpful in presenting the Mormons' belief in belief, their readiness to borrow from any other faith, new or old, whatever tenet seems pleasant or requisite, and their consequently inevitable reply, "We believe practically the same thing," to almost any doctrine of any other faith that a member of that other faith presents to them in attractive or logical form.

> *Article X. We believe in the literal gathering of Israel and in the restoration of the Ten Tribes; that Zion will be built upon this continent; that Christ will reign personally upon the earth, and that the earth will be renewed and receive its paradise glory.*

In connection with this article it should be noted that not only was Zion, the capital city of God, to be built in America, first in Missouri and then in Utah, where it is now established, but the Garden of Eden had also been in the western hemisphere, being located, in fact, in Jackson County, Missouri. It is from this place, the first site chosen for Zion, that the paradisaic glory is to spread over all the earth. Meantime, the Saints were admonished that Christ would never return if his city was not built, but that, once it was prepared, the Second Coming would not be long delayed and the temporal reign of the Messiah over all the world begin. Salt Lake City being now an achieved fact, many Mormon calculations declare that the millennium cannot be far away. Flanigan has further stated[1] that the Saints believe in the literal resurrection of the body, in the rising first of those

[1] *Mormonism Triumphant.*

who died in the faith, and in the postponement of the resurrection of all the rest of mankind until the thousand years have expired and Christ's temporal rule is at an end.

Articles XI., XII., and XIII.

We claim the privilege of worshipping Almighty God according to the dictates of our consciences, and allow all men the same privilege, let them worship how, where, or what they may.

We believe in being subject to kings, presidents, rulers, and magistrates, in obeying, honouring, and sustaining the law.

We believe in being honest, true, chaste, benevolent, virtuous, and in doing good to all men; *indeed, we may say that we follow the admonition of Paul. "We believe all things, we hope all things"; we have endured many things, and hope to be able to endure all things. If there is anything virtuous, lovely, or of good report or praiseworthy, we seek after these things.*

These articles seem innocent enough, and probably were intended merely to show the Saints' acceptance of the moral codes accepted, if not practised, by the rest of the world. It must, however, be observed that a Mormon woman accused of dishonesty in her testimony in court regarding polygamy is reported to have answered, "I lied only to the Gentile God, not to the Mormon," thereby possibly demonstrating what is to many Saints the advantage of polytheism for the protection of their faith against the infidel.[1] And in the more interesting matter of polygamy, one must

[1] "The Mormon Revival of Polygamy," Burton J. Hendrick, *M'Clure's Magazine,* January 1911.

bear in mind that, as we shall presently see, the Woodruff manifesto, issued to obtain statehood, though it pretends to abolish plural marriage, may be read in more ways than one; that polygamy was at least at one time an essential part of the Mormon faith and "a means of the highest heavenly exaltation"; and that, finally, the Mormons still call the practice of polygamy "living one's religion." So much is certain: when Smith wrote these articles and his followers, accused of polygamy, denied it—to the Gentile God, perhaps—the revelation in which Mormon polygamy originated was already written.

Of the doctrine of "Blood Atonement," of which much has been printed, something will be said when we come to treat more particularly of the political activities of the Mormon Church. The assertion of anti-Mormons is to the effect that murder of Gentiles dangerous to the faith is a means of grace and a way of saving the Gentiles' souls; and these critics add that this particular method of evangelization is enjoined by oath, and under penalties, upon all the faithful that pass through the Endowment House, the spirit of the doctrine being directed especially against the representatives of the Government of the United States, as a vengeance for the martyrdom of Mormons.

This brings us to the Endowment House. According to Mr Utter,[1] Smith, outgrowing his earlier belief that secret societies were a wicked thing, joined a fraternity, and it is commonly said that there is a resemblance between the "degree-work" of such fraternities and the rites in the Mormon temples called "taking the endowments." Says Mr Utter:

"In spite of their oaths, many who 'have gone

[1] *Mormonism To-Day.*

through the temple' have described these ceremonies, and their agreement is such as to leave little doubt as to the general facts. Endowments are usually taken at the time of marriage, though they may be taken at any time, but only in a temple, or an 'endowment house,' which is a substitute for a temple. The ceremonies continue for several hours, and consist of a sort of miracle play, embracing the whole subject-matter of the Bible, or at least the scheme of redemption as understood by the Latter Day Saints. There is, first, baptism or washing, or both; then anointing; and then the putting on the endowment robes, or the 'garments,' as they are popularly called. Then the couple are told that they personate Adam and Eve, and a guide or interpreter answers for or prompts them, and the drama begins. First, they are taken into a room whose walls (in the Salt Lake Temple) are magnificently painted to represent the Garden of Eden, or the natural world before the fall of man. Here the lessons are

> 'Of man's first disobedience, and the fruit
> Of that forbidden tree, whose mortal taste
> Brought death into the world and all our woe.'

Then the candidates are taken into a room representing the world as it now is, where many other lessons are given. Satan is said to be one of the chief characters. Elohim, Jehovah, and Jesus are heard talking behind screens. The marriage occurs in one of the rooms into which they pass after the grips and passwords and the grand secrets of the different priesthoods have been given.

"Every woman who 'goes through the temple' is 'sealed' to some man as his spiritual wife for eternity. Many are sealed to Jesus, some to Joseph Smith, many to Brigham Young, many to one man for time and to another for eternity. The 'endowments' pertain to exaltation in the life to come. One who should live and die a Mormon without going through this ceremonial would not belong to any particular family in heaven, and would in reality have only a servant's place; but if one is sealed to a prominent man or leader, she is already established in an exalted position in the society of heaven. Endowments are also substantially 'taken' for the dead, and this adds greatly to the temple 'work.' It is the hope and the deliberate intention of many of the most self-sacrificing of these people to save the whole world in this way. Any person who has a Mormon for a friend is likely, after death, 'to have his work done for him' by that friend, or by a hired worker paid by that friend, and so his salvation and exaltation will be secured.

"The 'garments' put on during these ceremonies are to be worn during life, and when changed, the person is careful to put off the soiled linen, part at a time, and put on the fresh garments in a similar way, so as never to be wholly unclothed. At death the garments serve as burial robes; and some people are quite superstitious in regard to their use in this way, believing that in the morning of the resurrection such robes will be useful and prevent shame and exposure."[1]

Fortunately we have a full description of this endowment-taking. It is that of Mrs Fanny Stenhouse, and because her book[2] is out of print we here reproduce her account in full.

Mrs Stenhouse was an Englishwoman, who married and went to Utah in the early days of Mormondom.

1 See also the admissions of witnesses in the case before the United States District Court previously quoted in this volume.

2 *The Tyranny of Mormonism.*

She and her husband, at that time devout believers, were persuaded to "take the endowments." She says:

"So I agreed to go, trying to persuade myself that it was a sacred duty; for, although my faith in Mormonism had been roughly shaken, I still believed that its origin was divine.

"The Temple robe, which is a long, loose, flowing garment, made of white linen or bleached muslin, and reaching to the ankle, had been placed upon us just before we took the oaths. It was gathered to a band about twelve inches long, which rested on the right shoulder, passed across the breast, and came together upon the left arm, and was then fastened by a linen belt. This leaves the left arm entirely free. The veil consists of a large square of Swiss muslin, gathered in one corner so as to form a sort of cap to fit the head; the remainder falls down as a veil. The men wear the same kind of under garment as the women, and their robes are the same, but their head-dress is a round piece of linen drawn up with a string and a bow in front, something after the fashion of a Scotch cap. All good Mormons, after they have received their first endowments, get whole suits of Temple robes made on purpose for them, so that they may be ready for use at any time when they are needed. All marriages in the Endowment House are performed in these robes, and in them all Saints who have received their endowments are buried. Besides our robes, we were instructed to take with us a bottle of the best olive-oil.

"At seven o'clock in the morning of the day appointed, we presented ourselves at the door of the Endowment House, and were admitted by Brother Lyon, the Mormon poet. Everything within was beautifully neat and clean, and a solemn silence pervaded the whole place. The only sound that could be heard was the splashing of water, but whence the sound proceeded we could not see. In spite of myself, a feeling of dread and uncertainty respecting what I had to go through would steal over my mind, and I earnestly wished that the day was over.

"We waited patiently for a little while, and presently a man entered and seated himself at a table placed there for that purpose, upon which was a large book. He opened the book, and then, calling each person in turn, he took their names and ages, and the names of their fathers and mothers, and carefully entered each particular in the book. Our bottles of oil were then taken from us, and we were supposed to be ready for the ceremony.

"First, we were told to take off our shoes and leave them in the anteroom, and then to take up our bundles and pass into another room beyond. This was a large bathroom, which was divided down the middle by a curtain of heavy material placed there for the purpose of separating the men from the women. Here my husband left me—he going to the men's and I to the women's division. In the bathroom were two or three large bathing-tubs supplied by streams of hot and cold water. We were as much concealed from the men as if we had been in an entirely separate room, and everything was very quiet and orderly.

"Miss Eliza R. Snow, the poetess, and a Mrs Whitney were the officiating attendants on that occasion. The former conducted me to one of the bathing-tubs, and, placing me in it, she proceeded to wash me from the crown of my head to the soles of my feet. As she did this she repeated various formulas to the effect that I was now washed clean from the blood of this generation and should never, if I remained faithful, be partaker in the plagues and miseries which were about to come upon the earth. When I had thus been washed clean, she wiped me dry, and then, taking a large horn filled with the olive-oil which we had brought, she anointed me. The oil was poured from the horn by Mrs Whitney into the hand of Eliza Snow, who then applied it to me. The horn was said to be the horn of plenty, which, like the widow's cruse of oil, would never fail as long as the ordinance should continue to be administered. In addition to the crown of my head, my eyes, ears, and mouth were also anointed: my eyes that they might be quick to see, my ears that they might be apt at hearing, and my mouth that I might with wisdom speak the words of eternal life. She also anointed my feet, that they might be swift to run in the ways of the Lord I was then given a certain garment to put on.

"Now, this garment is one peculiar to the Mormon people. It is made so as to envelop the whole body, and it is worn night and day. I was told that after having once put it on, I must never wholly take it off before putting on another, but that I should change one half at a time, and that if I did so I should be protected from disease, and even from death itself; for the bullet of an enemy would not penetrate that garment, and that from it even the dagger's point should be turned aside. It has been said that Prophet Joseph carelessly left off this peculiar garment on the day of his death, and that, had he not done so, the rifles of his assassins would have been harmless against him.

"When thus arrayed, I proceeded to put on a white nightdress and skirt, stockings, and white linen shoes. A new name was then whispered into my ear, which I was told I must never mention to any living soul except my husband in the Endowment House. This name was taken from the Bible, and I was given to understand that it would be the name whereby I should be admitted into the celestial kingdom. This was of course very gratifying. A circumstance, however, occurred which took from me all the pride which might have been mine in the possession of a new name. There was among our number a deaf woman; Mrs Whitney had to tell her her name once or twice over, loud enough for me to hear, and thus I found that her new name, as well as mine, was Sarah. To make the matter worse, another sister whispered, 'Why, that is my name too.' This entirely dispelled any enthusiasm which otherwise I might have felt. I could well understand that I might yet become a Sarah in Israel; but if we were all Sarahs, there would not be much distinction or honour in being called by that name. As a matter of course, I supposed that the men would all become Abrahams.

"Our washing and anointing being now over, we were ready for the initiation—there were about fifteen couples in all.

"A voice from behind the curtain asked Miss Snow if we were ready, and was answered in the affirmative. We were then arranged in a row, the curtain was drawn aside, and we stood face to face with the men, who had, of course, on their side of the curtain, been put through the same ordeal. I felt dreadfully nervous, for I did not know what was coming next, and I could not quite dismiss from my mind the stories that I had heard about these mysteries. But in spite of my nervousness, curiosity was strong in me at that moment, as it was, I suppose, in the others; for, as soon as the curtain was drawn aside, we all cast our eyes in the direction of the men. They, as might be expected, were looking in our direction, and when I beheld them I must say that my sympathies were drawn out towards the poor creatures. However little vanity or personal pride they possessed, they must have felt it unpleasant to have to appear in the presence of ladies in such a dress—or rather *un*dress; and notwithstanding the solemn meaning of the ceremony, there was just the ghost of a smile upon our faces as we looked at each other and dropped our eyes again. To anyone who did not feel as we did the religious nature of the initiation, the scene must have appeared perfectly ludicrous. In fact, some of us felt it so. One sister, just as the curtain was drawn up and we came in full view of our lords, cried out, 'Oh dear, oh dear, where shall I go? What shall I do?' This, as may be supposed, caused a laugh, which was, of course, immediately suppressed.

"We could see how the men looked, but of our own appearance we could not so easily judge. Certainly, we must have looked anything but handsome in our white garments, and with the oil trickling down our faces and into our eyes, making them smart and look red. There was nothing, however, for us to do but to submit quietly and make the best of it we could. Ashamed as I was, I thought I might venture to look at my husband—there could be no harm in that; but when I saw his demure-looking countenance and his efforts to keep his clothing in order, I thought I should be compelled to laugh outright, for I could see that his thoughts were more occupied about his personal appearance than with the solemnity of the occasion. The men were all dressed in the same garment as the women—drawers and shirt all in one, very much like those which are used for children to sleep in, and over that an ordinary white shirt, such as men always wear; that, with socks and white linen shoes, completed their toilet.

"Clad after this interesting fashion, we sat opposite to each other for several minutes, and then my husband and myself were instructed to come forward and kneel at the altar while all the rest remained standing. It is the custom thus to select two persons, and we were either picked out by chance, or it might be, as my husband was thought a good deal of by the authorities, that they considered he would feel honoured by the preference.

"Suddenly a voice was heard speaking to someone, who also replied. This voice from the unseen was supposed to be the voice of Elohim in conversation with Jehovah, and the words that were used were much the same as those contained in the first chapter of the book of Genesis, describing the creation of the world. Finally, Jehovah and Elohim declare their intention to come down and visit the earth. This they do, and pronounce all that they behold very good; but they declare that it is necessary that one of a higher order of intelligence than the brute creation should be placed in the world to govern and control all else.

"Michael the Archangel is now called, and he is placed upon the earth under the name of Adam, and power is given him over all the beasts of the field, the fowls of the air, and the fishes of the sea. Moreover, the fruits of the earth are all given to him for his sustenance and pleasure; but he is strictly charged, as in the Bible story, not to eat of one particular tree which stands in the midst of the garden. This tree is represented by a small real evergreen, and a few bunches of dried raisins are hung upon it as fruit.

"It is now discovered that it is not good for man to be alone; Elohim and Jehovah, therefore, hold another conversation upon that subject, and they finally determine to give a companion to Adam. They therefore cause a deep sleep to fall upon Michael—or Adam, as he is now called—and they prepare to operate upon him. Here we were all instructed to assume the attitude of deep sleep by dropping our heads upon our breasts. Elohim and Jehovah then come down and go through the motions of removing a rib from the side of the sleeper, which said rib appears immediately upon the scene in the person of Eliza R. Snow. Elohim and Jehovah are generally represented by two of the Twelve Apostles. When Brigham is present he plays a prominent part.

"And now the devil makes his appearance in the person of W. W. Phelps. Phelps used always to personate the devil in the Endowments, and the *rôle* suited him admirably. . . . The devil wears a very tight-fitting suit of black muslin, with knee-breeches and black stockings and slippers. The dress had all the appearance of a theatrical costume, and the man looked as much like what one might imagine the devil would look as he possibly could. He began by trying to scrape an acquaintance with Eve, whom he meets while taking a walk in the garden. The innocent, unsuspecting woman is fascinated by his attentions. Father Adam—who seems to have had a touch of the Mormon about him—perhaps was not the most attentive of husbands; or he may have made the same mistake as that which so many of his sons have since made—neglecting to pay the same attentions after marriage as he was wont to before—and left his young wife to the mercy of the tempter. However that may be, Satan and Eve are soon discovered in conversation together, and Eve appears to be particularly pleased with Satan. At length he offers her some of the fruit of the forbidden tree, and after some little demur she accepts it and eats thereof.

"Then the devil leaves her, Adam makes his appearance, and Eve persuades him also to eat of the fruit of the tree. After this they make a dumb show of perceiving their condition, and an apron of white linen is produced, on which are sewn pieces of green silk in imitation of fig-leaves, and in these they both attire themselves.

"Then all the brethren and sisters produced similar aprons which they had brought with them on purpose, and these they put on as Adam and Eve had already done. Elohim now appeared again and called Adam; but Adam was afraid and hid himself in the garden with Eve. The curse was now pronounced upon the serpent—the devil—who reappears upon his hands and knees making a hissing noise. . . . We were then all driven out of the Garden of Eden into another room which represented the world—and this ended the 'First Degree.'

"We were now supposed to be out in the world earning our daily bread by the sweat of our brows, and we were informed that, although we had been driven out from the presence of the Lord, yet a plan of salvation would be devised for us by which we should be enabled to return to our first estate. We were to wait patiently until this plan should be disclosed to us.

"There was such a mixture of persons and events that I could not exactly follow the idea that was intended to be conveyed. . . . Men representing the ancient prophets entered and gave instructions to the people to prepare themselves for the first coming of our Saviour upon earth. Then we were taught certain passwords and grips; and then we were all arranged in a circle. The women covered their faces with their veils, and we all kneeled down, and with our right hands uplifted towards heaven we took the solemn oath of obedience and secrecy. We swore that by every means in our power we would seek to avenge the death of Joseph Smith, the Prophet, upon the Gentiles who had caused his murder, and that we would teach our children to do so; we swore that without murmur or questioning we would implicitly obey the commands of the priesthood in everything; we swore that we would not commit adultery—which with reference to the men was explained to mean the taking of wives without the permission of the holy priesthood; and we swore that we would never under any circumstances reveal that which transpired in the Endowment House.

"The penalty for breaking this oath, which was worded in the most startling and impressive way, was then explained to us. His bowels were—while he was yet living—to be torn from him, his throat was to be cut from ear to ear, and his heart and tongue were to be cut out. In the world to come everlasting damnation would be his portion. . . .

"After these fearful oaths had been taken with due solemnity, we were instructed in the various signs representing those dreadful penalties, and we were also given a 'grip' peculiar to this degree.

"We were next entertained by a long address from the Apostle Heber C. Kimball. . . . The subject of which he discoursed was the married life in the 'Celestial

Order'; he also laid great stress upon the necessity of our keeping silence concerning all that we had witnessed in the Endowment House—even husbands to wives and wives to their husbands, we were not to utter a single word. With the sermon ended our 'Second Degree.'

"We were now taken to another room for the purpose of passing through the 'Third Degree' of the Order of the Melchisedec (*sic*) Priesthood. When we were all arranged on one side against the wall, a number of individuals entered who were supposed to represent the ministers of every denomination and religion upon the face of the earth. The devil also makes his appearance again. The ministers set forth the various claims of their respective creeds—each one striving to show that his is the purest and the best,—but the devil sows division and hatred among them, and a good deal of confusion ensues.

"Then came in the personages representing Peter, James, and John, the Apostles; and they commanded ministers, devil, and all to depart. They then appeared to organize a new Church in which the true principles of the Gospel were to be taught; our Temple robes were also all changed from the right shoulder to the left, indicating that we were now in the true Church, and that we were to be absolutely and in every way dependent upon the priesthood. Another grip was then given, and thus we received the 'Third Degree' of the Order of the Melchisedec (*sic*) Priesthood. In that room was a division made of bleached muslin; in the division a door; and in the door a hole, with a flap of muslin over it, through which to pass the hand. Whoever was on the other side could see us, but we could not see them. The men first approached this door. A person representing the Apostle Peter appeared at the opening in the muslin curtain, and mysterious fingers cut a mark on the left breast of the men's shirts—one mark also over the abdomen, and one over the right knee; which marks the women religiously imitated upon their own garments when they got home. The applicant was then told to put his hand through the opening and give the last grip belonging to the 'Third Degree,' and mention his new name. He was then permitted to enter. This was called 'going behind the veil.' When the men were all admitted, the women were suffered to approach, and were passed through by their own husbands. When a woman has no husband she is passed through by one of the brethren; and to those who are not going to be married or sealed for eternity, here the ceremonies end.

"Now, as I before stated, according to Mormon ideas we had never before been legally married. It was therefore necessary that we should now pass through that ceremony. We accordingly were conducted to a desk, where our names were entered, and we were then passed into another room. In that room was a long, low altar covered with red velvet, and an armchair placed at one end of it, in which sat Brigham Young. My husband knelt at one side of the altar and I at the other, with our hands clasped above it in the last grip which had been given to us. Then the ordinary formula of marriage was gone through with, and we were informed that we were sealed for time and for eternity.

"Thus we passed through the mysteries of the Endowment House, and at three o'clock in the afternoon we found ourselves at liberty to return home. The various ceremonies had occupied eight hours."[1]

[1] The naïve quality of these ceremonies characterizes the Mormon hymns. Thus we have the saints singing:

"I never knew what joy was
Till I became a Mormon."

And again to the air of the *Marseillaise*:

"The Spirit of God is like a fire burning!
The latter-day glory begins to come forth;
The visions and blessings of old are returning,
The angels are coming to visit the earth.
We'll sing and we'll shout with the armies of heaven,
Hosannah! Hosannah to God and the Lamb;
All glory to them in the highest be given
Henceforth and for ever: Amen, and Amen."

Still another note of triumph sounds in this hymn:

"The morning breaks, the shadows flee;
Lo! Zion's standard is unfurled!
The dawning of a brighter day
Majestic rises on the world.

The clouds of error disappear
Before the rays of truth divine;
The glory bursting from afar,
Wide o'er the nations soon will shine!

The Gentile fulness now comes in,
And Israel's blessings are at hand;
Lo! Judah's remnant, cleansed from sin,
Shall in the promised Canaan stand.

Angels from heaven and truth from earth
Have met, and both have record borne;
Thus Zion's light is bursting forth
To bring her ransomed children home."

And the entire Mormon spirit, whatever may be said of the poetic virtues of the verse, is summed up in these lines on the murder of Joseph Smith:

"Unchanged in death, with a Saviour's love
He pleads their cause in the courts above.
His home's in the sky, he dwells with the Gods,
Far from the furious rage of mobs! . . .

He died! he died for those he loved;
He reigns! he reigns in the realms above."

The church services of the Latter Day Saints do not, it may be added, differ greatly from those of the larger non-ritualistic sects.

X

POLYGAMY BEGUN AND SUSPENDED

In *The Book of Mormon* it is written:

"This people seek to excuse themselves in committing whoredoms because of the things which were written concerning David, and Solomon . . . truly had many wives and concubines, which thing was abominable before me, said the Lord. . . . I will not suffer that this people shall do like them of old. . . . There shall not any man among you have save it be one wife, and concubines he shall have none; for I the Lord God delighteth (*sic*) in the chastity of women."[1]

Thus Joseph Smith, when he wrote *The Book of Mormon* in 1827, or the god of Joseph Smith when he delivered this message to the patriarch who set it down for Smith's ultimate "translation." But between that time and 1843, either the god of Joseph Smith or that god's prophet suffered a change of heart, for in the latter year the head of the Latter Day Saints received from heaven the following revelation:[2]

[1] Jacob ii.

[2] Revelation of 12th July 1843, once omitted from *The Doctrine and Covenants,* then published in its chronological place, and, in the latest editions, printed at the end of the volume.

"Revelation on the Eternity of the Marriage
"Covenant, including Plurality of Wives.

"*Given through Joseph the Seer, in Nauvoo, Ill.,*
"*July* 12, 1843.

"Verily, thus saith the Lord unto you, my servant Joseph, that inasmuch as you have inquired of my hand to understand wherein I the Lord justified my servants Abraham, Isaac, and Jacob as touching the principle and doctrine of their having many wives and concubines: Behold, I reveal unto you an everlasting covenant; and if ye abide not that covenant, then are ye damned; for no one can reject this covenant and be permitted to enter into my glory. . . . The conditions of this law are these: All . . . oaths, connections . . . that are not made and entered into and sealed by the Holy Spirit of Promise of him who is anointed (and I have appointed unto my servant Joseph Smith to hold this power in the last days, and there is never but one on earth at a time on whom this power and the keys of the priesthood are conferred) are of no efficacy, virtue, or force in and after the resurrection from the dead. . . . Therefore, if a man marry him a wife in the world, and he marry her not by me . . . they are not bound by any law when they are out of the world. Therefore, when they are out of the world, they neither marry nor are given in marriage, but are appointed angels in heaven . . . to minister for those who are worthy of a far more and an exceeding and eternal weight of glory. Again, verily . . . if a man marry a wife by my word and by the new and everlasting covenant, and it is sealed to them by the Holy Spirit of Promise by him who is appointed . . . then shall it be written in the Lamb's Book of Life . . . it shall be done unto them in all things whatsoever my servant hath put upon them in time and throughout eternity; . . . and they shall pass by the angels and the Gods which are set there in their exaltation and glory in all things, as hath been sealed upon their heads. Then shall they be Gods, because they have no end . . . and the angels are subject to them."

This, though condensed, is the revelation from on high on which the Mormon doctrine of polygamy is founded, and upon it, cunningly devised as it is, has been erected a structure of dogma which amounts to this: that to commit polygamy in this world is the one way to obtain pardon for terrestrial sins and at the same time to ensure heavenly exaltation in the life to come. Whatever may now be said to the contrary, no unprejudiced student of the faith of the Latter Day Saints can doubt that Mormonism, at least in the form in which it attained its present power, was built upon polygamy.[1]

For the Church proceeded to teach that Adam, the

[1] English readers, or some of them, may still recall how the argument of Dr Colenso, Anglican Bishop of Natal, in favour of polygamy for his converts stirred the Established Church of England. His wish was that this Church should formally declare polygamy not an evil *per se*, but a practice that, in particular circumstances, might be permitted of converts from heathendom. As *The Spectator* later (1862) put it, he argued against the hardship of compelling a polygamous convert to put away plural wives married under the sway of his former faith; to which it was replied that such a course was a trial no more than the compulsory renunciation of caste required of Hindoo converts. When there seemed to be an inclination to justify the toleration of polygamy and the "civil immunity which polygamy has always enjoyed in heathen countries governed by British law," the Established Church responded that polygamy could not be recognized by the faith because it "enslaves half the human race" and "cannot

god of this earth and of the men on it, his children, was a polygamist in heaven before he came to earth, bringing Eve, "one of his wives," with him. "The question has been and is often asked," said Brigham Young,[1] "who it was that begat the Son of the Virgin Mary. The infidel world have concluded that if what the Apostles wrote about his father and mother be true, and the present marriage discipline acknowledged by Christendom be correct, then Christians must believe that God is the father of an illegitimate son, in the person of Jesus Christ! I will tell you how it is. Our Father

be worked at all without sharp and stern laws pressed down on the women's necks."

Nevertheless, there was a time when, in England, plural marriage, at least on the part of the wife, seems not to have been so harshly regarded, as one sees from this entry in the register of St Mary's Church, Bermondsey, in the year 1604: "The forme of a solemne *vowe* made betwixt a man and his wife, having been longe absent, through occasion the woman beinge married to another man, took her again as followeth:—*The Man's Speach.*—'Elizabeth, my beloved Wife, I am right sorie that I have so longe absented mysealfe from thee, whereby thou shouldest be occasioned to take another man to be thy husband. Therefore I do now vowe and promise in the sight of God, and this companie, to take thee againe as mine owne, and will not only forgive thee, but also dwell with thee, and do all other duties unto thee, as I promised at our marriage.' *The Woman's Speach.*—'Ralphe, my beloved Husband, I am right sorie I have in thy absence taken another man to be my husband; but here, before God and this companie, I renounce and forsake him, and do promise to keape mysealfe unto thee during life, and to perform all duties which I first promised unto thee in our marriage.'" Then follows a short occasional prayer, the entry thus concluding: "The first day of August, 1604, Ralphe Goodchild, of the parish of Barkinge, in Thames Street, and *Elizabeth* his wife, were agreed to live together; and thereupon gave their hands to one another, making either of them a solemn vow so to doe in the presence of us, William Steve, Parson; Edward Coker, and Richard Eives, Clerk."

[1] Brigham Young, *Journal of Discourses,* vol. i. p. 50.

in Heaven begat all the spirits that ever were, or ever will be, upon this earth; and they were born spirits in the eternal world. Then the Lord by his power and wisdom organized the mortal tabernacle of man. We were first made spiritual, and afterwards temporal. Now hear it, O inhabitants of the earth, Jew and Gentile, saint and sinner! When our father Adam came into the garden of Eden, he came into it with a celestial body, and brought Eve, *one of his wives*,[1] with him."[2] This god's first affair was to "increase and

[1] The italics are Young's.

[2] Brigham continues: "He is Michael, the Archangel, the Ancient of Days, about whom holy men have written and spoken. He is our Father and our God, and the only God with whom we have to do. Every man upon the earth, professing Christians or non-professing, must hear it, and will know it sooner or later. When the Virgin Mary conceived the child Jesus, the Father had begotten him in his own likeness. He was not begotten by the Holy Ghost. And who is the Father? He is the first of the human family; and when he took a tabernacle, it was begotten by his Father in heaven, after the same manner as the tabernacle of Cain, Abel, and the rest of the sons and daughters of Adam and Eve; from the fruits of the earth, the first earthly tabernacles were originated by the Father, and so on in succession. I could tell you much more about this; but were I to tell you the whole truth, blasphemy would be nothing to it, in the estimation of the superstitious and overrighteous of mankind. However, I have told you the truth as far as I have gone." Later (p. 51), the same authority continues: "I was in conversation with a certain learned professor upon this subject, when I replied . . . 'If the Son was begotten by the Holy Ghost, it would be dangerous to baptize and confirm females, and give the Holy Ghost to them, lest he should beget children, to be palmed off upon the Elders by the people, bringing the Elders into great difficulties.'" This amazing doctrine is the doctrine of the Mormon Church. In *The Mormon Doctrine of Deity* we read (pp. 42–43): "Some sectarian ministers are saying that we Mormons are ashamed of the doctrine. . . . No, my friends, it is not that we are ashamed. . . . If you see any change coming over the countenance when this doctrine is named, it is surprise, astonish-

multiply" and replenish the earth. It was his task in sinless state, it was his task after the fall; and now, in the star to which he has been exalted and from which he governs this world, the god continues to multiply, begetting in heaven celestial instead of terrestrial children that must have for their salvation an earthly birth, which can be procured for them only by man's earthly productiveness.

God the Father, the Mormons teach, is, then, a polygamist;[1] but they do not stop there. The Latter Day Saints are at least no people for half-way measures. They taught and teach that God the Son was also a polygamist, that Mary and Martha were his wives, and that they were "sealed" to him at the wedding at Cana.[2]

ment that anyone at all capable of grasping the largeness and extent of the universe, the grandeur of existence, and the possibilities in man for growth, for progress, should be so lean of intellect, should have such a paucity of understanding, as to call it in question at all."

1 And all the pantheon of gods: "If none but gods will be permitted to multiply *immortal* children, it follows that each god must have one or more wives." (Orson Pratt.)

2 "I will next call your attention to the marriage practice of Jacob, one of the most illustrious prophets, and a grandson of Abraham. Jacob had several wives, and by them were born unto him the Twelve Patriarchs, after whom all the tribes of Israel were named. Now, sir, one of these wives was honoured with being the lineal mother of Jesus Christ, according to the flesh. What! Jesus Christ descended from a man who advocated the doctrine of a plurality of wives, and actually had many wives! Why, he was as bad as Mahomet! 'I wonder,' says one, 'that God ever kept a record of such a lineage, seeing it favours the doctrine of a plurality of wives.' Why, sir, this was one object of keeping the record of Christ's lineage, that it might sustain this very doctrine." (Orson Spencer's *Letters*, p. 197, 1891 edition.)

"'Then you really mean to hold to the doctrine that the Saviour of the world was married; do you mean to be understood so? And, if so, do you mean to be understood that he had more than one wife?' . . . Now, suppose I should set out myself, and travel through the

From this point progress was easy. What God the Father (Adam) had done on earth, and what God the Son (Jesus) had done on earth, it was the duty of man to do on earth in order to release on earth God's

cities of the nation as a celebrated reformer, preaching revelations and sentiments as lofty as the skies, and rolling out ideas strange and new, to which the multitude were entirely unaccustomed; and wherever I went, suppose I had with me three or four women, one combing my head, another washing my feet, and another shedding tears upon them, and wiping them with the hair of her head. Suppose I should lean upon them, would it not appear monstrous in the eyes of the world? Would they ride me into Jerusalem upon an ass's colt, and cast branches of the palm tree beneath my feet, shouting: 'Hosannah! blessed is he that cometh in the name of the Lord; hosannah in the highest!'? I guess they would give me a coat of tar and feathers and ride me on a rail; and it is my opinion they would serve the Saviour the same, did he go about now as he did eighteen hundred years ago.

"There is an old prophecy of Isaiah, which I cannot stop to read, but you will find it in the 53rd chapter of his prophecies; read the whole of the chapter. This particular prophecy speaks of Christ all the way through. It is there said, 'When thou shalt make his soul an offering for sin, he shall see his seed.' . . . If he has no seed, how shall he see them? . . . By and by, the prophet goes on to say, 'And who shall declare his generation?' for his life is taken from the earth. If he had no generation, who could declare it? . . . Who shall declare it? He could not, for he was cut off from the earth.

"How was it with Mary and Martha, and other women that followed Him? In old times, and it is common in this day, the women, even as Sarah, called their husbands lord; the word lord is tantamount to husband in some languages; master, lord, husband, are about synonymous. In England we frequently hear the wife say, 'Where is my master?' She does not mean a tyrant, but as Sarah called her husband lord, she designates hers by the word master. When Mary of old came to the sepulchre on the first day of the week, instead of finding Jesus she saw two angels in white. 'And they say unto her, Woman, why weepest thou? She said unto them, Because they have taken away my Lord (or husband), and I know not where they have laid him. And when she had thus said, she turned herself back, and saw Jesus standing, and knew not that it was Jesus. Jesus

heavenly children, who were clamouring for that terrestrial birth and its subsequent state of probation in this world whereby alone the children of God may gain place in God's kingdom after the end of the earth.[1] Man must do what God had done before him, men

saith unto her, Woman, why weepest thou? Whom seekest thou? She, supposing him to be the gardener, saith unto him, Sir, if thou have borne him hence, tell me where thou hast laid him, and I will take him away. Jesus saith unto her, Mary. She turned herself, and saith unto him, Rabboni; which is to say, Master.' Is there not here manifested the affection of a wife? These words speak the kindred ties and sympathies that are common to that relation of husband and wife. Where will you find a family so nearly allied by the ties of common religion? 'Well,' you say, 'that appears rather plausible, but I want a little more evidence. I want you to find where it says the Saviour was actually married.'

"Gentlemen, that is as plain as the translators, or different councils over this Scripture, dare allow it to go to the world, but the thing is there; it is told; Jesus was the bridegroom at the marriage of Cana of Galilee, and he told them what to do.

"Now, there was actually a marriage; and if Jesus was not the bridegroom on that occasion, please tell me who was. If any man can show this, and prove that it was not the Saviour of the world, then I will acknowledge that I am in error. We say it was Jesus Christ who was married, to be brought into the relation whereby he could see his seed before he was crucified. 'Has he indeed passed by the nature of angels, and taken upon himself the seed of Abraham, to die without leaving a seed to bear his name on the earth?' No. But when the secret is fully out, the seed of the blessed shall be gathered in, in the last days; and he who has not the blood of Abraham flowing in his veins, who has not one particle of the Saviour's in him, I am afraid is a stereotyped Gentile, who will be left out and not be gathered in the last days; for I tell you it is the chosen of God, the seed of the blessed, that shall be gathered. I do not despise to be called a son of Abraham, if he had a dozen wives; or to be called a brother, a son, a child of the Saviour, if he had Mary, and Martha, and several others as wives; and though he did cast seven devils out of one of them, it is all the same to me." (Orson Hyde, *Journal of Discourses*, vol. ii. pp. 81, 82.)

1 Compare Maeterlinck's *The Blue Bird.*

must do for men to come what men that have gone did for those who are. It was so in the days of the patriarchs, who were near to God;[1] even the fathers of the Christian Church were quoted to plead for the theory that when God establishes any part of his kingdom on earth it should be modelled after his polygamous kingdom on high.[2]

In any event, the thing must be done. The Mormons,

[1] "Here let me say that the family order which God established with Abraham and the Patriarchs was the order observed among celestial beings in the celestial world. And this family order is not the only one at which God sits as the Head and first pattern in the series of matrimonial examples; but it is of perpetual duration, both in and beyond this world. It is utterly absurd to suppose the anomaly of such an existence as a father without a mother. Everything in the analogy of nature forbids such an idea. The analogy of birds, fish, quadrupeds, creeping things, and vegetables forbids it. Have not we all one Father? We are all his offspring. A large family to be ascribed to one father! But where is the Scripture that ascribes the origin of all diverse sons to one and the same mother? When God sets up any portion of his kingdom on earth it is patterned after his own order in the heavens. When he gives to men a pattern of family organization on the earth, that pattern will be just like his own family organization in the heavens. The family of Abraham was a transcript of a celestial pattern. Abraham's family was a fresh organization, designed to effect the perpetuity and increase of God in an endless succession of families. And every family which God institutes upon the earth is fashioned like his own original family in the heavens." (Orson Spencer's *Letters*, p. 192, 1891 edition.)

[2] "When God permits a thing in certain cases, and to certain persons, or in regard to certain nations, it may be inferred that the thing is not evil of its own nature." (Grotius, B., i. c. ii., sec. 17.)

"It is objected against Jacob that he had four wives . . . which, when a custom, was not a crime." (St Augustine, lib. xxii., *Contra Faustum*, chap. 47.)

Compare also Theodoret, St Ambrose, and St Chrysostom, all of whom are cited by George I. Cannon in his defences of Mormon polygamy.

who hated the Presbyterian version of infant damnation, yet in their own faith had an infant damnation of sorts in that belief of theirs about their god and his wives begetting countless children on high, whose only chance of ultimate salvation lay in the chance of qualifying upon earth through a birth provided by human men and women. That was the masterstroke of the Saints' theologians. You and I and all mankind had once needed and had been given such a birth: obviously, it was all mankind's duty to do as much as might be in the same way for all the numberless yet-unborn. Nothing else could save them. As Mr Burton Hendrick has pointed out,[1] "unless they come to earth, reborn, these souls are doomed to an eternal life as homeless spirits; they must go wailing through eternity, with no abiding-place in any of the Mormon heavens—the cast-off, neglected children of the eternal Father. Consequently they have but a single purpose—they are irrepressibly seeking to be born. Every woman is constantly surrounded by thousands, millions of them, pleading for an opportunity to get into the world. The prime object, of course, is to capture the most desirable human parents. Especially blessed are those who are born in Utah and the other Mormon states, in the families of the Saints. The supply of human parents is so small, however, and the multitude of homeless spirits so large, that many are constrained to enter the world under less desirable conditions. Some even submit willingly to a humiliating parentage; the fact that there are so many illegitimate children is due to their incessant pleadings. And the competition is now waxing acute, as there is only a little time left; in a

[1] "The Revival of Polygamy," Burton Hendrick, *M'Clure's Magazine*, 1911.

few years the millennium will be here, the first resurrection will come, the reign of earthly man will be over, and there will be no further opportunity to enter the flesh."

The duty of the Mormons follows naturally. Women must be mothers, men fathers. Nearly all that live will reach heaven, but only the parents of many children will be "exalted" there. Whoso "releases" the most of God's children most pleases God—and, Mormonism not being a woman-made religion, it was argued that the more wives a man has the more easily he may thus do his duty to God. Hence the marriage customs of the Latter Day Saints.

These customs are not at all so simple as they may at first appear. In the first place, one may be "married for time," that is, until death ends the contract; but as a man may marry for eternity, and in that case will continue to produce spiritual children by the wife or wives that he has married "for eternity" in this world—children that will then, by the same process gone through by Adam and Adam's seed, people the world that the man, thus become a god, will govern—the wives that he has here married only "for time" will be strangers to him, as will also the children that they have borne him—will, in fact, be upon another star, where the "wife for time" may be the "wife for eternity" of another apotheosized man governing another earth.

Consequently, for the Mormon, the important marriage is the marriage "for eternity," which is called "sealing" because the contracting couple is "sealed up unto eternal life."[1] The greater number of Mormon marriages are, as a matter of fact, made both "for

[1] See the Mormon ritual for this rite.

time" and "for eternity";[1] but sometimes a woman will have one temporal and another eternal husband, or the widow of a man to whom she has been sealed for eternity, or for time and eternity, may take a second husband for time only, when her children belong to her eternal spouse. It is therefore not surprising to learn that Joseph Smith's several "eternal" wives, many of whom had no earthly relationship with him, were taken over for time, half of them by Brigham Young and half by Apostle Heber C. Kimball. Nor yet can it be denied as logical, admitting the strange premise, that, as often does happen, many beneficent Saints should permit unmarriageable spinsters to be sealed to them in this manner, which has no validity until the sealed reach heaven, since no unmarried man or woman may enter the celestial kingdoms. It is at least a simple and, the Saints assure us, a satisfactory way of consoling the ineligible, not a few of whom the obliging Church "seals" to persons of eminence already deceased.[2]

1 Hendrick.

2 We hear of poor, aged, and decrepit females being "sealed" to young and prosperous Mormon Saints. (*The Athenæum,* quoted in Littell's *Living Age,* vol. xlix. p. 602.)

"If plural marriage be unlawful, then is the whole plan of salvation through the house of Israel a failure, and the entire fabric of Christianity without foundation."—*A Compendium of the Doctrine of the Gospel* (issued for Mormon missionaries, 1898).

"This doctrine of eternal union of husband and wife, and of plural marriage, is one of the most important doctrines ever revealed to man in any age of the world. Without it man would come to a full stop; without it we never could be exalted to associate with and become gods, neither could we attain to the power of eternal increase, or the blessings pronounced upon Abraham, Isaac, and Jacob, the fathers of the faithful." (Joseph F. Smith, present head of the Mormon Church, *Journal of Discourses,* vol. xxi. p. 10.)

Remember, then, that *The Book of Doctrine and Covenants* is accepted as binding authority.[1] Remember that the authority has said:

1. In the celestial glory there are three heavens or degrees.
2. And in order to obtain the highest a man must enter into this order of the Priesthood (*i.e.* must receive the "new and everlasting covenant of marriage").
3. And if he does not, he cannot obtain it.
4. He may enter into the other degrees, but that is the end of his kingdom; he cannot have an increase.

Nothing could be plainer. The unmarried will be angels, the married with children will reign together as kings and queens, and, after enough children have been born to them to people an earth, they will reign over that earth as Adam, their father, reigns over this one. In a word, the Mormon with an increase will be a god.[2]

[1] Testifying in 1903 before a Congressional Committee in the Smoot investigation, which will be treated of later, Charles W. Penrose, former editor-in-chief of *The Deseret Evening News*, an official Mormon paper, added that this book had been even formally accepted by vote among the Saints.

[2] "I wish to be perfectly understood here. Let it be remembered that the Prophet Joseph Smith taught that man—that is, his spirit—is the offspring of Deity: not in any mystical sense, but actually; that man has not only a Father in Heaven, but a Mother also. And when I say that the Prophet taught that the resurrection is a reality, that the relationship of husband and wife is intended to be eternal, together with all its enduring affections, I mean all that in its most literal sense. I mean that in the life to come man will build and inhabit, eat, drink, associate and be happy with his friends; and that *the power of endless increase will contribute to the power and domination of*

And now consider this further portion of the revelation that established Mormon polygamy, and you have the final touch for the finished product:

"Verily, verily, I say unto you, If a man marry a wife according to my word, and they are sealed by the Holy Spirit of promise, according to mine appointment, and he or she shall commit any sin or transgression of the new and everlasting covenant whatever, and all manner of blasphemies, and if they commit no murder, wherein they shed innocent blood—yet they shall come forth in the first resurrection, and enter into their exaltation."

In brief, therefore, a Mormon may do what he pleases, may commit any sin in the calendar, and yet, so long as he does not shed innocent blood—and the blood of the unbeliever is not innocent in the eyes of the zealot—he has but to take a few plural wives to save his soul alive.

It has been urged that Joseph Smith founded this system, or that, at any rate, Brigham Young expanded and enforced it, because the heads of the Church saw in its results a sure means of increasing the numbers of the Saints and securing the temporal prosperity of Mormondom. When, however, we examine this theory closely, we see, what even the early Mormon

those who attain by their righteousness unto these privileges. What a revelation is here! Instead of the God-given power of procreation being one of the chief things that is to pass away, it is one of the chief means of man's exaltation and glory in the great eternity which like an endless vista stretches out before him." (*A New Witness for God,* by Brigham H. Roberts.)

It may be added that, to obtain a share in such glory, many of the marriageably ineligible above referred to have, it is said, had themselves sealed to various dead kings of England, Hebrew prophets, and even to Jesus.

polygamists must have seen, that it did not hold good in fact. The case of the prolific Young himself is surely a fair example. Young had a dozen wives, who bore him forty-eight children. But if we suppose each Mormon woman to be the mother of four children, the women being twice the number of the men, the increase would be but from three to eight, and that, though rapid, is scarcely worthy of consideration when it is compared with the actual growth of Mormonism by proselytising, which, in thirty years, increased the membership of the Church from six to two hundred thousand.[1]

What, on the other hand, polygamy could do and did, when Utah was reached, was to supply the polygamist with cheaper labour than he could otherwise obtain, and thus the growth of the capitalistic system in Zion[2] was favourable to the continuance of polygamy. Labour was scarce and high-priced, and the labourer had many opportunities to work, either as farmer or mining-prospector, in the capacity of "his own boss." So long as Utah was cut off from the rest of the Union, home manufacture, which the east had long left behind, was the rule, and that set an especial value on female labour and made children economically useful at an unusually early age. "It was," says Schick,[3] "cheaper for the embryo capitalist to marry help and to raise it than to hire it. The economic inducements to marriage in early Utah corresponded more nearly to the situation of the Israelites than to the affairs of the eastern states and Europe. Logic and history unite in testifying

[1] "The Passing of the Mormon," A. L. Mearkle, *The Arena*, April 1900.

[2] See Chapter XII.

[3] "Mormon and Mammon."

that the commercial advantages of polygamy played an important part in popularizing the institution."

When the first Prophet had his revelation, he, of course, did not see polygamy as a wage-lowering institution. In the circumstances, it is far safer to assume that here the severer critics of Smith are correct, and that polygamy was at least originated, only in part to increase the numbers of the Saints in the territory where they were to build Zion, and mainly to appeal to the instinct for promiscuity in male converts and to give sanction to the indulgence of that instinct on the part of the heads of the faith. Possibly, as has been hinted, the American Joseph did not in all things resemble the Joseph of Israel. At any rate, it is well, just here, to recall the gossip that led to the publication of *The Expositor*, as narrated in a previous chapter, and to consider the story of the beginning of Mormon polygamy as given by Mrs Stenhouse and others.[1]

"One very pleasant morning, early in January 1858," writes Mrs Stenhouse, ". . . my husband handed me a copy of *The Millennial Star*, a Mormon paper. . . . I copy exactly what I then read:

"'Verily, thus saith the Lord, unto you, my servant Joseph, that inasmuch as you have inquired of my hand, to know and understand wherein I, the Lord, justified my servants Abraham, Isaac, and Jacob, as also Moses, David, and Solomon, my servants, as touching the principle and doctrine of their having many wives and concubines: Behold! and lo, I am the Lord thy God, and will answer thee as touching this matter: Therefore prepare thy heart to receive and obey the instructions which I am about to give unto

[1] *The Tyranny of Mormonism.*

you; for all those who have this law revealed unto them must obey the same. . . .[1]

"'I am the Lord thy God, and I give unto thee, my servant Joseph, an appointment, and restore all things. . . . I have conferred upon you the keys and power of the priesthood, wherein I restore all things, and make known unto you all things, in due time. And verily, verily I say unto you, that whosoever (*sic*) you seal on earth shall be sealed in the heavens . . . and whosesoever sins you remit on earth shall be remitted eternally in the heavens; and whosesoever sins you retain on earth shall be retained in heaven. . . . And again, verily I say unto you, my servant Joseph, that whatsoever you give on earth, and to whomsoever you give anyone on earth, by my word, and according to my law, it shall be visited with blessings. . . .

"'Verily I say unto you, a commandment I give unto mine handmaid, Emma Smith, your wife . . . *let mine handmaid Emma Smith receive all those that have been given unto my servant Joseph,* and who are virtuous and pure before me; *and those who are not pure, and have said they were pure, shall be destroyed, saith the Lord God!* . . .

"'And I command mine handmaid, Emma Smith, to abide and cleave unto my servant Joseph, and to none else. But if she will not abide this commandment, she will be destroyed, saith the Lord; for I am the Lord thy God, and will destroy her if she abide not in my law; . . . and I will bless him, and give unto him a hundredfold in this world, *of fathers and mothers, brothers and sisters, houses and lands, wives and children, and crowns of eternal lives in the eternal world.* And again, verily I say, *let mine handmaid forgive my servant*

[1] Here follows the text of the general revelation.

Joseph his trespasses, and then shall she be forgiven her trespasses wherein she has trespassed against me.[1]

"'*If any man espouse a virgin, and desire to espouse another, and the first give her consent; and if he espouse the second, and they are virgins, and have vowed to no other man, then is he justified. He cannot commit adultery, for they are given him; for he cannot commit adultery with that that belongeth unto him, and to none else;* and *if he have ten virgins given unto him by this law, he cannot commit adultery,* for they belong to him; and they are given unto him—therefore is he justified. But *if one or other of the ten virgins, after she is espoused, shall be with another man, she has committed adultery and shall be destroyed;* for they are given unto him to multiply and replenish the earth, according to my commandment, and to fulfil the promise which was given by my Father before the foundation of the world; and for their exaltation in the eternal worlds, that they may bear the souls of men; for herein is the work of my Father continued, that he may be glorified.

"'And again, verily, verily I say unto you, if any man has a wife who holds the keys of this power, and he teaches unto her the law of my priesthood, as pertaining to these things, then shall she believe and administer unto him, or she shall be destroyed, saith the Lord your God; for I will destroy her; for I will

[1] Compare this revelation and the apparent cause of it with the similar revelation made to Mahomet for a similar reason.

It reminds one of the story of the devout husband in Christendom, whose wife wanted a new Easter bonnet. "And I want you to have one," he made answer, "but of course I must first lay the matter before the Lord." He retired for a while to pray, and returned with a long face. "I am sorry, my dear," he said, "but the Lord doesn't seem to see this matter as you and I do."

magnify my name upon all those who receive and abide in my law. Therefore it shall be lawful in me, if she receive not this law, for him to receive all things whatsoever I, the Lord his God, will give unto him, because she did not believe and administer unto him, according to my word; and she then becomes the transgressor, and he is exempt from the law of Sarah, who administered unto Abraham according to the law, when I commanded Abraham to take Hagar to wife. And now, as pertaining to this law: Verily, verily I say unto you, I will reveal more unto you hereafter: therefore let this suffice for the present. Behold, I am Alpha and Omega. Amen. . . .'

"I was" (this is some years later) "told that Eliza R. Snow, one of Young's wives, was the first woman married in polygamy after Joseph Smith received the revelation, and I believed it was so.[1] People who lived in Nauvoo, respectable people, and not one or two either, have assured me that for four years before Joseph is said to have received the revelation he was practising polygamy, or something worse, and that the revelation was given to justify what was already done."

But there is further evidence to the same effect. Although the revelation in regard to polygamy was not received until 1843, there was published in Boston in 1842, one year short of a day before that revelation was received, the following letter and affidavit:[2]

"ST LOUIS, MISSOURI, *July* 13, A.D. 1842.

"DEAR SIR,—I left Warsaw a short time since for this city, and having been called upon by you, through

[1] Left a widow by the murder of Smith, this woman was one of those spouses of the Prophet taken over "for time" by Young.

[2] *Mormonism Exposed,* J. C. Bennett.

the *Sangamo Journal*, to come out and disclose to the world the facts of the case in relation to certain propositions made to me, at Nauvoo, by some of the Mormon leaders, I now proceed to respond to the call, and discharge what I consider to be a duty devolving upon me as an innocent, but insulted and abused female. I had been at Nauvoo nearly three weeks, during which time my father's family received frequent visits from Elders Brigham Young and Heber C. Kimball, two of the Mormon Apostles; when, early one morning, they both came to my brother-in-law's house, . . . and particularly requested me to go and spend a few days with them. I told them I could not at that time, as my brother-in-law was not at home; however, they urged me to go the next day and spend one day with them. The day being fine, I accordingly went. When I arrived at the foot of the hill, Young and Kimball were standing conversing together. . . . After several flattering compliments, Kimball wished me to go to his house first. . . . We had not, however, gone many steps when Young . . . said he would go to that brother's (pointing to a little log hut but a few yards distant). . . . When he had gone, Kimball . . . said, 'Martha, I want you to say to my wife, when you go to my house, that you want to buy some things at Joseph's store (Joseph Smith's), and I will say I am going with you to show you the way. You know you want to see the Prophet, and you will then have an opportunity.' . . . I remained at Kimball's nearly an hour; when Kimball, seeing I would not tell the lies he wished me to, told them to his wife himself. . . . So Kimball and I went to the store together. As we went along, he said, 'Sister Martha, are you willing to do all that the Prophet requires you to do?' I said

I believed I was. . . . 'Then,' said he, 'are you ready to take counsel?' I answered in the affirmative, thinking of the great and glorious blessings that had been pronounced upon my head if I adhered to the counsel of those placed over me in the Lord. 'Well,' said he, 'there are many things revealed in these last days that the world would laugh and scoff at: but unto us is given to know the mysteries of the kingdom.' He further observed, 'Martha, you must learn to hold your tongue.' (Then followed a wait in a small room.) . . .

"'Now, Martha,' said Kimball (after this wait), 'the Prophet has come; come upstairs.' . . . I was introduced to the Prophet by Young, who arose, locked the door, closed the window, and drew the curtain. He then came and sat before me and said, 'This is our private room, Martha. . . . Sister Martha, I want to ask you a few questions; will you answer them?' 'Yes, sir,' said I. 'And will you promise me not to mention them to anyone?' 'If it is your desire, sir,' said I, 'I will not.' 'And you will not think any the worse of me for it; will you, Martha?' said he. 'No, sir,' I replied. 'Well,' said he, 'what are your feelings toward me?' I replied, 'My feelings are just the same toward you that they ever were, sir.' 'But to come to the point more closely,' said he, 'have you not an affection for me, that were it lawful and right, you would accept of me for your husband and companion?' . . . If I say *No*, they may do as they think proper; and to say *Yes*, I never would. So I considered it best to ask for time to think and pray about it. I therefore said, 'If it was lawful and right, perhaps I might; but you know, sir, it is not.' 'Well, but,' said he, '*Brother Joseph has had a revelation from God that it is lawful and right for a man to have two wives ; for, as it was in the days of Abraham, so it shall be in these last days, and whoever is the first that is willing to take up the cross will receive the greatest blessings ;* and, if you will accept of me, I will take you straight to the celestial kingdom; and if you will have me in this world, I will have you in that which is to come, and Brother Joseph will marry us here to-day, and you can go home this evening and your parents will not know anything about it.' 'Sir,' said I, 'I should not like to do anything of the kind without the permission of my parents.' 'Well,' said he, 'you are of age, are you not?' 'No, sir,' said I: 'I shall not be until the 24th of May.' 'Well,' said he, 'that does not make any difference. You will be of age before they know, and you need not fear. If you will take my counsel it will be well with you, for I know it to be right before God; and if there is any sin in it, I will answer for it.' . . . 'Well, I want you to say something,' said he. 'I want to think about it,' said I. 'Well,' said he, 'I will have a kiss anyhow,' and then rose, and said he would bring Joseph. . . . 'Well, Martha,' said Joseph, 'it is lawful and right before God—I *know* it. Look here, sis: don't you believe in me?' I did not answer. 'Well, Martha,' said Joseph, 'just go ahead, and do as Brigham wants you to; he is the best man in the world, except me.' 'Oh!' said Brigham, 'then you are as good.' 'Yes,' said Joseph. 'Well,' said Young, 'we believe Joseph to be a Prophet. I have known him near eight years, and I have always found him the same.' 'Yes,' said Joseph, 'and I know that this is lawful and right before God, and if there is any sin in it I will answer for it before God; and I have the keys of the kingdom, and whatever I bind on earth is bound in heaven, and whatever I loose on earth is loosed in heaven; and if you will accept of Brigham, you shall be blessed—God shall bless you, and my blessing shall rest upon you; and, if you will be led by him, you will do well; for I know that Brigham will do well by you, and if he don't do his duty to you, come to me and I will make him; and if you do not like it in a month or two, come to me and I will make you free again; and if he turns you off, I will take you on.' 'Sir,' said I, rather warmly, 'it will be too late to think in a month or two after. I want time to think first.' 'Well, but,' said he, 'the old proverb is "Nothing ventured, nothing gained," and it will be the greatest blessing that was ever bestowed upon you.' 'Yes,' said Young, 'and you will never have reason to repent it—that is, if I do not turn from righteousness, and that, I trust, I never shall; for I believe God, who has kept me so long, will continue to keep me faithful. Did you ever see me act in any way wrong in England, Martha?' 'No, sir,' said I. 'No,' said he; 'neither can anyone else lay anything to my charge.' 'Well, then,' said Joseph, 'what are you afraid of, sis? Come, let me do the business for you.' 'Sir,' said I, 'do let me have a little time to think about it, and I will promise not to mention it to anyone.' 'Well, but look here,' said he; 'you know a fellow will never be damned for doing the best he knows how.' 'Well, then,' said I, 'the best way I know of is, to go home and think and pray about it.' 'Well,' said Young, 'I shall leave it with Brother Joseph, whether it would be best for you to have time or not.' 'Well,' said Joseph, 'I see no harm in her having time to think, if she will not fall into temptation.' 'Oh, sir!' said I, 'there is no fear of my falling into temptation.' 'Well, but,' said Brigham, 'you must promise me you will never mention it to anyone.' 'I do promise it,' said I. 'Well,' said Joseph, 'you must promise me the same.' I promised him the same. 'Upon your honour,' said he, 'you will not tell.' 'No, sir; I will lose my life first,' said I. 'Well, that will do,' said he; 'that is the principle we go upon. I think I can trust you, Martha,' said he. 'Yes,' said I, 'I think you ought.' Joseph said, 'She looks as if she could keep a secret.' I then rose to go, when Joseph commenced to beg of me again. He said it was the best opportunity they might have for months, for the room was often engaged. I, however, had determined what to do. 'Well,' said Young, 'I will see you to-morrow. I am going to preach at the schoolhouse opposite your house. I have never preached there yet; you will be there, I suppose?' 'Yes,' said I. The next day being Sunday, I sat down, instead of going to meeting, and wrote the conversation, and gave it to my sister, who was not a little surprised; but she said it would be best to go to the meeting in the afternoon. We went, and Young administered the sacrament. After it was over, I was passing out, and Young stopped me, saying, 'Wait, Martha; I am coming.' I said, 'I cannot; my sister is waiting for me.' He then threw his coat over his shoulders and followed me out, and whispered, 'Have you made up your mind, Martha?' 'Not exactly, sir,' said I; and we parted. I shall proceed to a justice of the peace and make oath to the truth of these statements, and you are at liberty to make what use of them you think best.—Yours respectfully, MARTHA A. BROTHERTON.

"Sworn to and described before me this 13th day of July, A.D. 1842. DU BOUFFAY FREMON,

"Justice of the Peace for St Louis County."

One point, at anyrate, is clear. Mrs Stenhouse first learned of the doctrine of polygamy as a foundation-stone of the Mormon faith in 1858, which was six years after it was adopted by a conference of the heads of the Church in Salt Lake City,[1] and fifteen years after the revelation had been vouchsafed to Joseph Smith. In other words, then, for some reason, the revelation was not made public in America for nine years after it had been received, and was kept from the missionary fields for fifteen years.[2]

Just how jealously the secret was guarded is shown in this excerpt from a biography of Lorenzo Snow by his sister Eliza, the Mormon poetess, and, as has been

[1] *The Mormons Unmasked,* C. Sheridan Jones.

[2] "The history of polygamy furnishes an excellent illustration of what the non-Mormon mind must regard as ecclesiastical duplicity. From the beginning the Church has invariably taught one thing in the matter of plural marriage, and practised another. The revelation itself bears internal evidence of this state of mind. It says, almost in so many words, that polygamy was being practised by Joseph Smith before he received any commandment from God. 'And let mine handmaid, Emma Smith, receive all those that have been given unto my servant, Joseph, and who are virtuous and pure before me,' reads this revelation. Emma was the wife of the Prophet Joseph; this quotation pretty clearly implies that Joseph had already begun taking plural wives, and that the revelation was promulgated chiefly as a divine endorsement of his practices. Most Mormon historians now assert that the Prophet received the first intimation concerning the sacred ordinance in 1832, and began its observance about 1838. As a matter of fact, however, Joseph Smith himself never publicly acknowledged that polygamy was an article of the Mormon religion. It was not until 1852, eight years after the Prophet's death, that Brigham Young first published the fact to the world. But the evidence is abundant that Joseph Smith, Brigham Young, and other members of the inner circle had been practising polygamy for years. Only the other day a woman died in Salt Lake City—Lucy Walker Smith—who was officially recognized as one of the plural wives of the Prophet."—Hendrick.

noted, one of the wives of Brigham Young. Writing of the years 1840 to 1843, she says:

"While my brother was absent on a mission to Europe, changes had taken place with me, one of eternal import, of which I supposed him to be entirely ignorant. The Prophet Joseph had taught me the principle of plural or celestial marriage, and I was married to him for time and eternity. *In consequence of the ignorance of most of the Saints, as well as people of the world, on this subject, it was not mentioned, only privately between the few whose minds were enlightened on the subject.* Not knowing how my brother (he came back in April 1843) would receive it, I did not feel at liberty, and did not wish to assume the responsibility of instructing him in the principle of plural marriage. . . . I informed my husband (Smith) of the situation and requested him to open the subject to my brother. A favourable opportunity soon presented, and, seated together on the bank of the Mississippi River, they had a most interesting conversation. The Prophet afterward told me he found that my brother's mind had been previously enlightened on the subject in question. That comforter which Jesus says shall 'lead unto all truth' had penetrated his understanding, and, while in England, had given him an intimation of what at that time was to many a secret. This was the result of living near the Lord.

"It was at the private interview referred to above that the Prophet Joseph unbosomed his heart, and described the trying ordeal he experienced in overcoming the repugnance of his feelings, the natural result of the force of education and social custom, relative to the introduction of plural marriage. . . . Yet the Prophet hesitated and deferred from time to time, until an angel of God stood by him with a drawn sword, and told him that, unless he moved forward and established plural marriage, his priesthood would be taken from him and he should be destroyed."

That the Saints publicly denied that they practised polygamy, we have already seen. When, however, one of them, J. C. Bennett, Smith's candidate for the Vice-Presidency of the United States, quarrelled with the Prophet, left the Church, and published a book exposing this practice, it clearly became incumbent upon the Mormon officials to take some official action to counteract the allegations thus given, even though Bennett was a man of notoriously bad character. Consequently, nineteen Mormon women gave out, on 1st October 1842, this statement, the "Secretary" being that Eliza R. Snow who has in her biography of her brother confessed herself a plural wife of Joseph Smith, and who, also, the Latter Day Saints *Biographical Encyclopedia* says, was married to Smith on 29th June 1842:

"We, the undersigned members of the Ladies' Relief Society, and married females, do certify and declare that we know of no system of marriage being practised in the Church of Jesus Christ of Latter Day Saints save the one contained in *The Book of Doctrine and Covenant*, and we give this certificate to show that J. C. Bennett's 'secret wife system' is a disclosure of his own make.

"EMMA SMITH, President.
"ELIZABETH ANN WHITNEY, Councillor.
"SARAH M. CLEVELAND, Councillor.
"ELIZA R. SNOW, Secretary."
(Fifteen other names.)

[1] *Mormonism Exposed.*

Further to quiet adverse criticism, and perhaps to keep the truth from the converts overseas, some of whom were deserting because of the mere rumours of polygamy,[1] a scapegoat was chosen, and this bull of excommunication issued against him eight months after Joseph Smith had received his god's revelation establishing plural marriage:

"As we have been credibly informed that an elder in the Church of Jesus Christ of Latter Day Saints, by the name of Hyrum Brown, has been preaching polygamy and other false and corrupt doctrines in the county of Laper and state of Michigan, this is to notify him and the Church in general that he has been cut off from the Church for his iniquity, and he is further notified to appear at the special conference on the sixth day of April next, to make answer to these charges.

"JOSEPH SMITH.
"HYRUM SMITH."

Permitted by their religion to deny in public what their religion privately enjoined them to practise, the Saints then scattered the seed of polygamy. The heads of the Church married plural wives and quietly "sounded" their followers and prepared the minds of the faithful, so that, five years after the Utah migration, the Church, in its mountain stronghold, publicly adopted and proclaimed the system. Smith was dead, Young was in tyrannical control. It mattered little that the first wife of the first Prophet, who survived him, should, with the four sons that she had borne to Smith, deny that her husband had ever received the revelation. The thing was established; it became the custom of Mormon Utah.

1 When polygamy was pronounced a duty, four thousand converts in England recanted. (Linn.)

Over that period, the period of polygamy's perfect sway, when interference from without failed to shake the prosperity of the institution, one may pass after giving a single illustration. Not many Gentiles, as we have already seen, were in those days, when East was East and West was West, permitted to see the inside of Mormondom; but one traveller overcame the jealousies of the Saints and has left a vivid description of them. This was Fitz-Hugh Ludlow, from whose remarkable account of the Saints and their greatest leader it is well worth while to quote at length:[1]

"Contrasting the Mormon settlements with their surrounding desolation," says this writer, "we could not wonder that their success had fortified this people in their delusion. The superficial student of rewards and punishments might well believe that none but God's chosen people could cause this horrible desert, after such triumphant fashion, to blossom like the rose. . . .

"The first Mormon household I ever visited belonged to the son of the famous Heber Kimball, Brigham Young's most devoted follower, and next to him in the Presidency. It was the last stage station but one before we entered Salt Lake, situated at the bottom of a green valley in Parley's Cañon (named after the celebrated elder, Parley Pratt); and as it looked like the residence of a well-to-do farmer, I went in, and asked for a bowl of bread-and-milk—the greatest possible luxury after a life of bacon and salt-spring water, such as we had been leading in the mountains. A fine-looking, motherly woman, with a face full of character, grey-haired, and about sixty years old, rose promptly to grant my request; and while the horses

[1] *The Atlantic Monthly*, April 1864.

were changing I had ample time to make the acquaintance of two pretty young girls, hardly over twenty, holding two infants, of ages not more than three months apart. Green as I was to Saintly manners, I supposed that one of the two young mothers had run in from a neighbour's to compare babies with the mistress of the house, after our eastern fashion, universal with the owners of juvenile phenomena. When the old lady came back with the bread-and-milk, and both of the girls addressed her as 'mother,' I was emboldened to tell her that her daughters had a pretty pair of children.

"'They are pretty,' said the old lady demurely; 'but they are the children of my son'; then, as if resolved to duck a Gentile head and heels into Mormon realities at once, she added, 'Those young ladies are the wives of my son, who is now gone on a mission to Liverpool—young Mr Kimball, the son of Heber Kimball; and I am Heber Kimball's wife.' . . .

"The one dreadful thought which persistently kept uppermost, so that I felt they must read it in my face, was, "How *can* these young women sit looking at each other's babies without flying into each other's faces with their finger-nails, and tearing out each other's hair?' Heber Kimball afterward solved the question for me, by saying that it was a triumph of grace.

"Such another triumph was Mrs Heber Kimball herself. She was a woman of remarkable presence, in youth must have been very handsome. . . . Here was this strong-minded woman, as her husband afterwards acknowledged to me, his best counsellor and right-hand helper through a married life reaching into middle age, witnessing her property in that husband's affections subdivided and parcelled out until she owned but one-thirtieth share, not only without a pang, but with the acquiescence of her conscience and the approbation of her intellect. . . . I am half inclined to think that she embraced Mormonism earlier than her husband, and by taking the initiative secured for herself the only true wifely place in the harem—the marital afterthoughts of Brother Heber being her servants rather than her sisters. She was most undoubtedly his favourite. . . .

"Heber and I got talking of the *potpourri* of nationalities assembled in Utah. Heber waxed benevolent, and expressed his affection for each succeeding race as fast as mentioned.

"'I love the Danes dearly! I've got a Danish wife.'

"A moment after—'The Irish are a dear people. My Irish wife is among the best I've got.'

"Again—'I love the Germans! Got a Dutch wife, too! . . . She couldn't scarcely talk a word of English when she came.'

"I happened to touch upon the earliest Mrs Heber, . . . referred to the interview I had enjoyed with her on the afternoon before entering the city. His whole manner changed to a proper husbandly dignity, . . . he replied gravely, 'Yes! that is my first wife, and the best woman God ever made.'

"All of the Saints within half a day's ride of the city come flocking into it to spend the Fourth of July. A well-to-do Mormon at the head of his wives and children, all of whom are probably eating candy (sweets) as they march through the metropolitan streets in solid column, looks to the uninitiated like the principal of a female seminary, weak in its deportment, taking out his charges for an airing. . . .

"Morality in this world is so mainly a matter of convention that I dreaded to appear (at a Fourth of

July ball) in decent polygamous society, lest respectable women, owning their orthodox tenth of a husband, should shrink from the pollution of my presence. . . . But they were very polite, and received me with as skilfully veiled disapprobation as is shown by fashionable eastern belles to brilliant seducers immoral in *our* sense.

"I sought out our entertainer, Brigham Young. . . . He was standing in the dress circle of the theatre, looking down on the dancers with an air of hearty kindness and feudal ownership. I could excuse the latter, for Utah belongs to him of right. He may justly say of it, 'Is not this great Babylon which I have built?' His sole executive tact and personal fascination are the keystone of the entire arch of Mormon society. . . . Brigham Young is the farthest remove from a hypocrite; he is that grand, yet awful sight in human nature, a man who has brought the loftiest Christian self-devotion to the altar of the Devil, who is ready to suffer crucifixion for Barabbas, supposing him Christ. . . .

"Like any eastern party-goer, he is habited in the 'customary suit of solemn black,' and looks very distinguished in this dress, though his daily homespun detracts nothing from the feeling, when in his presence, that you are beholding a remarkable man. He is over seventy years old, but appears very little over forty. His height is about five feet ten inches; his figure very well made and slightly inclining to portliness. His hair is a rich curly chestnut, formerly worn long, in supposed imitation of the apostolic coiffure, but now cut in our practical eastern fashion, as accords with the man of business, whose *métier* he has added to apostleship with the growing temporal prosperity of Zion.

Indeed, he is the greatest business man on the continent, the cashier of a firm of eighty thousand silent partners, and the only auditor of that cashier; besides, . . . the hand of the Church holds the soul of the Saints by inevitable purse-strings. . . . Over all these matters Brigham Young has supreme control. His power is the most despotic known to mankind. . . . Thus everything vital, save the air he breathes, reaches the Mormon only through Brigham's sieve. . . . I never heard Brigham's worst enemies accuse him of peculation, though such immense interests are controlled by his one pair of hands.

"His eyes are a clear blue-grey, frank and straightforward in their look; his nose a finely chiselled aquiline; his mouth exceedingly firm, and fortified in that expression by a chin almost as protrusive beyond the rest of the profile as Charlotte Cushman's, though less noticeably so, being longer than hers; and he wears a narrow ribbon of brown beard, meeting under the chin. There are few courtlier men living. His address is a fine combination of dignity with the desire to confer happiness—of perfect deference to the feelings of others, with absolute certainty of himself and his own opinions. . . .

"Heber Kimball, Second President (*proximus longo intervallo!*), Brigham's most devoted worshipper, and in all respects the next most important man, . . . is the latter's equal in years, but in all things else his antipode. His height is over six feet, his form of aldermanic rotundity, his face large, plethoric, and lustrous with the stable red of stewed cranberries, while his small, twinkling black beads of eyes and a satyric sensualism about the mouth would indicate a temperament fatally in the way of any apostleship save that of polygamy, even without the aid of an induction from his favourite topics of discourse and his patriarchally unvarnished style of handling them. . . . Most of us in the east would feel that we were insulting the lowest member of the *demi-monde* if we uttered before her a single sentence of the talk which forms the habitual staple of all Heber Kimball's public sermons to the wives and daughters who throng the Sunday Tabernacle.

"Peter Rockwell is a man whom my readers must have heard of in every account of fearlessly executed massacre committed in Utah during the last thirteen years. He is chief of the Danites—a band of Saints who possess the monopoly of vengeance upon Gentiles and apostates. . . . Peter Rockwell has slain his forty men. This is historical. His probable private victims amount to as many more. He wears his hair braided behind, and done up in a knot with a back comb, like a woman's. He has a face full of bull-dog courage, but vastly good-natured and without a bad trait in it. . . . He was everywhere known as the Destroying Angel, but he seemed to have little disagreement with his toddy, and took his meals regularly. He has two very comely and pleasant wives. Brigham has about seventy, Heber about thirty. The seventy of Brigham do not include those spiritually married or 'sealed' to him."

It was a state of things that inclines one to believe the story told of a Mormon Elder, who one Sunday came upon a little lad smoking a stolen cigarette.

"I am surprised, my boy," said the Elder—"surprised and shocked. Smoking at your age! And on a Sunday, too! What would your father say if he knew of this?"

The offender burst into tears.

"Don't you know me, papa?" he wailed.

Woman was, indeed, in this form of society of small importance save in her capacity of wife. When, twice a year, on 6th April and 6th October, the Saints assembled in conference from far and near and met in the great Salt Lake Tabernacle, that will comfortably hold 12,000 people and that can hold 15,000, woman, for the four days of those meetings, was in one respect equal to man: she had a vote in the gathering; but a man amounted to little at such times, unless he was a member of the hierarchy, because the hierarchy had decreed that every officer of the Church must be at least once re-elected to each and every position that he held, and because the hierarchy always saw to it that its own candidates were originally chosen. Some women, of course, like that Amazon of Mormondom, Eliza R. Snow, of whom we have just heard, assumed the pose of pride in polygamy,[1] and during the later inquiries made by Congress gravely perjured themselves and in effect illegitimatized their children by swearing that those children had unmarried fathers; but how far such attitudes were the result of fanatic zeal and how far the result of terror may never definitely be decided.

Certain it is that the wife was in complete subjection to her husband, through whom alone she could attain

[1] Mrs Snow, after once denying the existence of polygamy, said, in a moment of terrestrial exaltation: "I am proud to say that I believe in the principle of plural marriage, just as sacredly as I believe in any other institution which God has revealed. I believe it to be necessary for the redemption of the human family from the low state of corruption into which it has sunken. . . . Virtue is the foundation of the prosperity of any nation; and this sacred principle of plural marriage tends to virtue, purity, and holiness!"

eternal life,[1] and that, in such cases as those in which woman rebelled against polygamy, the result of her rebellion was always the ruin and sometimes the end of her mortal existence.[2] The horrors of polygamy as it obtained in Utah have been sufficiently exploited; sometimes they have undoubtedly been exaggerated; but they were bad enough in the reality, and our task here has been not so much to depict them as to tell

[1] Apostle Kimball, speaking in the Tabernacle in the later 'fifties, said: "*I have no wife or child that has any right to rebel against me.* If they violate my laws and rebel against me, they will get into trouble just as quickly as though they transgressed the counsels and teachings of Brother Brigham. Does it give a woman a right to sin against me because she is my wife? No; but it is her duty to do my will, as I do the will of my Father and my God. It is the duty of a woman to be obedient to her husband; and unless she is, I would not give a damn for all her queenly right and authority, nor for her either, if she will quarrel and lie about the will of God and the principles of plurality. If you oppose the spiritual wife doctrine, the patriarchal order, which is of God, . . . you will go overboard. Go ahead upon the right principle, and God bless you for ever and ever, and make you fruitful, that we may fill the mountains and then the earth with righteous inhabitants."

[2] Not only were women forced into polygamy; the Mormon husband of one wife was "persuaded" to take at least one other, as Mrs Stenhouse has pointed out in her book, and critics of the system were severely silenced. Thus a certain Dr Robinson would not be "counselled" to refrain from censuring the polygamy that he saw about him in Salt Lake City: "One beautiful moonlight night a man came to his house and told him that a man had been kicked by a mule 'down on the state road,' and that his leg was broken. He was suffering the greatest agony, needed the services of a surgeon; would the doctor not come to his relief? Mrs Robinson pleaded with her husband not to go. He laughed at her fears, and went. One block from his house he was assassinated by a blow on the head with some dull instrument, and shot from a pistol. His murderer was never apprehended." ("Woman's Life in Utah," Ruth Everett, *The Arena*, February 1899.)

how they came to be, and how, being, they were defended.

The end of the absurd "Mormon War" left the Saints, of course, just about where the beginning of that war had found them. They had to be a trifle more careful to conceal their treatment of Gentile travellers and even Gentile settlers, but so far as polygamy was concerned they were to all intents and purposes free to go their own road, and they went it with a sublime and contemptuous disregard for the wishes of Congress to the contrary, even complaining that the presence of Federal soldiers in Utah was bad for the morals of plural wives of Mormondom.[1]

The national Government at Washington passed several laws against polygamy in the territories that were, by the terms of the Constitution of the United States, directly under its control, but all these efforts were futile. The death of Brigham Young, if it at all affected the attitude of the Saints in the matter of polygamy, seemed to have confirmed them in their marriage practices, because death, among zealots, adds a new sanctity to the character of the dead, and because Brigham had stood, above all else, for polygamy. John Taylor, who became Prophet, in due time publicly announced that he would never yield to the Govern-

[1] In *The New York Times* of this period one reads: "One of the charges which Young has most vehemently urged against the Federal officers, both civil and military, which (*sic*) have been sent among them, has been that they seduced their wives away, broke up their marriage system (!)—and there has undoubtedly been abundant foundation for the reproach. There is no doubt at all that the presence of these men among them has greatly disturbed the established system of society among the Saints. The sentiment of constancy, where it is divided among twenty or thirty wives, must lose much of its force, while the passions certainly lose none of their power."

ment in this matter, and held to his announcement until the day of his death.[1]

Representing the Gentile influence in Utah, James H. Beatty, the Federally appointed United States District Attorney for the territory, wrote to *The New York Tribune* in 1881 declaring "the impossibility of enforcing existing laws against polygamy." He pleaded for the adoption of more stringent methods by Congress.

Moved at last by the causes stated in a previous chapter, Congress, in the 'eighties, entered upon its open fight against the Utah social conditions. Having found that, because of the allegiance which the Saints held to their Church and to one another, it was difficult to prove polygamous marriage, laws were passed making a specific offence in the territories of "the outward manifestation of polygamous relations,"[2] and, under the Edmunds law, it was required merely to prove that a man "by common habit and repute" lived as man with wife with more than one woman at the same time. The Government of the United States for the first time made a crime of the act of "unlawful cohabitation."

What followed was a period that the Mormons still refer to as their "Diocletian Persecutions." The Edmunds law required voters to take oath "faithfully to obey the laws" of the United States, which of course included the law against unlawful cohabitation. It created an Electoral Commission that purged the Utah voting-lists of from 12,000 to 15,000 actual voters. It deprived, in effect, the polygamist of the franchise.

This Act was passed in 1882. In 1884 the Government began to put into effect its penal provisions. Chester A. Arthur, who was chosen President of the

[1] Taylor died in 1887.

[2] Hendrick.

United States under the belief that he would be the tool of his faction, but who proved to be a man of force and independence, sent out to administer the Act in Utah Chief Justice Zane, of Illinois, who, at Springfield, Illinois, had succeeded Lincoln in the law firm of Lincoln & Herndon; and at Zane's arrival in Salt Lake City all the leaders of the Mormon Church immediately went abroad or into hiding, so that for several years following only three or four of the Twelve Apostles were present at the semi-annual conferences of the Church, the rest being frankly fugitives from the law.

Zane brought with him a little army of United States marshals, who began a thorough scouring of the territory in the pursuit of what they called "cohabs," so that "cohab-hunting" was the sport of the hour. What followed was not an elevating spectacle. All the Gentiles in Utah aided in the sport even more actively than the law required. Women and children, bankers, merchants, newspaper reporters, and a host of Christian clergymen took part.[1] When a stranger appeared in a Mormon town, that town was at once in a turmoil of apprehension. Disguised as pedlars, tramps, and book-agents, the officers of the law and their volunteer assistants ransacked churches and houses, searched cellars, looked under beds and between mattresses, explored the caves of the mountains and the shadows of the cañons. Dwellings were "routed out," and the doors of residences broken down at midnight with axes.

The courts were congested, even more congested than the average American court is at this day, and the justice dispensed was not infrequently equal to the amazing brand commonly delivered at the present day.

[1] Hendrick.

Plural wives, with their babies in their arms, would be called as witnesses and urged to testify against their husbands, generally swearing that they were not married, or else refusing to answer any of the questions that were put them, filling the prisons with female prisoners committed for contempt of court. Fathers of plural wives made answer to the prosecution's questions as to whether their daughters were plural wives: "I never had the curiosity to inquire"; "It's none of my business"; "My girl is able to take care of herself." Even the children were put upon the stand, and, for the most part, formally illegitimatized themselves.

Nevertheless, and in spite of the fact that the Mormon press went on its even way openly defending polygamy,[1] considerably more than a thousand polygamists were sent to the Federal prison. Many of the convicts were prominent in the Church. Some of them were very near its head. The situation was acute.

What immediately followed the reader already knows. Congress disincorporated the Church of Jesus Christ of Latter Day Saints on the ground that it was a law-defying institution, and, the Saints failing in their endeavour to prove this action unconstitutional before the Supreme Court of the United States, the confiscation of the Church's property ensued. Meanwhile the Federal Courts continued their disenfranchisements, and refused to naturalize alien-born Saints on the ground that such Saints were members of the law-defying institution aforesaid; and then, after Congress had taken the vote from all polygamists, a carefully thought-out movement was begun to deprive all members of the Mormon Church,

[1] See, for instance, *The Evening News*—then edited by the polygamist Charles W. Penrose—for 5th December 1885.

whether aliens or natives, monogamists or polygamists, of the right to the ballot. The territory of Idaho, a neighbouring division of the country, of the population of which one-third was Mormon, having already come under such an Act, a representative named Strube in the Lower House of Congress, and Shelby M. Cullom in the Upper, introduced a bill, which had the support of such men as Senator Orville H. Platt, of Connecticut,[1] and Congressmen William M'Kinley[2] and Thomas B. Reed, for the disenfranchisement of all Mormons in all the territories.

The Church saw destruction ahead. The passage of the Strube Bill meant that, while the Federal offices of the territory would continue in the hands of the Gentiles by appointment from Washington, the elective offices would go entirely out of Mormon control. The Church's property had been confiscated. Hundreds of the Church leaders were in prison, and the Government had ominously begun building an annex to the penitentiary in which they were confined. Such leaders as were not in jail were in hiding. And on all sides, as we have already seen, the Mormons were informed that the one way to escape annihilation was to give up polygamy and so knock from under their persecutors the chief prop of the persecution.

Several men prominent in the faith, but still at liberty, went to Washington to see if a compromise could be arrived at. This was early in 1890, and the Mormons were received by John W. Noble, Secretary of State under President Harrison. They suggested and pleaded, but the Government was firm. They must

[1] Not to be confused with Senator "Tom" Platt, a notorious "boss" of New York.

[2] Afterwards President of the United States.

give up their marriage customs. The representatives of Mormondom protested, what was perfectly true, that, as a result of the persecutions, the Mormon priesthood had already considerably modified its attitude in regard to this matter, no longer openly "persuading" its members toward polygamy, and they added that they could never alter their religious convictions regarding the basis of the doctrine. In vain. The delegation was sent back to Utah with a clear understanding that the persecutions would not cease until polygamy was wiped out, or until, polygamy having been officially abandoned by the Church, Utah was admitted to the Union as a self-governing state.[1]

The time had come for action of a positive sort. The Church took that action at the next semi-annual conference of the Latter Day Saints, held in the great Tabernacle at Salt Lake City on the 6th of October 1890. There, when there were about 2451 male members of the faith who were maintaining polygamous families, Wilford Woodruff, the mild-mannered Connecticut Yankee who had succeeded to the office of Prophet of the Church, and who was one of the few Prophets of Mormondom to make friends among the Gentiles, rose and, speaking in his official capacity, asked the question:

[1] The Government at this time shared the opinion of the Utah Gentiles that the modification of the Mormon Church's attitude in regard to polygamy was a mere makeshift and farce. That it was indeed a farce may be seen by running down the records of the numerous plural marriages that were taking place in Utah at this time. For instance, in the Smoot investigation, later to be referred to, Josiah Hickman, Professor at the (Mormon) Brigham Young University in Provo, testified that he had taken a plural wife in June 1890, and had received the necessary permission to do so from Apostle Francis M. Lyman.

"What do the Latter Day Saints believe?"

He called on Bishop Orson F. Whitney to read the articles of the Mormon faith, in which, as the reader now knows, there is no specific mention of polygamy. When the reading of this creed was over, Prophet Woodruff, then eighty-three years old and a man of impressive presence, who believed or pretended to believe in divine guidance by revelation and vision for his everyday action,[1] directed the reading of the following now famous manifesto, issued in his prophetic character, and received, at least by the Gentile world, as something that the Mormons must accept as the voice and will of God:

"OFFICIAL DECLARATION.

"*To whom it may concern:*

"Press despatches having been sent for political purposes from Salt Lake City, which have been widely published, to the effect that the Utah Commission, in their recent report to the Secretary of the Interior, allege that plural marriages are still being solemnized, and that forty or more such marriages have been contracted in Utah since last June or during the past year; also that in public discourses the leaders of the Church have taught, encouraged, and urged the continuance of the practice of polygamy;

"I, therefore, as President of the Church of Jesus Christ of Latter Day Saints, do hereby, in the most solemn manner, declare that these charges are false. We are not teaching polygamy, or plural marriage, nor permitting any person to enter into its practice; and I deny that either forty or any number of plural mar-

[1] Hendrick.

riages have during that period been solemnized in our temples or in any other place in the territory.

"One case has been reported in which the parties alleged that the marriage was performed in the Endowment House in Salt Lake City in the spring of 1889.

"But I have not been able to learn who performed the ceremony. Whatever was done in the matter was without my knowledge. In consequence of this alleged occurrence, the Endowment House was, by my instructions, taken down without delay.

"Inasmuch as laws have been enacted by Congress forbidding plural marriages, which laws have been pronounced constitutional by the court of last resort, I hereby declare my intention to submit to those laws, and to use my influence with the members of the Church over which I preside to have them do likewise.

"There is nothing in my teachings to the Church, or in those of my associates, during the time specified, which can be reasonably construed to inculcate or encourage polygamy, and when any elder of the Church has used language which appeared to convey any such teaching he has been promptly reproved; and I now publicly declare that my advice to the Latter Day Saints is to refrain from contracting any marriage forbidden by the laws of the land.

"WILFORD WOODRUFF,
"President of the Church of Jesus Christ
"of Latter Day Saints."

Even the will of God, as thus revealed, must, in Mormondom, be "confirmed" or "sustained" by a vote of the conference of the Church. Accordingly, when the manifesto had been read, Lorenzo Snow, then President of the Board of Twelve Apostles, rose and moved its acceptance. He said:

"I move, recognizing Wilford Woodruff as the President of the Church of Jesus Christ of Latter Day Saints, and the only man on earth at the present time who holds the keys of the sealing ordinances, we consider him fully authorized by virtue of his position to issue the manifesto which has been read in our hearing, and which is dated 25th September 1890, and that, as a Church in general conference assembled, we accept his declaration concerning plural marriage as authoritative and binding."

There was a moment's pause. Then, according to the Mormon custom, Snow continued:

"All who accept this document will signify it by raising the right hand."

The conference had been prepared and instructed. From all over the body of the tabernacle rose a legion of hands.

"Contrary minded, by the same sign," said Snow.

Not one vote was cast in the negative. Within the few following weeks conferences were called in all the stakes and wards of Mormondom, and at every conference the manifesto was accepted without a dissenting voice.

XI

POLYGAMY REVIVED

THE Federal Government accepted this manifesto as fatuously as it had accepted the Mormons' seeming acquiescence in the confiscation of their property. The Prophet of the Latter Day Saints had apparently said that polygamy was at an end, and the Government was as eager to accept his word as if the President and Congress were themselves Mormons and believed Woodruff's promises to be the everlasting covenants of God. Orders went out from Washington to the effect that, though the laws forbade men from contracting new polygamous unions and living in polygamy with wives formerly married, there must no bar be put in the way of those men who, already polygamists, desired properly to support their plural wives and the children that such wives had borne them.

Then someone began to examine the manifesto and to ask questions. Just what, exactly, did it mean? Its opening statement that polygamy had not recently been taught or practised was false and generally known so to be. Did this message of the Prophet merely prohibit new plural marriages, or did it put an end to old ones? Did it, indeed, really prohibit polygamy at all? Was it issued simply as an "official statement," which was what it was called, or as a revelation?

Was it the advice of the Prophet on a matter of expediency? Was it the advice of Deity on a matter of expediency, which might be followed or not as the individual elected, and not followed at all when there came a change in the temporary situation that made an end of polygamy expedient? Or was it the voice of the Most High for ever revoking what had once been set down as an everlasting law for the exaltation of the Saints and the salvation of the countless children of God?

It is difficult to see how the Mormons could accept the manifesto in this last sense without entirely denying their religion. It is more difficult to see how the Government could believe the Mormons when they said that they did so accept it. And yet the Mormons made the declaration, and the Government believed them.

Before a Master in Chancery, in October 1891, Prophet Woodruff, when the Church was applying for a restoration of its confiscated property, gave this testimony, and Lorenzo Snow, George Q. Cannon, Joseph F. Smith,[1] and Anthon H. Lund, all members of the Board of Twelve Apostles, followed him on the witness-stand and corroborated him:

"Q. Did you intend by that general statement of intention (the manifesto) to make the application to existing conditions where the plural marriages already existed?

"A. Yes, sir.

"Q. As to living in the state of plural marriage?

"A. Yes, sir; that is, to the obeying of the law."

Before the examination was over, this company of witnesses had sworn that the manifesto "meant not only no more plural marriages, but no more cohabitation with plural wives taken previous to that date."

[1] The present Prophet (1912).

Was this merely "lying only to the Gentiles' God"? It seemed not when, a few days later,[1] the Prophet Woodruff said in the Mormon Tabernacle at Logan:

"I have had some revelations of late, and very important ones to me, and I will tell you what the Lord said to me. Let me bring to your minds what is termed the manifesto. . . . I should have let all the temples go out of our hands, I should have gone to prison myself and let every other man go there, had not the God of Heaven commanded me to do what I did do, and when the hour came it was all clear to me. I went before the Lord, and I wrote what the Lord told me to write. I laid it before my brethren, . . . the Twelve Apostles. These men agreed with me. . . . Why? Because they were moved upon by the Spirit of God . . . to do it."

That sounded convincing, but still a few doubters asked embarrassing questions. What, after all, had the Mormon God "moved upon" his Prophet and his Prophet's disciples to have them do? Merely publicly to "declare" a piece of "advice."[2] The Adam God is a man, and, even when he speaks in a Mormon tabernacle, diplomacy is not beneath him.

Nevertheless, the leaders of the Church were careful that, until independent statehood had been secured, the deception of the Government should be maintained. To the day of his death Woodruff took precaution to avoid "even the appearance of associating with his

[1] 1st November 1891.

[2] "This declaration is regarded as being divine authority, since it was given by Wilford Woodruff, the head of the Church. And yet, since it gives a reason for refraining from polygamy other than the divine will, it is seen to be a suspension rather than a repeal, so to speak, of the law of celestial marriage as revealed through Joseph Smith." (*Mormonism To-Day.*)

plural wives."[1] Lorenzo Snow, once in jail for refusing to obey the civil law by disobeying the law of God, went to his youngest wife, Minnie Henson, and lived only with her until his life's end, and a similar course was pursued by George Q. Cannon and other conspicuous Mormons.

So the Government was hoodwinked. The courts forgot their established precedent and began to naturalize alien-born Saints. Benjamin Harrison, as President of the United States, pardoned all the polygamists in prison "on the express condition" that the pardoned should "in future faithfully obey the laws." Within a few months the laws had restored the confiscated property to be held by the Prophet of Mormondom and his successors as "trustee in trust."

Then the Saints asked for statehood. They would put into their state's constitution a clause forbidding polygamy and a clause forbidding the former clause's repeal. They would re-enact as a state all the anti-polygamy laws that they had fought and suffered for as a territory. They promised to do whatever was demanded of them.

Judge Zane, who had headed the courts' advance upon polygamy, told Congress that polygamy was now a "dead issue." Judge Judd, who had been an anti-Mormon Jeffreys under Zane, added: "I do not believe to-day that we could any more, by the consent of the people of the territory of Utah, re-establish polygamy there than you could re-establish slavery in Georgia or Tennessee." So the Act that made Utah a state was passed; a convention, in which the majority were Mormons, and thirty of the seventy-seven Mormons were polygamists, met in 1895 and drafted a state

[1] Hendrick.

constitution officially prohibiting polygamy for ever, and the first legislature of the new state re-enacted all the Federal laws against plural marriage. Then, when these formalities had been solemnly gone through, Utah, a state with a population two-thirds Mormon, proceeded to ignore in practice what it had enacted in theory, and the Church passed the word:

"Live your religion."

The revelation that established polygamy, though it has been relegated to an appendix and is now called, as in the manifesto, an "official declaration," has never been removed from *The Book of Doctrine and Covenants*, and *the Woodruff Manifesto was not included in that volume at all.*[1] The Mormons feel with one of their writers that has said: "Not to admit the purity of polygamy is to pin the scarlet letter on my mother's breast." More than this, they still believe in the revelation, and they live, in part, accordingly.

In 1907 the Mormon member of the United States Senate, Reed Smoot, said that the number of Mormon polygamists had decreased until at that date these did "not exceed five hundred householders." He continued, referring to the effort to unseat him from the Senate: "The testimony taken tends to show that there have been some polygamous marriages since the manifesto, (but) I sincerely believe that such cases are rare, (and) they have not received the sanction or the encouragement of the Church."

Yet in 1899 *The New York Journal* had published the following table:[2]

1 "Under the Prophet in Utah," ex-Senator Frank J. Cannon, *Everybody's Magazine*, 1911.

2 Issue of 30th April.

FAMILIES OF MORMON SAINTS AND PLURAL WIVES WHO ARE LIVING IN DEFIANCE OF THE LAW

Name of Husband.	Residence.	Position in Church.	Name of Plural Wife.	Number of Children born since 1890.
Joseph E. Wilson	Logan	Bishop's Counsellor	Esther Wilson	3
William Bassett	Provo	Elder	Kate Smith	3
James Thomson	Logan	Bishop's Counsellor	Mrs Thomson	1
John Larson	Coreville	Bishop	Mrs Larson	1
William Murray	Wellsville	Bishop's Counsellor	Three plural wives	1
S. Roskelly	Logan	Temple Devil	Mollie Roskelly	...
	Smithfield		Mary Jane Roskelly	1
			Maggie Roskelly	1
W. B. Parkinson	Logan	Elder	Maud Burton	...
			Clara	...
			Gertie	1
Charles Spierman	Logan	Elder	Edith Benson	1
John Thomas	Logan	Elder	Clara Johnson	1
Richard Jessop	Millville	Elder	Carrie Jensen	2
			Three plural wives	2
C. C. Amussen	Logan	Elder	Barbara	3
Thomas H. Merrill	Logan	Elder	Martha	3
			Mrs Merrill	2

Orson Smith	Logan	Stake President	Mary E. Wright Smith	1
O. C. Ormsby	Logan	Superintendent Sunday Schools	Rebecca Langton Ormsby	2
F. Bitters	Logan	Elder	Mrs Bitters	1
C. W. Nibley	Logan / Baker City	Elder	Julia Rudge Nibley	1
			Ellen Ricks Nibley	1
			Carrie Rigby	...
C. O. Card	Logan / Cardston	Elder	Sarah S. Painter	...
			Zina Y. Card	...
			Lavinia R. Card	3
Moses Thatcher	Salt Lake	Ex-Apostle	E. Snow's daughter	1
Moses Thatcher	Salt Lake	Ex-Apostle	Lydia Ann Clayton	2
W. H. Maughan	Wellsville	Bishop	Three wives	...
B. M. Lewis	Logan	Bishop	Eliza Jenks	1
F. A. Neuberger	Logan	Elder	Mrs Neuberger	1
George L. Farrell	Smithfield	Bishop	Four wives	2
P. Nielsen	Smithfield	Elder	Two wives	1
T. Stirland	Providence	Elder	Maria Christensen	1
F. Theurer	Providence	Bishop	Mary Hockstrausser	1
John Jenkins	Newton	Elder	Four wives	2
John Griffin	Newton	Bishop	Two wives	2
Paul Cardon	Benson	Elder	Two wives	2
T. B. Cardon	Benson	Elder	Ella	5
Isaac Smith	Logan	Stake Counsellor	Lizzie Furman	2
Joseph C. Knowles	Logan	Bishop's Counsellor	Thirsie Conrad Knowles	1

These families were all found in the vicinity of Logan, Cache County, Utah, and only the most notorious cases were given. Wilson, besides being a Bishop's Counsellor, was secretary of the Logan Agricultural College, supported jointly by the state and Federal governments. Bassett, secretary of the Provo woollen mills, when his first wife objected to a second, obtained a fraudulent divorce, which was set aside by the Supreme Court. Roskelly played the part of Satan in the "Endowment" ceremonies, or masques. Parkinson was a physician, Amussen a man of wealth, Orson Smith a postmaster, Ormsby another physician, Nibley a rich mining operator, and Knowles a justice of the peace. As for Moses Thatcher, he is mentioned in connection with Logan, although he was then living in Salt Lake City with his plural wives. He became a candidate for the Senatorship without asking the Church's consent, and was finally defeated by the efforts of the Church authorities. He was then disciplined by the High Council, deposed from the apostolate and degraded to the ranks. In his speech at Logan in justification of his cause, he said: "Before I will break the laws of the United States, I will declare my children bastards."

And have things changed since 1899? Not for what monogamists believe the better. In 1910 Mr Benton J. Hendrick, one of the most careful of journalists in the United States, was sent to Utah to investigate the growth of polygamy. He travelled through the Mormon towns, talked with scores of people, and derived his information largely from Mormon sources. "Everywhere he finds that not only are the old polygamous relations that existed before 1890 still maintained, but that hundreds of young men and women—young people in their twenties and thirties—have contracted plural marriages. More important, these 'new polygamists,' as the people of Utah call them, receive special favours at the hands of the Church—many of them hold the highest ecclesiastical offices, are teachers in the Church educational institutions, and are prominent in business and social life."[1]

How did this condition arise? It began with the heads of the Church and worked down—or up—to the laity. Woodruff died. His place was taken by Snow. Snow died, and, in 1901, Joseph Fielding Smith, politician, and bitterly uncompromising polygamist, became the chief of the Mormon Church and the voice of God.

Smith is a reactionary. He is the son of Hyrum and the nephew of Joseph the Founder. Though he was then but six years old, he can still remember the day when the bodies of his murdered father and uncle were brought home from the scene of their assassination. He drove an ox-team across the prairies in the great migration of 1846. He sucked the faith with his mother's milk. The flesh of the First Prophet is his flesh, the blood of the First Martyrs flows in his veins. To Joseph F. Smith every letter of *The Book of Mormon*, *The Pearl of Great Price*, and *The Doctrine and Covenants* is a direct and binding inspiration from God; and the foundation of God's kingdom and man's salvation is polygamy.

Upon the question of polygamy this Smith is, therefore, an uncompromising bigot. "Some people," he thundered in one of his sermons,[2] "have supposed that the doctrine of plural marriage was a sort of super-

1 *M'Clure's Magazine*, December 1910.

2 Sermon preached 7th July 1878.

fluity or non-essential to salvation or exaltation of mankind. . . . I want here to enter my solemn protest against this idea, for I know it is false. . . . *I understand the law of celestial marriage to mean that every man in this Church who has the ability to obey and practise it in righteousness, and will not, shall be damned.* I understand it to mean this and nothing less, and I testify in the name of Jesus that it does."

Smith has lived his religion. His first wife was Levira A. Smith, whom he married in 1859; she went to California and secured a divorce on the ground of Smith's adultery, because, at the time of her application to the court, it was proved that her husband was living in polygamy; and when she died, thirty years later, this husband, who had himself obtained a Mormon divorce from her, made an unsuccessful effort at law to establish a claim upon her property. Smith's polygamous marriages seem to have been more happy. He has married five women, two of them sisters—Alice Rich, Edna Lamson, Juliana Lamson, Sarah Richards, and Mary Schwartz—among whose various establishments he divides his time, in open violation of the law. These wives have borne him forty-three children, of whom the eldest is about fifty years old and the youngest scarcely four,[1] arriving in Zion when the Prophet had passed his seventieth year. *Twelve of the children were born after the issuance of the manifesto.*

Before a Senate committee in March 1904, this supreme head of the Mormon Church gave the following testimony:—

"Q. Is the cohabitation with one who is claimed to be a plural wife a violation of the law or rule of the Church, as well as of the law of the land?

[1] Alfred Henry Lewis. Mr Lewis's dates are questionable.

"A. That was the case, and is the case even to-day . . . that it is contrary to the rule of the Church and contrary as well to the law of the land for a man to cohabit with his wives.

"But I am placed in this position: I had a plural family, if you please; that is, my first wife was married to me over thirty-eight years ago; my last wife was married to me over twenty years ago, and with these wives I had children, and I simply took my chances, preferring to meet the consequences of the law rather than abandon my children and their mothers; and I have cohabited with my wives — not openly, that is, not in a manner that I thought would be offensive to my neighbours — but I have acknowledged them; I have visited them; they have borne me children since 1890; and I have done it, knowing the responsibility and knowing that I was amenable to the law.

"Q. I wish to ask you a question right here. You speak of your unwillingness to abandon your children.

"A. Yes, sir.

"Q. Why is it necessary, in order to support your children, educate and clothe them, that you should continue to have children by a multiplicity of wives?

"A. Because my wives are like everybody else's wife. . . .

"Q. How many children have been born to you since 1890?

"A. I have eleven children born since 1890. . . . All my wives bore children.

"Q. Since 1890?

"A. That is correct. . . .

"Q. How many children have you in all?

"A. I have had born to me forty-two children, twenty-one boys and twenty-one girls; and I am proud of every one of them. . . .

"Q. Is there not a revelation that you shall abide by the laws of the state and of the land?

"A. Yes, sir.

"Q. If that is a revelation, are you not violating the laws of God?

"A. I have admitted that, Mr Senator, a great many times here."

Doubtless the voice of the Mormon God was again employing diplomacy, for there is small reason to believe that Smith had lost his faith in the divine institution of the doctrine of celestial marriage. He testified that he adhered to both the divine revelation instituting polygamy and the equally divine revelation suspending it. He said that he considered the former as "correct a principle" as when first revealed, but that the latter had brought to pause the "law commanding it." He swore that he believed the Woodruff manifesto to be a revelation from God, but, instead of calling it "a law of the Church," he insisted that it be called a "rule of the Church." He admitted that the revelation which founded polygamy was still printed in *The Book of Doctrine and Covenants* without any note of explanation or qualification, and the manifesto was not printed there or in any other doctrinal work given to Mormon missionaries. He pleaded that the manifesto had been sent out in circular form, but he granted that this pamphlet did not "state in terms" that its contents were a revelation. He concluded that it had been omitted from *The Book of Doctrine and Covenants* by an "oversight," and promised that it should be included in the next edition. This promise was broken, and the manifesto was not added until some time later, and then only after considerable agitation.[1] In short, the fact is established that Smith has ignored the manifesto from the hour of its appearance, and that he expressed his real sentiments when, in a sermon that he preached at the dedication of a Mormon church in Payson, Utah, in 1896, he cried:

"Take care of your *polygamous wives; we don't care for Uncle Sam now!*"

Ten years later,[2] one of Smith's own polygamous wives bore him a child, and an enterprising Gentile of Salt Lake City swore out a warrant for the Prophet's arrest, charging adultery. But Smith was not arrested. What member of a Mormon police force dared arrest him? Indeed, the prosecuting attorney changed the charge to one of unlawful cohabitation, for which the Prophet, through his lawyer, was fined £60, paid the fine, and ended the entire matter.

That is a picture of the man left to carry on the faith, practice, and business of the Mormon Church, after the Church had pretended to abolish polygamy. What hope for the future do we find in the men that are to succeed him?

Francis Marion Lyman is President of the Board of Twelve Apostles. If he survives Smith, he will succeed him. Here is an example of the testimony given by Mr Lyman before the same committee that Mr Smith testified before in 1904:

"Q. Did you think it would have been right to abstain from polygamous cohabitation with your plural wife?

"A. I think it would have been right.

[1] Frank J. Cannon.

[2] November 1906.

"Q. You did not do that, though?

"A. No, sir. . . .

"Q. So you violated both laws (*i.e.* the manifesto and the law of the land)?

"A. Yes, sir.

"Q. You are now continuing in this polygamous relation?

"A. Yes, sir.

"Q. And intend to?

"A. I had thought of nothing else, Mr Chairman.

"Q. So you say that you, an apostle of your Church, expecting to succeed, if you survive Mr Smith, to the office in which you will be the person to be the medium of divine revelation, are living, and are known to your people to live, in disobedience to the law of the land and the law of God?

"A. Yes, sir."

Another witness before the same committee was John Henry Smith, Second Counsellor to Prophet Joseph F. Smith. John Henry appeared in his official capacity as the next in succession to the supreme command after Francis Marion Lyman. An excerpt from his testimony is worth consideration:

"Q. In your own case, you understand that the rule of the Church is against polygamist cohabitation, do you?

"A. Yes, sir.

"Q. And the law of the land is against it?

"A. Yes, sir.

"Q. But you propose to continue to violate the law of the land and the rule of the Church as a purely personal matter with yourself, and to take such consequences as may be imposed upon you for it?

"A. *Neither the law of the land nor the Church can take away obligations and contracts, and relieve me of them, made between me and my God.*"[1]

The words of the Church leaders found adequate expression in action. Apostle Abraham H. Cannon had been publicly insisting on the observance of the manifesto, and, although he had three wives and had been in jail during the "Diocletian Persecutions" therefor, he came out as a preacher for obedience to the new law. Then, in 1896, his brother David, while on a mission, died in Germany. David had been engaged to Lillian Hamlin. Mindful of the injunction of Deuteronomy,[2] Abraham married Miss Hamlin, and had the ceremony performed on a steamer on the high seas so as to be beyond the jurisdiction of United States law. Joseph F. Smith denies that he officiated at this strange wedding, but one of Abraham Cannon's wives says that Smith was the priest, and John Henry Hamlin, brother of Lillian, testifying before the Senate committee of 1904, said that the family "understanding was that Joseph F. Smith" had read the service. Married she at any rate was; the child that was born of the union was called Marba;[3] the Cannon family, on Abraham's death, acknowledged her as a widow of Abraham and gave her child a share in the estate; the Church made her a teacher in the Brigham Young

[1] One of the First Seven Presidents of Seventies gave similar testimony. This was Brigham H. Roberts, elected to Congress, but unseated because he was a polygamist. Asked in committee whether, by continuing in polygamy, he was "disregarding the law of God and man," he calmly answered, "I suppose I am."

[2] Deut. xxv. 5–6.

[3] Abram reversed.

University, and not long since she became the wife of another Cannon.[1]

Apostle Abraham Owen Woodruff was the son of that Prophet who had issued the famous manifesto pretending to end polygamy. After the publication of the manifesto he contracted a polygamous marriage with Avery Clark, a woman twenty-four years old, who tenderly nursed her husband and his first wife when they were smitten with smallpox, of which they died, while seeking, in 1904, refuge in a Mormon colony from a subpœna issued for Woodruff in connection with the Smoot inquiry.

Apostle Marriner H. Merrill was another offender. Nor did he confine his belief in polygamy to his words or his own actions. He presided at the polygamous wedding of his son to Chloe Hendricks, six months after the manifesto was published.[2]

Apostle George Teasdale, an Englishman, and a friend of Brigham Young, junior,[3] had, so far as was generally known in 1896, four wives. At that time

[1] Lewis M. Cannon. Another Cannon, Angus, aged seventy, for twenty-eight years President of the Salt Lake State, confessed before the Senate committee that he had six wives, all living.

[2] See testimony given before the United States Senate Committee on Privileges and Elections, 1904.

[3] The manifesto in the eyes of the younger Brigham was nothing less than treason to his father's memory. Externally he suggested little of the religious bigot. He was a heavy man, fat, sensual, good-natured; among Gentiles he was not unpopular. On only one subject did Young have any enthusiastic convictions, and that was polygamy. How many times he himself had married no one now pretends to know. During the late 'eighties he spent most of his time running away from United States marshals; on one occasion, while the officers of the law were close on his trail over the hills of Arizona, he paused long enough to marry a new polygamous wife. (*The Mormon Revival of Polygamy.*)

there came to his place at Nephi, Utah, to act as housekeeper, an Englishwoman, whom Teasdale had years before converted in England, and who brought with her a daughter, Marion Scoles, a woman thirty-one years old. Teasdale was then sixty-seven. About eighteen months after Marion's arrival in Teasdale's house she died in childbirth, and half of the Twelve Apostles attended her funeral in the Nephi burying-ground, where her grave is now marked with a stone inscribed:

Sacred to the Memory
of
Marion E. Scoles,
Wife of Apostle George Teasdale.
Born in London, England, April 6, 1865;
Died December 17, 1898.

Apostles John W. Taylor and Matthias F. Cowley were close friends, and fanatics upon the necessity of polygamy. The former was a son of the former Prophet, John Taylor; neither he nor his friend was much over thirty years old at the time that the manifesto was issued, and to both it came as a severe blow. Cowley showed his opinion of Prophet Woodruff's proclamation by marrying two new plural wives, Luella Parkinson, of Preston, Idaho, and Hattie Harker, of Salt Lake City. Two of Taylor's three previously acquired wives, Nellie Todd and Nettie Wooley, took up, in 1898, separate residences in a small town called Farmington, fourteen miles from Salt Lake City. The wives of Taylor secured as servants two girls of Farmington, sisters, Rhoda and Roxie Welling, the former sixteen and the latter eighteen years of age.

Taylor then came to visit his wives, and married the sisters.[1]

Both Taylor and Cowley continued to travel through Utah and the neighbouring states and territories doing missionary work. Taylor had received visions and spoken in tongues as a boy, prophesying that he would become an Apostle. These visions continued when he was working in his father's sawmill. A man with a thin face and gleaming, deep-set eyes, he was clearly always near to madness. Eventually his absolute acceptance of the Old Testament, which began with a horror of pork, ended in strange hallucinations. Cowley was like him, was called "The Travelling Apostle," and would voice opinions such as this, given at a meeting in the Logan tabernacle in January 1901:

"None of the revelations of the Prophets, either past or present, has been repealed. . . . If you have a teacher in the Sunday schools who would encourage the young to disregard or disrespect a single doctrine of the Church—plural marriage and all—turn them (*sic*) out; they have no right in the priesthood. Parents, you must teach the whole doctrine to your children, or they will apostatize and be damned. . . . These revelations received by our Prophets and seers are all of God, and we cannot repeal or disannul (*sic*) them without making God out a liar, and God cannot lie. I wish to remind you of a certain revelation given you through President Taylor. The command was given to set our quorums and houses in order, and the promise was that if we should obey the command God would fight our battles for us; but we did not obey the command, so God did not fight our battles for us. If we had obeyed

[1] See also the article by the Rev. Dr S. E. Wishard in the *Homiletic Review* for March 1903.

that command given through President Taylor, there would have been no manifesto."

The Senate investigation of the Smoot case, already liberally referred to, brought out even more facts. Fifteen men go to make up the governing board of the Mormon Church, the so-called First Presidency and Apostles' Quorum. They are the Prophet, his two Counsellors, and the Twelve Apostles. The Smoot investigation showed that of the First Presidency, as it was then composed, eight men, with thirty wives among them, had been living in polygamy since the publication of the manifesto. Certain Apostles, in requesting statehood for Utah and pardon for former polygamists, had signed a petition addressed to President Harrison of the United States, in which they "pledged their faith and honour for the future" to cease polygamous living. The Smoot investigation showed that at least eight of the thirteen leaders of the Church that had signed that petition had broken the solemn promises they then made. Moses Thatcher was one of these; Lyman, Taylor, Merrill and Abraham H. Cannon were others. The remaining three were John Henry Smith, Joseph F. Smith the Prophet himself, and Heber J. Grant, an Apostle with great business interests throughout Utah, who, in a speech delivered in Salt Lake City, had openly declared:

"I am a law-breaker, and I don't care who knows it. . . . I will sustain the principles of the Gospel even to the extent of taking more wives, *if necessary.*"[1]

In the educational institutions of the Church affairs were no better. Early in 1898, Benjamin Cluff, junior, President of Brigham Young University, and a man that read and quoted Herbert Spencer and sought to

[1] *New York Herald*, 9th March 1899.

prove that *The Book of Mormon* was in accord with Darwinism, announced his intention of organizing a scientific expedition that would be to most scientific expeditions what that contradiction in terms, a Holy War, is supposed to be to other wars. He proposed to explore the unknown regions of Central and South America, through which the tribes described in *The Book of Mormon* were supposed to have proceeded, and there discover ruins and records that would prove the authenticity of the Mormon story beyond all possibility of doubt.

The Mormon Church immediately took the expedition under its wing. It enlisted as members its brightest and most zealous missionaries. It would have no person accompany Dr Cluff before having "gone through the Endowment House." It held prayer-meetings, to petition Heaven for Cluff's success, all over Utah. It gave money, and it saw to it that, even in the most remote Mormon settlements, dances and entertainments were held to raise more funds.

Dr Cluff said good-bye to his two wives and, in June 1898, with his twenty eager followers, anxious to prove the truth of their faith to a doubting world, set out southward. The good Doctor led the chanting of Mormon hymns, to which tunes the cavalcade moved forward under the blistering sun. Each morning and evening he led his company in prayer, and, assuring them that he guided them under direct revelation, admonished them that there must be no loud conversation and no jesting in the ranks. Then, at the Mexican border, he said that he must leave them to make certain arrangements with the Mexican customs officers. He was unaccountably missing for two months. When he did return to his encamped followers, he brought with him a young woman of about twenty-six years old, whom he presented as "Sister Cluff," but who was at once recognized as a former pupil at Brigham Young University, Florence Reynolds, the daughter of George Reynolds, a prominent Mormon. Cluff had simply married a third wife and had been passing his third honeymoon at Colonia Jaurez and other Mormon colonies in Mexico. Either because of disgust at the hardship of a long encampment thus put upon it by its leader, or because the leader weakened in his faith that there would be any evidences of Mormonism to be found in Central and South America, the expedition dwindled, disbanded, returned home. Its sole result was to secure Dr Cluff another wife.[1]

Other cases of what was called "the new polygamy" were rapidly brought to light, by the Senatorial investigation, by Government officials, by newspapers, orthodox missionaries in Utah and still other persons

[1] Hendrick vouches for this story. Before the Smoot Committee, George Reynolds gave the following testimony:

"Q. Have you any daughters married in polygamy?

"A. I believe I have one.

"Q. To whom is she married?

"A. If married, she is married to Benjamin Cluff, junior. . . . He was in charge of an exploring expedition. It was a few years ago, but I don't remember when. I had no particular interest in it. . . .

"Q. Did she go to Mexico about the time that Mr Cluff went?

"A. I think so. . . . She has two children, I believe.

"Q. Did she tell you anything about when she was married?

"A. No, sir; not a word.

"Q. Did you ask her anything about it?

"A. No, sir.

"Q. Why did you not?

"A. Because I was satisfied in my mind that she had been married, and she never wrote me or told me anything about it, and I made no inquiries."

with no decent ends to serve. Angus Cannon, president of the Salt Lake stake, had said of the anti-polygamy legislation passed by the Mormon legislature: "It can never be enforced. We never agreed to abandon our families. I never agreed to do it, and I never will do it." Since 1890 two of the stake presidents out of the seven in Salt Lake City are known to have taken plural wives: they are Hugh J. Cannon, brother of ex-Senator Frank J. Cannon, and Frank Y. Taylor. J. H. Grant, a brother of the Mormon Apostle Heber J. Grant, presides over Davis stake, not far from the state capital, and he has followed the example of Cannon and Taylor. Thomas Chamberlain, president of the Kanab stake, and called the most influential Mormon in southern Utah,[1] is said to have eight wives, at least one of whom, Mamie Woolley, he has married since 1890, and is further reported to be the father of fifty children, of whom the youngest was born when, not long since, Chamberlain was celebrating his fiftieth birthday. Bishops, counsellors, elders, all the divisions of the hierarchy, have contributed members of their respective orders to follow the lead of those apostles and educators that preached and practised disregard of the Woodruff manifesto.

Nor has the Church punished them. In 1904 the most that the polygamous Prophet, Joseph F. Smith, would say about this was that practitioners of polygamy "will be *liable* to be dealt with according to the rules and regulations (of the Church) and excommunicated therefrom." Nobody of any importance to the Church, nobody of any use to it, has as yet suffered. Hendrick notes one case, that of an Elder named Tolman, who was senile and useless, and who was judged by a board

[1] Hendrick.

among the members of which was Apostle Anthony W. Ivins, himself guilty of the very offence of performing a plural marriage that was charged against the miserable prisoner at that ecclesiastical bar. When it seemed likely that the talk of renewed polygamy in Utah might unseat Senator Smoot and thus lose for the Church a vote in the United States Senate, Taylor and Cowley, the Travelling Apostles above referred to, were "forced to resign" for the sake of the moral effect of such an action on the country at large; but what they resigned was not their Apostleship—it was merely their seats in the Apostles' Quorum. They are still members of the Church, still authorized speakers and preachers from Mormon pulpits, still Apostles.[1]

Indeed, instead of punishing new polygamists, there is evidence to show that the Mormon Church rewards them. Walter C. Lyman has been removed from the presidency of the San Juan stake; but he cannot suffer, because he is a brother of that Francis M. Lyman who will be Joseph F. Smith's successor. Haskell S. Jolley, Bishop of the Lovell ward in Wyoming, has also been dropped, but not until the Church had first advanced him satisfactorily both in office and financially. On the other hand, the heads of the Church have promoted a notorious polygamist, Josiah Hickman, to the principalship of the Church's Murdock Academy at Beaver. Then there is Joseph M. Tanner, of Salt

[1] "The dropping of Taylor and Cowley from the Quorum of the Twelve Apostles was so evidently done for popular effect that the act merits no consideration whatever, except as an admission by the First Presidency and Twelve Apostles that Apostles Taylor and Cowley have each taken one or more plural wives since the manifesto." (Report of the United States Senate Committee on Privileges and Elections, sitting in the Smoot case.)

Lake City. He studied at the law school of Harvard University for three years, and then, returning to Utah, was made head of the State Agricultural College, which is supported by public taxation. Gentile taxpayers objected to Tanner because he had six wives, three of whom he had married since 1890; so, though the Church "removed" him, or forced him to resign, it promptly made him superintendent of the Sunday schools of the Church of Jesus Christ of Latter Day Saints throughout the world!

What has happened to polygamy in Utah is simple enough to anyone that has studied the Mormon religion. Under the terms of the Mormon faith, man's salvation rests on the practice of polygamy. Under the terms of the Mormon faith, a member of the faith or the Church as an official representative of the faith may lie to the infidel world and its governments when those governments threaten the faith, for the faith must be protected at all costs, and, though it is well to obey established law, when there are established laws that assail the faith, then those laws must be circumvented or overcome. Finally, under the Mormon faith, though the Prophet is the voice of God, the manifesto of 1890 was merely a piece of advice given by the Deity to circumvent the inimical laws that were killing his Church, advice that was to be abandoned as soon as those laws, by the admission of Mormon-controlled Utah into self-governing statehood, ceased to harm the faith; and in the meantime, whereas the creed limits all revelation concerning matters of doctrine to the Prophet, it extends revelation upon matters of purely personal conduct to every believing and practising Mormon. The heads of the Church set the example and preached accordingly; the laity began to imitate, and are continuing to imitate, justifying themselves, if they think justification necessary, by revelations that permit them, personally, to "live their religion."[1]

Thus polygamy was renewed and spread from the hierarchy to the laity. The women are fed with the ancient lie that the greatest sexual love is the love that gives all and asks nothing, the men with the assurance of heavenly exaltation in proportion to their progeny on earth. Clarice Thatcher, a woman of refinement and education, the daughter of the only Apostle that ever dared to fight the Church's domination in politics,[2] becomes the plural wife of Henry S. Tanner, a graduate of the law department of the University of Michigan, and Gentile Salt Lake will not believe the rumour until it sees the funeral of a child take place from Miss Thatcher's house.[3] Men and women holding Federal appointments enter polygamy.[4] Devoted sisters refuse to be divided at the altar and therefore marry one

1 Not a few Mormons have been quoted as saying that God has told them that the manifesto was "an attempt to beat the devil at his own game." Before the Smoot Committee, Professor Walter M. Wolfe quoted Apostle John Henry Smith as saying: "It (the manifesto) is a trick to beat the devil at his own game"; and John Wilson of Logan, "a prominent Mormon," as saying: "The manifesto enables the Church to exclude men who ought not to have more than one wife, and gives to worthy men an opportunity to take plural wives." Both of these statements were made in Wolfe's church.

2 Moses Thatcher.

3 Hendrick.

4 M. C. Forbes, Post Office Inspector, reported officially, 10th December 1904: "John Maughan, postmaster at Weston, aged seventy-four, appointed 18th March 1898, had two plural wives at one time; one of them left him and married another man. . . . Alnora N. Austin, postmistress at Liberty, was one of the plural wives of a bishop. . . . Nephi J. Bates, postmaster at Beach, married a plural wife," etc. etc.

man.[1] And as far away from Utah as Philadelphia, a Mormon preacher publicly says: "Under certain conditions we believe that God has justified a man in marrying more than one wife: the worse evil is not too much marrying, but too little."[2] Is it any wonder that, with plural marriages thus re-established, Dr Mattie Hughes Cannon, a plural wife of Angus M. Cannon, should in 1904, with a committee of Mormon women, call on the National Convention of the Democratic party to omit from its platform a proposed plank directed against polygamy?

In 1902 the Prophet Joseph F. Smith said, through *The Salt Lake Telegram*, that there were then only eight hundred and ninety-seven men living in "unlawful cohabitation" in Mormondom. If the Prophet was not mentally defining "unlawful cohabitation" in Mormon terms, he was either woefully misinformed or wilfully lying.[3] Mr Hendrick, a far

[1] The following list shows the "sister love" propensity of men high in the Church: Brigham Young married two sisters; Andrew Jansen, Church Historian, two sisters (and their mother "for eternity"); Lorenzo Snow, late President, two sisters; Joseph F. Smith, President, two sisters; Francis Marion Lyman, Apostle, two sisters; George Teasdale, Apostle, two sisters; Angus M. Cannon, Stake President, two sisters (at one time); Bishop Johnson, five sisters; Stephen Moat, three sisters; William Maughan, *three pairs of sisters*; Emanuel Bayley, three sisters; George Stranger, three sisters; Alma Merrill, son of an Apostle, two sisters; Ole Berg, two sisters; S. R. Parkinson, two sisters; Hyrum Watson, two sisters (who each bore him twins a year later). (*Philadelphia Press,* 23rd March 1904.) These are but a few examples.

[2] The Rev. J. G. M'Quarrie, President of the Eastern States Missions of the Mormon Church, as quoted in the *Philadelphia Press* (1902).

[3] Senator Kearns, in a speech in the United States Senate, 28th February 1905, spoke of the renewed spread of polygamy, the laws against which, he said, were violated by all but a few Apostles.

more reliable authority, writing in 1911, has thus put the case. We condense his version:

A large number of specific instances could be added to those already cited.[1] About two years ago *The Salt Lake Tribune*[2] began industriously to collect and publish the names of "new polygamists." Up to date, it has published detailed records of two hundred and twenty-four polygamous marriages. The Mormon Church has made no attempt to deny the substantial accuracy of the *Tribune's* list. The Mormon Church organ, *The Deseret News*, has remained silent in face of this accumulating evidence. The men and women whose names the *Tribune* has printed, though publicly and repeatedly accused by a responsible journal of committing criminal acts, have not attempted to secure legal redress—in only a very few cases have even taken the trouble to make denials. It may safely be assumed, therefore, that the facts are definitely known concerning at least two hundred cases of polygamous marriages since the manifesto. If so many cases can be reasonably proved, how many must there be of which nothing is known? Plural marriages have always been performed with the utmost secrecy, and only those which are most open and notorious reach the public attention. The Mormon people are, for the most part, farmers. They live in compact villages, generally remote from railways. All natural conditions, therefore, favour concealment.

1 "A two-column notice of the death of a leading Mormon (was) published in the Gentile papers the morning I struck town. The papers registered the old patriarch's age—seventy-nine,—his civic usefulness, his wealth, and then stated without emotion or apology that, all sorrowing in the mournful wake of the old hero's hearse, rode his four widows and thirty-five children—fifteen boys and twenty girls." (Alfred Henry Lewis.)

2 An anti-Mormon newspaper.

If we reckoned on the basis of ten plural marriages to every one known, we should thereby have more than fifteen hundred probable marriages since 1890. Should these figures be fair, it would mean that polygamy is almost as prevalent now as it was before the manifesto, the only essential difference being that it is more hidden.

It must be remembered that, even in the palmiest days of Mormonism, only a comparatively small number of Mormons were allowed to be polygamists. Plural marriage, under the Mormon system, was intended only for those who had advanced to a certain stage of grace. Even at present, should polygamy suddenly cease renewal, there have enough young men and women entered this relationship to keep the institution alive for fifty years or more.

The Mormons fear one thing from the United States Government: they fear some sort of constitutional amendment that will make it possible for Congress to reduce Utah to the condition of a territory under Federal control, although such an amendment is far from likely of accomplishment. But should it be made, they would be ready for it; and polygamy *will not* thereby be given up. The Church of Jesus Christ of Latter Day Saints already owns and has populated great tracts of land in Alberta and the Canadian North-west, where it has established two stakes; it has still greater tracts[1] in Chihuahua and Sonora, Mexico,[2] where polygamy was permitted by Diaz,[3] and is not yet forbidden

[1] Some 300,000 acres were bought not very long since.

[2] See also *The New York Sun* for 1st March 1903.

[3] "Before establishing these colonies, the Mormons talked with Diaz, and that astute dictator said 'Yes' with emphasis. Diaz welcomed the Mormons; they might be as polygamous as they

to the Mormon. To some such haven Zion may yet have to flee, but not until the United States has ended its political partnership with Mormondom; and how the United States can, under its capitalistic government, free itself from that partnership must be a mystery to anyone that will take the trouble to see how the Mormon Church has made itself a power among the financial forces that combine to rule the Republic.

pleased. He bade the Mormons come to Mexico, and make a bulwark of themselves between him and his American neighbours north of the Rio Grande.

"The Mormons, thousands of them, by command of the Prophet, migrated to Mexico. There they dwell to-day in many a rich community, as freely polygamous as in the most wide-flung hour of Brigham Young. Diaz smiles as he reviews those prodigal crops of corn and cattle and children which they raise. They make his empire richer in men and money—commodities of which he has only too often felt the want.

"Once when a Methodist clergyman remonstrated against that polygamy which he permitted, and spoke of 'immoralities,' Diaz snapped his Mexican fingers.

"'Do you see their children?' he cried. 'Well, I think more of their children than of your moralities!'" ("The Viper's Trail.")

XII

MONEY-BAGS

MORMON Utah is a perfect *imperium in imperio.* Under a territorial governor appointed by the President of the United States, matters were different, for a territorial governor is empowered to veto "all acts of the territorial legislature" of which he does not approve; and over him, as he existed in Utah, Congress could, and eventually did, legislate against polygamy, which is the basis of the Mormon faith, and could and did send Gentile officers into Utah to enforce those laws. Even under its territorial government, indeed, Mormondom was generally treated by the authorities in Washington with a degree of respect that must have been inspired, in part at least, by fear;[1] but when the Woodruff manifesto had been issued, when there came the petition for sovereign statehood,

[1] This was generally recognised as long ago as 1881. In that year a correspondent of *The Chicago Tribune* remarked: "Since we partially recovered the courts from them (the Mormons) in 1874, we have tried to punish some of their old criminals—but without success. John D. Lee (leader of the Mountain Meadow Massacre) was the single expiation for a thousand religious murders; there has been none for 10,000 religious robberies and 100,000 religious adulteries; and we have had to 'treat' with this foreign Power we have ourselves planted and nourished, the same as we would (*sic*) have had to with any other foreign Power, for the surrender of Lee."

followed later by the amnesty proclamation of President Harrison, a Republican, and President Cleveland, a Democrat, upon the oath of Mormon Apostles that their Church had abandoned polygamy [1]—when, in short, the Mormon Church had made Utah a state, then the authority of Congress ended, and the Mormons, numbering a two-thirds majority of the population, came, as a religious, financial, and virtually legislative body, into both *de jure* and *de facto* control.[2] It is the control of a sect numbering, after less than a hundred years of growth, 750,000 members,[3] who have turned, since the early 'forties, a wilderness into a garden, who touch no tobacco, tea, coffee, alcoholic liquor,[4] and to whom, as Chief Justice White declared, in an address from the bench to a Grand Jury, "industry, frugality, temperance, honesty, and, in every respect but one, obedience to law, are the common practices of life." The Chief Justice's single exception is this: that the Mormon puts the sovereignty of his religious rulers above all other sovereignty in his every word, deed, and possession; and the result is that we have in present-day Utah, "as represented by the managers of the Mormon organization, a power that is monarchical in its assumption and exercise of authority, . . . which believes itself strong enough to deny interference with its schemes," [5] and the head of which, a year or two ago, received an at least semi-official visit from the President of the United States, the Chief Magistrate of that Government which

[1] See article by the Rev. S. E. Wishard in *The Homiletic Review* for March 1903.

[2] Hendrick.

[3] Alfred Henry Lewis.

[4] *Under the Prophet in Utah,* Frank J. Cannon.

[5] *Illiteracy and Mormonism,* p. 38.

had forbidden his polygamy, and serenely presented the Executive[1] to two of the Prophet's wives.

This sort of statement sounds incredible. Few foreigners would believe it, and not many citizens of the United States. In order to bring it home to doubters and to show how tightly the Mormon Church is hand in hand with the capitalistic system in America, it is well to tell the story of the election of Senator Reed Smoot.

When the Mormon Church divided its numbers between the Republican and Democratic parties, it did so with the double purpose of making the nation believe that the Church was "out of politics" and of placing Mormons in high positions with both of what were then the only leading national parties.[2] It then, in 1899, had its members in one Congressional district cast their majority-vote for the Democratic nominee for Congress, Brigham H. Roberts, a native of Warrington, England, the author of *The Mormon Doctrine of Deity* and other Mormon works, and one of the most active controversialists in the ranks of Zion. The economic battle between the Mormons and the Utah Gentiles was at that time, however, sharp, and the consequent anti-polygamy agitation, hereinbefore accounted for, resulted in the Federal Congress unseating Roberts, after his constituency had elected him, on the ground that he was a polygamist.

[1] See Alfred Henry Lewis's "The Viper's Trail." This President was Mr Taft, while on an excursion to Saltair, at about the time of his journey to the Mexican frontier, where he took pains to associate on friendly terms with Diaz, in order to discourage the revolutionists in Mexico. There, under Diaz, Taft's brother was said to have large financial interests.

[2] This was before the Socialist party had grown to its present national strength in the United States. The constitution of that party makes impossible the interference of any Church.

The hierarchy, therefore, bided their chance and in 1902 nominated, this time on the Republican ticket, not for the Lower National House, but for the United States Senate, Reed Smoot, a millionaire in his own right, the son of a plural wife,[1] and, though charges of polygamy could never be proved against him, an Apostle of the Mormon Church.

Mr Smoot has thus described himself in the American *Who's Who?*

"Born Salt Lake City, Jan. 10, 1862; *s.* Abraham O. and Anne K. S.; grad. Brigham Young Acad., Provo, Utah, 1879; *m.* Alpha M. Eldredge, of Salt Lake City, Sept. 17, 1884. Pres. Provo Commercial and Savings Bank, Smoot Investment Co., Smoot Drug Co., The Electric Co., Provo, Provo Woollen Mills Co., etc.; dir. of Salt Lake corpns.: Zion's Co-operative Mercantile Co., Deseret National Bank, Deseret Savings Bank. Apptd. one of the Presidency Utah Stake of the Ch. of Jesus Christ of Latter Day Saints, Apr. 1895; Apostle, 1900. . . . Republican."

It will be observed that the gentleman is a man of wide interests and a thorough Mormon. Let us now see how these things worked together for the greater glory of the Mormon god.

In 1901, a year before Smoot's Senatorial candidacy was announced, and a year after he had been made an Apostle, it was known in Salt Lake City that Mr Smoot had been commissioned by the hierarchy to negotiate a sale of the Church's sugar holdings to the Sugar Trust. These negotiations were successfully concluded on 13th May 1902, when the president of the Trust announced to the Trust's executive committee that he had come to an agreement whereby the

[1] "The Viper's Trail."

Trust was to purchase a half-interest in the consolidation of the Mormon factories at Logan, Ogden, and Le Grande, the Trust thus openly becoming the partner of the Mormon Church.[1] On the next day, 14th May 1902, Smoot was called to the office of Prophet Smith, and, when the interview that took place there had been ended, Smoot's candidacy for the U.S. Senate was announced.

The partnership between the Mormon Church and the Sugar Trust was then cemented. On the 24th of June of the same year the Trust made public its purchase of half the stock of the Church companies already mentioned. Eleven days later, that is, on 5th July 1902—a wonderfully short time for such an amalgamation to be effected, if it had not been elaborately planned before,—the three companies were made one under the title of the Amalgamated Sugar Company. David Eccles, a trustee of Mormon Church bonds, a polygamist, and a *protégé* of the Prophet, was made president of the new concern,[2] and the Sugar Trust, which controls enough of Congress to shape tariff legislation to its desires, accepted half the stock in exchange for its shares in the original companies.

It was the man that had, in Trust slang, "engineered the deal," who was now put forward by the Church to serve it in another capacity, a capacity in which he could also be of service to the Sugar Trust. Smoot was to be rewarded and given a chance of further usefulness. Although the Democratic ticket would have done as well (but for the fact that the Republican party stood for the tariff which protected the Sugar

[1] Synopsis of these minutes of the Trust's executive committee in *Hampton's Magazine,* January 1910.

[2] *Under the Prophet in Utah.*

Trust), he was put forward as the Republican candidate for United States Senator.

Members of the Roman Catholic Church have, before now, served in the United States Senate, but the candidacy of Smoot was scarcely similar to theirs. To parallel it, one would have to imagine the Pope of Rome promising and giving his Church's support—as Prophet Smith now promised and gave to an Apostle the Mormon support—to an American-born member of the College of Cardinals who was wanted by the Vatican to represent it in the Higher House of the United States national legislature. Smoot assumed the *rôle* of candidate not to represent Utah the state, although of course that was the necessary fiction. Once an Apostle in Zion, always an Apostle. Smoot was a candidate in the only way in which his apostolic office allowed him to be, and that was to represent the Mormon Church and the Mormon hierarchy.

On the Democratic side, Joseph H. Rawlins had been nominated. The announcement of his candidacy had preceded the announcement of Smoot's, and no sooner did it become known that, on the Republican side, an Apostle of the Church would be in the field against Rawlins than the Democratic State Chairman noticed a sudden torpor settling upon all his Mormon adherents.[1] This chairman, Frank J. Cannon, a

[1] In every state of the United States each political party has a "State Committee," which looks after the interests of its party's nominee in that state. The head of the State Committee is the State Chairman. In the present instance, the Democratic State Chairman for Utah was Frank J. Cannon. From his narrative of the following campaign, as given in *Everybody's Magazine* for May 1911, the facts now set forth are derived. It should, in fairness, be remembered that Mr Cannon is a partisan, having himself been a United States Senator (1896-99), and that the contest of which he

Mormon that was on bad terms with the Prophet, called his lieutenants together. He pointed out to them that his party "was not making war on the Church," and he proceeded to Prophet Smith's office to ask the Prophet whether the hierarchy were indeed using their power in favour of Smoot.

Quick as he was about this visit, the news, or suspicion, of his mission had preceded him. Probably some Mormon in his confidence had betrayed him: he was refused admission to the Prophet's presence.

A few days later the hierarchy sent an ambassador to Cannon in the person of Apostle Cowley. This is the same Cowley whom we have already seen as a polygamist, violating the manifesto and the law and preaching such violation to his congregations. He was chosen for his present task because he had been a boyhood friend of Cannon, and he told Cannon that Smoot was the Prophet's choice for the Senatorship, and that such Mormons as opposed him would oppose him at their peril.

Cannon realized the difficulties of his situation. "The Mormon Church," as he wrote,[1] "is so constituted that the Apostle carries with him the power of the Church wherever he appears. The whole people recognize in him the personified authority of the Church; and if an Apostle were allowed to make a political campaign without a denunciation from the

speaks brought upon him, a Mormon of some independence of mind, the displeasure of his Church. He is a man, however, of probity; and he wrote for a magazine of good repute. Nevertheless, in an address read at the General Conference of the Church of Latter Day Saints at Salt Lake City, 9th April 1911, the truth of practically everything he said was flatly denied by the Presidency.

[1] *Everybody's Magazine*, May 1911.

other Church authorities, it would be known that he had been selected for political office by 'the mouthpiece of the Almighty.'" Cannon recalled the instance of Moses Thatcher[1] as proof of how the Church acted in politics. "If," he argued, "the Church failed now to rebuke Smoot, this very failure would be an affirmative use of its power in his behalf; all Mormons who did not wish to raise their hands against 'the Lord's anointed' would have to support Smoot regardless of their political convictions; and all Gentiles and independent Mormons would have to fight the intrusion of the Church into open political activities."

Cowley ended the interview with one significant statement.

"Well," he said, "the Prophet has spoken. That's enough for me. I submit cheerfully when the will of the Lord comes to me through His appointed servants. The matter has been decided, and it does not lie in your power—or anyone else's—to withstand the purposes of the Almighty. . . . I hope you are not going to be found warring against the Lord's anointed. He has been consecrated to the Apostleship."

The election campaign that followed resolved itself into a fight between the Church and the Church's enemies, and of course the strength was all on the Church's side. Openly the hierarchy said nothing; secretly "Visiting Apostles" carried to the presidents of stakes the word that Smoot must be elected and Rawlins defeated. The presidents of stakes passed this order to the bishops under them; the bishops accordingly instructed their inferiors, and so the command

[1] Thatcher, it will be remembered, was one of the few Mormons that attempted independence in politics. The Church defeated him and severely disciplined him.

went down the Church, always received from a person in authority, until all the laity were instructed, and even the mother of Rawlins, Smoot's antagonist, herself a Mormon, was warned by her ecclesiastical superior that if she voted for her son[1] she would do so so "at the peril of her immortal soul." Smoot's election was secured by an overwhelming majority.

Within the week following that event a protest, signed by Gentile citizens of Utah, was sent to Theodore Roosevelt, then President of the United States, and to the United States Senate, asking that Smoot be forbidden to take his seat in the Upper House of the national Legislature. The protest alleged that the Mormon Church, through its hierarchy, which was breaking the anti-polygamy laws, amounted to a treasonable organization, and that Smoot, like all Mormons, sworn to blind obedience,[2] was its representative, not the people's.

The Senate, properly influenced by the great capitalistic powers with which the Mormon Church was in financial partnership, postponed the hearing of these charges for one year, and the hierarchy openly boasted of their success. "I knew," writes Cannon,[3] "that if Smoot were excluded from the Senate, his exclusion would be argued as proof that the wicked and unregenerate nation was still devilishly persecuting God's anointed servants, to its own destruction; if he were permitted to take his seat, that this fact would be cited to the faithful as proof that the Prophet had been called to save the nation from the destruction that threatened

[1] Both women and men vote in Utah.

[2] "The Viper's Trail." The reference is to the Endowment House oaths.

[3] *Under the Prophet in Utah.*

it!" However that was to be, the Apostle-Senator was permitted to assume his seat pending the inquiry. He took his oath of office on the 5th of March 1903; not until January 1904 did the Senate Committee on Privileges and Elections begin its investigation; not until February 1907 was the case ended, and by then Smoot had been in Washington for two-thirds of the term of six years to which he had been elected.

Much of what those weary three years of investigation uncovered has already been told;[1] more will be set down when the reader's attention is called to the Church's alleged animosity to the United States Government.[2] Many Mormons, high in authority in Zion, had fled the country[3] to escape subpœnas, and the Senate expressed its unwillingness to transport polygamous wives and their children in any great number to Washington to give testimony;[4] but enough Saints and to spare were put upon the witness-stand, where some of them quibbled, and some of them lied, and some refused to answer important questions, and some defied their inquisitors by telling the truth and so, as Brigham H. Roberts boasted, "carried the gospel to the benighted nation."[5] It was shown that the Mormon Church in Utah:

Taught and practised polygamy;
Taught its religion in the state schools;
Controlled the state courts;

[1] See the chapters on Polygamy.

[2] See Chap. XIII.

[3] Hendrick.

[4] Some of Joseph F. Smith's (the Prophet's) several wives even complained feelingly that they "were not allowed to testify for Papa" (Cannon).

[5] Cannon.

Exacted implicit obedience to the hierarchy;

Made all Mormons seeking political honours secure its permission before appealing to the electors;

Administered oaths of fatal vengeance to be inflicted upon certain of its enemies;

Imposed vows that set it above all temporal governments and were directed against the United States Government in particular.

On any one of these proved charges Smoot could legally have been unseated. Yet he was confirmed; he was given his place in the Senate of the United States, and he has since been re-elected and re-admitted.

Why?

On the floor of the Senate, in 1907, Senator Dubois, of Idaho, declared:

"The President of the United States[1] is an open friend of the Senator from Utah.[2] You all know it. The country knows it. He wants him seated. You[3] have got the Mormon vote.[4] You have every one of them, my friends, on the Republican side."

Mr Dubois, being a member of the Democratic party, was thus charging that the Republican party favoured Smoot so as to secure to itself the support of the Mormon Church at the polls. In this there is truth; but an examination of the vote on the Smoot case tells even more.

The Senate's action in seating Smoot, or rather in continuing him in his seat, was contrary to the report made by the majority of the committee that took the evidence in his case. That majority reported that

[1] Theodore Roosevelt, Republican, was then President.

[2] Smoot.

[3] That is, the Republican party.

[4] See the Congressional Record.

Smoot was a member of a self-perpetuating body of fifteen men, uniting in themselves authority in both Church and State—men that "so exercise this authority as to encourage a belief in polygamy as a divine institution, and by both precept and example encourage among their followers the practice of polygamy and polygamous cohabitation." The report declared that the Mormon hierarchy had "endeavoured to suppress, and succeeded in suppressing, a great deal of testimony by which the fact of plural marriages contracted by those who were high in the councils of the Church might have been established beyond the shadow of a doubt"; but that, "aside from this, *it was shown by the testimony that a majority of those who gave law to the Mormon Church are now, and have been for years, living in open, notorious, and shameless polygamous cohabitation.*"

This report noted the fact that the Woodruff "manifesto in no way declares the principle of polygamy to be wrong, or abrogates it as a doctrine of the Mormon Church, but simply suspends the practice of polygamy, to be resumed at some more convenient season." It placed upon Smoot a full share of the responsibility for all the actions of the Mormon Church; it branded him as having at least countenanced polygamy "by repeated acts and in a number of instances, as a member of the Quorum of the Twelve Apostles"; and it adds:

"The First Presidency[1] . . . exercise a controlling influence over the action of the members of the Church in secular affairs as well as in spiritual matters; . . . contrary to the principles of the common law under which we live, and the constitution of the State of Utah, . . . (they) dominate the affairs of the state and

[1] That is, the Prophet, his two Counsellors, and the Twelve Apostles.

constantly interfere in the performance of its functions. But it is in political affairs that the domination of the First Presidency is most efficacious and most injurious to the interests of the state. . . . Notwithstanding the plain provision of the constitution of Utah, the proof offered on the investigation demonstrates beyond the possibility of doubt that the hierarchy at the head of the Mormon Church has, for years past, formed a perfect union between the Mormon Church and the State of Utah, and that the Church, through its head, dominates the affairs of the state in things both great and small. . . . The said Reed Smoot comes here, not as the accredited representative of the State of Utah in the Senate of the United States, but as the choice of the hierarchy which controls the Church and has usurped the functions of the State in Utah. It follows, as a necessary conclusion from these facts, that Mr Smoot is not entitled to a seat in the Senate as a Senator from the State of Utah."

There was a minority report, which, in the face of the overwhelming evidence produced before the committee, declared that Smoot had "all the qualifications prescribed by the Constitution to make him eligible to a seat in the Senate; that 'the regularity of his election' had not been questioned; that his private character was 'irreproachable'; and that, so far as mere belief and membership in the Mormon Church are concerned, he is fully within his rights and privileges under the guaranty of religious freedom given by the Constitution of the United States." It found that the testimony as to whether he had taken an "Endowment oath," whereby "he obligated himself to make his allegiance to the Church paramount to his allegiance to the United States" was "limited in amount, vague, and indefinite in character and utterly unreliable, because of the disreputable character of the witnesses"; and it said that, as for polygamy, although Smoot had "silently acquiesced" in that, it was enough that he had, under oath, denied ever having "advised any person to violate the law," and that, anyhow, it was necessary to recall certain historical facts, among which are some that indicate that the United States Government is not free from responsibility for these violations of the law.

Of course, this report entirely ignored the fact that one of the witnesses to the Endowment House oaths had been called in *defence of Smoot*, his character not having been so much as questioned. Of course, it forgot that the other witnesses on this point were denounced by the Mormon bishop, Daniel Connolly, as "traitors who had broken the oaths of the Church," precisely because they had betrayed the secrets of the Endowment oath. Of course, it took no account of the truth that such Mormons as swore that the oath was not unpatriotic would not tell what it was. Of course, finally, the minority refused to see that an Apostle of the Mormon Church had to believe in polygamy and, by the very holding of his position, encourage it, and that such an official, if he were sincere in his faith, must have more than one woman, perhaps secretly, at least "sealed to him for eternity." These things were of no importance to the minority.

This minority consisted of but five persons, and yet it was its report that the Senate eventually adopted. The five men so hard to convince were Joseph Benson Foraker, of Ohio; Albert J. Hopkins, of Illinois; William Paul Dillingham, of Vermont; Albert Jeremiah Beveridge, of Indiana; and Philander Chase Knox, of

Pennsylvania. They were all lifelong supporters of the protective tariff that fostered the Sugar Trust, and the last named, the successor of the notorious Matthew Stanley Quay, not long after became Secretary of State and head of President Taft's cabinet.

Popular indignation in the east had been able, some years before,[1] to keep the Mormon Roberts out of the Lower House of Congress; but the economic forces that systematically fomented that indignation had now passed away, and there were stronger economic forces in alliance with Zion. The Woman's Christian Temperance Union, which has succeeded in influencing much legislation at Washington, fought its bitterest battle against Smoot; New England, the South, the Middle Atlantic and Middle Western states were roused, and there was sent to Congress a petition so large that one goods-car could scarcely hold it.[2] In vain. Smoot was retained in the Senate, where he has never since failed to defend the Mormon Church and its partners in the Trusts.

Did the Republican party bring this to pass? In one sense, yes. But that was merely because the Republican party was in a majority in the Senate. When the Democratic party is in the majority there, the Trusts find it quite as easy to influence. The final ballot in the Smoot case stood:

For seating Smoot	42
For unseating him	28

Of the favourable votes there were three Democratic, and of the adverse votes nine were Republican. "Take," says Mr Lewis,[3] "the roll-call of what senators sat

[1] 1900.

[2] Alfred Henry Lewis.

[3] "The Viper's Trail."

for (the states of) California, Oregon, Washington, Montana, Idaho, Wyoming, Nevada, Colorado, and Utah. These states, beginning at the western lines of Kansas, Nebraska, and the two Dakotas, make, *with Utah in the centre*,[1] a solid block of territory which is an empire in itself. But two senators in all that great region, almost if not quite in area a third of the whole country, voted to unseat Apostle Smoot.[2] . . . Senators Perkins and Flint, of California; Fulton and Mulkey, of Oregon; Ankeny and Piles, of Washington (not Washington, D.C., the capital, but the state); Heyburn, of Idaho; Clark, of Montana; Warren and Clark, of Wyoming; Nixon, of Nevada; and Sutherland, of Utah, voted to keep Apostle Smoot in his seat.[3] There were three dodgers, a hidden trio, namely, Senators Teller and Patterson, of Colorado, and Carter, of Montana, who heedfully refrained from voting at all, not daring to take either side. Apostle Smoot himself didn't vote. . . . (The senators that voted for Smoot) knew that they must have Mormon approval and consent in order to succeed themselves. Consider that Senate vote in conjunction with your map, and you will come by some impression of the fell radius of the Mormon shadow." That shadow, however, falls farther than even Mr Lewis here points. In the western states that he mentions there is a pro-Mormon vote, which is much; but in the eastern money-markets there is Mormon money, and that is more.

1 The italics are ours.

2 These were Fred T. Dubois, of Idaho, who held that the Mormon Church was treasonable, and Francis Griffith Newlands, of Nevada, who declared that Smoot held his Church superior to the State.

3 The Senate of the United States is composed of two senators from each state in the Union; the House of Representatives is made up of representatives from the several states according to their population.

The movement in this direction began long ago, and, so far as any alliance with eastern Gentile capital is considered, it was begun blindly. It was, in a phrase, merely making a corporation of the Church. Even when Utah was a territory and its legislature derived what power it had from the Federal Congress, the Church slipped through the legislature those beneficial laws which it could, and they were not a few.[1] Among these was the Act of 1850, which was skilfully amended in 1856, and is now to be found among the laws officially published in 1876. This statute made the Mormon Church an immigration company and gave over to it the whole immigration system of the territory "to promote, facilitate, and accomplish the immigration of the poor," one section of the original Act (1) even providing that "the Island of Great Salt Lake, known as Stansbury Island and Antelope Island, are hereby reserved and apportioned for the use and benefit of said company, and said islands shall be under the exclusive control of President Brigham Young." Grants of water-rights, timber, and cañon were made to Young and others of the Church hierarchy, and ferry privileges were given on condition that the recipient pay ten per cent. of his receipts (tithes) to the above-referred-to Mormon Immigration Fund Co.; and, in section 569 of the compiled Laws of Utah as published in 1876, we find it provided that all escheats must be turned over to this company by the probate judge, who was "empowered" thereby and "required to take possession of all property left by any deceased or abscondant person where there is no legal claimant known or sufficiently near to see to it in season"!

A great deal has been said about Mormon communism.

[1] See article by the territorial governor, Eli H. Murray, in *The North American Review* for January 1884.

There is no such thing. The Mormon Church is a government, but it began by modelling itself on the old patriarchal forms, and it is now merely paternalistic. It cares for its poor, and it promotes thrift among its members. But its tithing system does more than care for needy and ill Saints: the tithing system acts as insurance for the Mormon body, and the entire Church machinery enriches the Church in the Church's capacity of corporation.

In the early 'seventies, Brigham Young, in order to increase economic solidarity among his people, revived the Order of Enoch, an early Mormon co-operative society, and had all his clergy preach vigorously the doctrine of co-operation in production, manufacture, and distribution.[1] Application of this doctrine was rapid in the smaller communities, but in Salt Lake City, where there were the beginnings of Gentile competition, it was necessarily slower. Then came the incorporation of Zion's Co-operative Mercantile Institution, already referred to, into which the mercantile Saints were urged to turn their stocks, taking shares in the institution as payment. It was argued that, since they could be ordered in greater bulk, materials could be bought for lower prices, so that retail prices would be lowered, while fixed charges would be reduced and patronage consolidated. The merchants hesitated, but the Mormon tradesmen at last "came in," the control of the capital stock going to the hierarchy. Although the plan was not so successful as had been anticipated, the store grew to large proportions. Other stores of the same kind were started throughout Mormondom, and if some of these failed, others prospered, and their stock was gradually absorbed by the hierarchy.

[1] "Mormon and Mammon."

The Gentile competitors fought hard. They are even supposed to have supplied the money for the publication of a paper ironically called *Enoch's Advocate*, which assailed the Order of Enoch with violent ridicule;[1] but the Church's business interests continued to grow; the hierarchy increased its control; so-called co-operative societies expanded into larger enterprises; companies that were formed to run shops began to run salt-works, sugar-factories, mines, smelters, and to build railways or invest in railway stock and the bonds of irrigation companies.

The Church, to be sure, continued its care of its own people. From the tithing fund there was, and still is, provided relief for the poor, hospitals for the ill, homes for the crippled, the aged, and the infirm. New enterprises gave employment, and helped, perhaps, to maintain the wage standard and even to reduce somewhat the cost of certain commodities. Nevertheless, the hierarchy were slowly being transformed into a capitalistic class. Capitalism was gaining in Zion just the position that it held in the wicked world outside, and the accruing profits made the hierarchy largely in favour of the tariff that protected the "infant" industries in which they—and the Mormon Church—were now so heavily interested.

The economic stimulus to the growth of polygamy has already been noted;[2] that phase of the development of capitalism in Mormondom which we are now tracing also affected polygamy. In the early days of Utah, when there were no great differences in the financial standing of the various Saints, the labour-producing benefits of polygamy were perhaps equally distributed; but soon the practical application of the theory began

[1] Schick. [2] Chapter X.

to be of more help to the man that was acquiring more property than the mass of his neighbours, and of less help to that mass. One had to own property to have use for the labour of plural wives, and land was no longer free for the asking; one had to have property to support the children of polygamous marriages, and population was, from a variety of causes, increasing; finally, marrying-women preferred propertied husbands. Thus the voluntary practice of polygamy by the few soon began to mean the involuntary practice of celibacy by the many. The persecutions by the Government and the pleading of the zealots were needed to revive as a religious practice what had become an economic practice.

With the growth of its industrial life, and the advance of capitalism, the hierarchy had also to face the labour question, and in its attitude in this matter the Church has revealed its appreciation of the fact that its interests are identical with the interests of capital throughout the country: Zion is capitalistically class-conscious. When it was fighting Gentile industry, the Church encouraged Mormon employés of Gentile corporations to demand higher wages, since this disturbed the Gentile employers and increased tithes. It began opposing labour unions, however, because, when it was in competition with Gentile capital, it had to meet the advantages of its established rivals with the advantages of labour that was cheap because it was done by churchmen for the Church, and there the tithing of the Mormon worker was a differential of ten per cent. in favour of the Mormon as against the Gentile product, and a differential of ten per cent. against the Mormon worker seeking employment in competition with the Gentile worker. Now that it is working with the Trusts, the

Church continues to oppose labour unions because it wants no organization interfering with the Mormon labourers' dependence on Zion, and because Zion, being an employer of labour, wants long hours and low wages. On the other hand, when there is a strike in a Gentile-worked mine owned by a Mormon-Gentile Trust, the Church will send in as blacklegs the saintly unemployed, or call upon its farmers during the winter when the farmers are otherwise practically idle.

The lot of the Mormon labourer is therefore hard. In Salt Lake City and the other industrial centres of Mormondom the cost of living is high. "The Church employé of the Church sugar-factory," says Schick, "has to pay for his sugar the wholesale price in Chicago, plus the retailer's profit, *plus the freight* (goods) *rate from Chicago to Salt Lake City.* The worker in the Church salt-ponds pays more for his table-salt than the worker in Chicago. . . . The Church, either directly or through its officers, is interested in wool. Woollen goods are more costly in Salt Lake than in Denver, San Francisco, or Chicago. For his devotion to Church industry the Mormon wage-earner may get an assurance of continued employment at something less, the tithing deducted, than the going rate of wages, the vague promise of cheaper living when the industries are further developed, and the benefit of a fairly well-organized system of charity when he is crippled or superannuated."

The Mormon Church is, then, a capitalist; but if it shows a realization of that fact by its attitude toward labour, the fact itself has again and again been made evident by a word here and there dropped in a Congressional inquiry, a bit of data here and there betrayed in a court record. No close student of the industrial movements in the United States for the past quarter-century can have failed to note this. You have but to follow the trail of the Trusts for that period to find their trail more and more frequently crossing the trail of the Saints, and you have not to go far before you find the two trails merged into one. Other combinations of New York capitalists besides the sugar-barons were interested in the seating of Reed Smoot in the United States Senate, because with other trusts than the Sugar Trust the Mormon Church is in partnership.

The foundation of the Church's wealth is its land and its tithes.[1] The former, if added to the holdings of its members, who pay it one-tenth of the income they derive therefrom, would make a region larger than France, Portugal, and Spain combined.[2] All this was once the direct property of the Church, because it belonged to individual Saints by right of settlement in the eyes of the law, and to the Church by right of Church members' settlement in the eyes of the Church. As the latter view was superior in Zion, the Church kept what it wanted and disposed of the rest to its adherents upon advantageous terms, and has ever since received tithes of the earnings of all that it disposed of. The amount of the tithes from all sources—a tenth of the income of every Mormon—is, as we have previously seen, a matter of some doubt. Forced to give some estimate to a Government commission, Prophet Smith[3] has said that "in prosperous years"

[1] Before a House of Representatives committee inquiring into the Sugar Trust in 1911, Prophet Smith said that the income of his Church was derived "mostly from the tithes of its people."

[2] Alfred Henry Lewis.

[3] See *New York World*, 28th June 1911.

the total ran from £250,000 to £300,000; but as Prophet Smith perverted the truth in his testimony before the Smoot committee, there is no reason to believe him in the present instance, especially as he followed this estimate with the declaration that the tithes "are systematically accounted for," whereas they are accounted for, not to the people that pay them, but only to the First Presidency, or Board of Directors, of the Church. Opposed to Smith's estimate is that of Alfred Henry Lewis, which suggests a possible £4,000,000, and considers £3,000,000 conservative. Mr Lewis, however, is prejudiced on the opposite side, against the Church. Certainly somewhere between these widely differing figures the truth lies, and, as Mr Lewis had less reason to exaggerate[1] than Prophet Smith has to depreciate, the lower of the former's sums is likely not far from the facts. In any case, the tithes have been continuing almost steadily, increasing almost steadily, since the earliest days of the Church; in any case, as we have seen, they have been constantly and safely invested and re-invested, and in any case, deducting all expenditure, they must now form an enormous sum.

When, therefore, the "co-operative" institutions and what-not of the Church grew in wealth, and branched into other industries, they were backed by substantial capital. Co-operation had taught the hierarchy the value of combination, and the new industries became little, but growing, trusts. Then, as the railways extended and as the capitalistic system increased in other parts of the United States, the great eastern trusts invaded the Mormon field, and, although here and there a fight ensued, the end of the matter

[1] Mr Lewis frankly admits that definite knowledge is impossible.

was that the great trusts, seeing their Mormon rivals well enough moneyed and equipped to make war expensive, took the rivals into partnership on a basis beneficial to both sides.[1]

Something of how this sort of thing was done has been shown in our account of the Mormon Senator Smoot's efforts as go-between for the Church and the Sugar Trust; but more, of course, remains to be told, and an excellent example is provided by the instance of the Utah Sugar Company.

Brigham Young started the Church in the sugar industry within a short time after the founding of Salt Lake City. American sugar was then made from sugar-cane; but Utah was separated from the sugar markets by a wilderness of prairie and mountain, and sugar was a necessity. Mormon missionaries probably brought from France the details of how sugar was produced in Europe, and Young had machinery shipped across the Atlantic and carted to Salt Lake, where, by the time of its arrival, a crop of Utah-grown beets was ready for the experiment. The experiment succeeded, and its result was the Church-owned Utah Sugar Company, which had a monopoly of the sugar trade with all the faithful.

In 1902, the year in which Apostle Smoot had acted as the Church's agent in making Zion a partner of the Sugar Trust in the ownership and operation of the Mormon factories at Logan, Ogden, and Le Grande,

[1] Almost the last exception to this is shown by the struggle between the Mormon Smelter Trust and the "Gentile" Smelter Trust, the heads of the latter being Hebrews (the Guggenheims). Schick says that in this combat "the Church has lost approximately one hundred thousand dollars" in five years. There is reason, however, to believe that "an honourable truce" is now being concluded.

the Utah Sugar Company increased its stock in order to purchase the Garland sugar-factory, and it is now generally understood that there was an arrangement[1] whereby this new stock was sold to the Sugar Trust. During 1903, 1904, and 1905, the Idaho Sugar Company, the Freemount Sugar Company, and the West Idaho Sugar Company were formed and incorporated, and in 1906 these three companies were united to the Utah Sugar Company, the entire corporation trading under the name of the Utah-Idaho Sugar Company, of which Prophet Smith is president; T. R. Cutler, a prominent Mormon, vice-president; and Horace G. Whitney, general manager of the Mormon newspaper *The Deseret News*, is secretary and treasurer. Other officials of Zion are directors, and the Gentile Sugar Trust, which had long wanted to control the beet-sugar as well as the cane-sugar industry in the United States, holds fifty-one per cent. of the stock.

In June 1911 a committee of the Lower House of the United States Congress was investigating the Sugar Trust, and called Prophet Smith. What Smith there admitted serves to give at least some idea of the relations of the Mormon Church to the Trusts.

Escorted to the hearing by Senator Smoot, the Prophet began by saying that it was not "the general practice of the Church to make business investments,"[2] though the interests of the Mormon people were "safeguarded" by the Church "at all times," and that Zion's sugar-holdings were the largest that it had. He denied that the Church had any stock in the American Sugar Refining Company (the Sugar Trust), which is, of course, merely the title of the holding company, but

[1] Cannon.

[2] How little truth there was in this has already been made clear.

he confessed that the stock held in the Mormon companies under the control of the American Sugar Refining Company was a different matter. Then followed this testimony:

"Q. You knew Havemeyer[1] was a very powerful man in the business world, and you were glad to get him interested in your business, weren't you?

"A. We were only interested in getting his money.

"Q. Have you any official connection with the Utah-Idaho Sugar Company?

"A. I am president of the company.

"Q. Do you own any stock?

"A. Yes, sir, I own about 5000 shares individually.[2]

"Q. Do you own any stock in a representative capacity?

"A. Yes, I hold 49,815 shares for the Church. The title is held in the name of Joseph F. Smith, trustee."

The Prophet said that the company had been under bond to build a beet-sugar factory, and was in danger of defaulting, because many subscribers had failed to produce the promised money, when the Church, appealed to at this crisis, invested £10,000.

"Q. Does the Utah-Idaho company pay dividends?

"A. Yes; seven per cent.

"Q. How is that dividend used by the Church?

"A. In promoting its religious interests."

Mr Smith said Cutler had charge of the negotiations with the Trust, and he, though president of the company, knew little about them. He could not, or would not, give any figures as to the cost of beet-sugar per pound,

[1] Head of the Sugar Trust.

[2] Smith, according to Cannon, came to his prophetic office a poor man.

the cost of machinery, or the number of acres of ground controlled by his company.

"Q. Do you regard this combination (with the Trust) as being in restraint of trade?

"A. I regard it as being in extension of trade. It has enhanced the value of *our*" (italics ours) "farms; it has made possible the cheaper production of beets; and it has proved one of the greatest blessings ever visited upon Utah and Idaho. I do not think that the combine has increased the price of sugar to the consumer one bit."[1]

The Prophet added that he did not believe the Church had broken the United States anti-trust law by its combination with the Sugar Trust. He explained his references to the Church in business by saying that the Church itself has nothing to do with business, but that its trustees have "full power." The combination had been sought for the benefit of the Mormon people, and Mr Smith did not regard the head of the Trust as "an industrial pirate," but rather as a "benefactor."

Zion's railway interests are probably as large as its sugar interests. Time was when the Oregon Short Line Railroad made complaint to the effect that the Mormon Church had misappropriated to its own uses a ten-thousand acre tract of land in Cache County, Utah, which the railroad wanted. For reply the Church bought the Oregon Short Line, and Prophet Smith is now a member of its Board of Directors. That is one instance. Another is found in the fact that Mr Smith is an influential director in the great, but scarcely savoury, Union Pacific Railroad.[2]

[1] *New York World*, 28th June 1911.

[2] Prophet Smith is to-day the ruling influence in both these corporations (Alfred Henry Lewis).

"Joseph F. Smith was of course already (1905) a director of

The Union Pacific is one of the "Harriman interests," the creatures of the late Edward Henry Harriman,[1] which are not well loved in the western portion of the United States, and it was to these interests that the Church sold the tram system of Salt Lake City and its electric-power company. Through its Mormon votes in the Salt Lake City Council, the governing body of the municipality, the Church hierarchy, as the owners of the Utah Light and Railway Company, of which Prophet Smith was president, secured, for a song, a fifty years' franchise. That was on 5th June 1905, and the Prophet's company had, meantime, secured other franchises of value originally granted to D. F. Walker, the Salt Lake and Ogden Gas and Electric Company, the Pioneer Power Company, and the Utah Power Company. On 3rd August of the same year, the "deal" being thus prepared, the Mormon-controlled City Council passed an ordinance extending all these other franchises for fifty years. The rolling stock and equipment of the tramway company was worn out and antiquated; the combined properties of the whole group of companies were said to be worth no more than $4,000,000. But they were bonded for $6,300,000;

Harriman's Union Pacific Railroad, a position to which he had been elected after his accession to the First Presidency. And he was so elected not because of his railroad holdings—for he came to the Presidency a poor man; and not because of his ability or experience as a financier or a railroad builder—for he had not had any such experience and he had not shown any such ability. He was elected because of the partnership between the Church leaders and the Union Pacific Railroad—a partnership that was doubtless used in defence of Apostle Smoot's seat in the Senate, just as the power of the Sugar Trust was used, and the influence of the whole financial confederation, in politics." (Cannon.)

[1] He died in 1909.

their franchises all ran to 1st July 1955; and as this meant a monopoly of the Salt Lake City tram service, electric power, and gas supply for an uninterrupted half-century, with full opportunity to extort from the public at pleasure, they were sold to the Harriman interests for $10,000,000.

The story might doubtless be carried further. Before the Smoot committee, C. A. Somerthwaite, who was contradicted by the Mormon witnesses, testified that the Mormon Church was so actively engaged in the salt business as to have gained a control amounting to a monopoly, and that he had been excommunicated because he would not capitulate to this control. The Church has been charged with selling liquor,[1] although the Saints are total abstainers. It is a part-owner of at least one large hotel. It is said to draw a hundred per cent. dividend from money invested in the Rubber Trust, formed by Senator Aldrich; to have an interest in the great National City Bank at 52 Wall Street, New York, and in many other banks; and to be in greater or less degree a partner with the trusts that control in the United States the wool, beef, tin, oil, tobacco, iron, and farming-implement industries.[2]

All of these trusts are protected, and therefore infinitely enriched, by the United States tariff law. The United States tariff law was framed by the Senate Finance Committee. One of the members of the Senate Finance Committee is the Mormon Senator-Apostle Reed Smoot.

[1] This also in the Smoot case, where the allegations were made against the Zion Co-operative Mercantile Institution and the Smoot Drug Company of Provo, Utah.

[2] Alfred Henry Lewis.

XIII

TEMPORAL POWER

THESE alliances of the Mormon Church with the trusts and other combinations of capital centred in the eastern part of the United States are made, of course, the more conveniently and thoroughly to govern the Church's own kingdom. Of the extent and resources of that kingdom, of the men that have governed and govern it, and of their theory of government, we come now to treat.

The State of Utah has an area of 84,970 square miles. Its land area is 52,601,600 acres, and its water area 1,779,200. It is thus, by 16,000 square miles, or 10,240,000 acres, larger than the six New England States combined,[1] and 3864 square miles larger than England, Scotland, and Wales. The population, according to the twelfth census, was 277,000; and the industries, apart from the beet-sugar industry already mentioned, are, in the order of their wealth:

(*a*) Mining.
(*b*) Agriculture.
(*c*) Sheep and wool.
(*d*) Manufacturing.
(*e*) Live stock.

(*a*) The mineral resources of Utah have not even yet

[1] See *Bradstreet's* for 3rd November 1894.

been developed to their fullest extent of productiveness, and this in spite of the fact that, so long ago as 1893, Utah's mineral product was $7,926,601 per annum, a sum that, if the gold and silver were reckoned at their mint valuation and the other metals at their value upon arrival at the shipping centres of the east, would become at least $12,832,074. Silver leads the list, followed in order by lead, gold, and copper, with the other metals crowding like racehorses for "place."

One county of the state has an iron belt fifteen miles long and averaging three miles in width, which ends in an iron mountain towering 1500 feet over the valley at its foot. The deposit is computed to contain 50,000,000 tons of ore that is ninety per cent. pure, and it lies in the centre of large beds of coal. The sulphur deposits in the southern part of the state are said to exceed, in size and quality, those of Sicily; there is a great deal of gypsum, from which plaster-of-paris is made; asphaltum in at any rate two counties; excellent potter's clay, asbestos, graphite, selenite, and mica. Bismuth, soda, nitre, and alum are produced; there are various mineral springs; marble and onyx of great beauty and variety, as well as much other excellent building and ornamental stone, are plentiful, and slate and lithographic stone. There is rock-salt brought from mines; and that made, by evaporation, from the waters of Salt Lake, containing in solution about twenty per cent. pure salt, is from the largest deposit known.

(*b*) Made easy by the proximity of the watersheds, the immigration of the early days has been developed from the numberless rivers rising in the mountain ranges that traverse the state from north to south, and agriculture, horticulture, manufacturing, and sheep and stock raising are prosperously carried on everywhere.

Farms of from ten to twenty acres support large families. The average cereal yield is as follows:

Oats, . . .	40 to 50	bushels	to the acre.
Barley, . .	40 to 45	,,	,,
Wheat, . .	25 to 35	,,	,,
Rye, . . .	25 to 30	,,	,,
Indian corn,	20 to 25	,,	,,

Potatoes have a rate ranging from a hundred to two hundred and fifty bushels per acre. Two, three, and sometimes four crops of alfalfa[1] are harvested in one season. The fruit includes apples, plums, pears, prunes, nectarines, and a wide variety of grapes. Nuts and the smaller berries are much in evidence, and the southern counties produce lemons, oranges, figs, and pomegranates. The mulberry tree flourishes throughout the state, and the cultivation of the silk-worm is becoming important.

(*c*) Sheep-raising is yearly increasing in extent. It is estimated that about $8,000,000 are now invested in it, and that the income from wool-clip and mutton is increasing in proportion to the general wealth of the state.

(*d*) Flour manufactured from native wheat is exported in large quantities. Cotton and woollen mills are busy, and woollens, blankets, dress materials, and hosiery, made in Utah from Utah wool, find a ready market throughout the Pacific seaboard. Boots, shoes, overalls, and clothing are growing factors in the industrial statistics. The beet-sugar industry is rich, and the smelters have made Utah the home of the Smelter Trust.

(*e*) Utah beef has won for itself a place that commands

[1] Spanish, from the Arabic *alfacfacah:* the lucern (*Mediago sativa*), in parts of England called *purple medic.* In the western portions of the United States it is of high value for pasture and forage, and has great drought-resisting qualities.

for it high prices from the Beef Trust, and large shipments are regularly made to Kansas City and Chicago. Pasturage is excellent on the southern slopes, and there are even some successful horse-breeders.

The state, once so isolated, is now bound to San Francisco and New York by some of the best-equipped and worst-financed railways in the world. After Salt Lake City, its chief cities are Ogden, the centre of a rich agricultural district and the junction of several transcontinental railroads; Provo and Logan, also at agricultural centres; and Park City, a mining town near the Ontario silver mine, which, in seventeen years, from 1877 to the end of the free-silver agitation, paid a hundred and ninety-seven dividends aggregating $13,175,000.

Situated on a plateau four thousand feet above the sea and at the foot of the Wasatch Mountains, Salt Lake City, the capital of the state, and the place prepared by the Saints for the temporal residence of God, is eighteen miles directly west of the lake, which is a hundred miles long, and from which the town derives its name. It has a dry and extremely healthy climate, in which many of the diseases of the eastern cities of the United States are unknown, and in which not a few are successfully brought for cure. The whole town is, so far as outward appearances go, thoroughly modern. It boasts of more foliage than any other city of its size in the world. Its dwelling-houses are substantial, its shops large, its streets clean and well-paved. It is busy and amused. The chimneys send out their clouds of smoke by day, the electric signs of the theatres blaze by night. Tram-cars rattle, taxi-motors toot, the tape records the actions of the London and New York markets, the telegraph and the telephone make instant connection with the world of to-day. The people offer no visible difference from the people of Denver or Butte. Unless you force yourself to recall some of the sensational stories that you have read, you might very well imagine yourself in any other of a hundred western American cities, save that not many of them would seem quite so pleasant.

If you fall into conversation with one of the Saints, he will show his amusement when you show your surprise at all this. He will point out to you with pride the handsome Eagle Gate and the Bee Hive and the Lion House, the home of Brigham Young, near which, under five tons of stone to foil grave-robbers, the second Prophet lies in a private burying-ground. The saintly native may omit to call to your attention Amelia Palace, built for Young's favourite wife, because it is a rather dingy place, but he will scarcely fail to tell you that the woman for whom it was built was an aunt of the wife of Grover Cleveland, a President of the United States. He will show you, too, the Mormon theatre and the cottage where one of the most popular of New York's living actresses was born in the days when her mother was the best player in the west.

From a hedge of high stone wall in Temple Square rises the Mormon Temple, which seats a multitude and is said to house the best organ in the world. Begun in 1853, dedicated in 1893, and built without nails or iron, this temple rose almost as silently as the Temple of Solomon. Its walls are nine feet thick at the base and six at the top, and the tallest of its six towers is surmounted by a golden statue of the angel Moroni, of heroic proportions,[1] heralding to man the

[1] Twelve feet, five and a-half inches.

coming of the new dispensation.[1] Into this temple no Gentile may enter.

[1] A souvenir of the dedication, issued by the Union Pacific Railroad (of which Prophet Smith is a director), gives an interesting history of this temple: "According to the original design, Temple block was to contain forty acres, but later on this area was reduced to ten acres, its present size. On 6th April 1853, the twenty-third anniversary of the Church, work was advanced sufficiently to allow the laying of the cornerstone. . . . The capstone of the temple was laid 6th April 1892. . . . The figure (of the angel Moroni) is admirably proportioned, and . . . is made of hammered copper, is gilded with pure gold leaf, and surmounting its crown is an incandescent lamp of 100-candle power. The placing of the ornamental spires on the other towers was continued till all were in place, each being provided with electric lights; the tower walls were washed, and gradually the scaffolding was removed, leaving the building with nothing to mar its magnificent beauty. . . .

"It should be remembered that until the completion of the railway from Salt Lake City south, and the completion of the Union Pacific Railway, each stone had to be hauled by ox-team from the quarries, twenty miles distant. . . . It frequently took four days to bring a single rock from the quarries to the Temple block, and the road was strewn with the wreckage of wagons and carts unable to bear the strain put on them. . . .

"The principal dimensions of this edifice are worthy of note. Its whole length, including towers, is 186½ feet, and the whole width 99. There are six towers, three on the east and three on the west end of the structure. Other measurements may be summarized as follows:—

	To end of rock work.	To top of spires.
	Feet.	Feet.
Height of central east tower	210	222½
Height of central west tower	204	219
Height of side east towers	188	200
Height of side west towers	182	194
Height of walls	167½	
Thickness of walls at bottom	9	
Thickness of walls at top	6	
Thickness of buttresses	7	

The whole rests on a footing-wall 16 feet thick and 16 feet deep.

This is the heart of the town, but about it lies the living body, eager, resourceful, cunning, rich. Salt

The building covers an area of 21,850 feet, and has cost upwards of $3,500,000.

"A circular stairway in each corner tower extends from the basement to the very top; the steps, upwards of 200 in number, are all of solid granite cut by hand, built into the massive walls, and the gigantic newel-post of solid masonry; the only woodwork is a wainscoting of heavy oak, crowned with moulding and relieved by a hand-rail. . . . The building is lighted by electricity, heated by hot water, and equipped with fire-apparatus.

"The marble-tiled baptismal room in the basement is . . . impressive. . . . The capacious bronze font rests upon the backs of twelve life-size bronze oxen, a reminder of a like feature in the house built by Solomon, which 'stood upon twelve oxen, three looking toward the north, and three looking toward the west, and three looking toward the south, and three looking toward the east, and the sea was set above them, and all their hinder parts were inward.' This large room has a pavement and base of fine white marble. A smaller room on an upper floor, resplendent in blue and gold, is paved with artistically designed native-wood mosaic, the blocks being no more than an inch square and finely polished. White and gold are the prevailing colours throughout, and harmonious tints, judiciously distributed, remove every suggestion of too dazzling brightness. Notably is this the case in the overhead and side decorations of a large high room on the north side, which is exquisitely chased, harmonious and natural in colour, as well as in every appointment. . . .

"There are four floors, counting the basement, and each one, excepting the top, is divided into rooms of varying sizes. This upper or assembly-room occupies the whole extent of the building, except the towers, being 120 feet long, 80 feet wide, and 36 feet high, with a seating capacity, including the gallery, of nearly 3000 persons. The gallery is of graceful sweep; it is railed with bronze, and is reached with circular stairways in each of the four corners. The elevated stands for the priesthood at either end, the . . . hand-carved decorations of daïs and balcony, the broad auditorium, the artistically panelled ceiling and frescoed frieze, with innumerable permanent lights . . . in the cornice, and five dependent chandeliers, all combine in presenting a scene which will be equally imposing by day or by night." (*Omaha*, Nebraska, *Daily Bee*, 2nd April 1893.)

Lake City is the supply centre of all that empire which extends from Denver to San Francisco; and as the capital of a state with resources such as Utah's its destiny can be no small thing.

Who are the men that have that destiny in their hands? Let us look for a moment at the line from which they descend.

Brigham Young, the successor of the first Prophet, came of English stock, and was born at Whittingham, Vermont, on 1st June 1801. His family removed to Sherburne, in New York State, but were poor, and up to his sixteenth birthday Brigham had scarce a fortnight's schooling. Before he was seventeen the lad was put to work in a joiner's shop, and later became a joiner-painter in Mendon, New York. In those days he was an ardent Wesleyan and something of a preacher, but in 1830 he read *The Book of Mormon*, and a year later was converted to the Mormon faith by Samuel Smith, one of the Prophet's brothers. Baptized in 1832, he preached Mormonism for a short time in Mendon, and then went to Kirtland, where he soon became so much of a favourite with Joseph Smith that he was ordained an elder and advanced to the Apostleate in 1835, and became President of the Board of Twelve Apostles in 1836. By the faithful he is said, in spite of the poor beginnings of his education, now to have undertaken the study of Hebrew. Certainly he was active in the foundation of Nauvoo. In 1840 he came to England, and was immediately successful. Although he arrived penniless, he lived well, and soon secured the publication of 5000 copies of *The Book of Mormon*, 3000 Mormon hymnals, and 50,000 tracts. These were sold and distributed under his supervision, and

Young sent a thousand English converts to America. When he heard of the murder of the Prophet, he had returned to his own country and was on a mission to New Hampshire, but he at once hastened to the scene of the assassination, restored order in the ranks of the frightened Saints, secured, as we have seen, the leadership, organized the great exodus to Salt Lake,[1] and founded the Mormon empire.[2]

Young went his own way. In the conduct of his domestic affairs he was scrupulously patriarchal, living in the so-called Lion House, the shape of a huge lion carved on its portico, surrounded by his many wives and children,[3] and at his death, 29th August

[1] An excellent account of this exodus is given in *The Great Salt Lake Trail*, by Colonel Henry Inman and Colonel William F. Cody ("Buffalo Bill"), chap. vi.

[2] Here is another picture of Young at the height of his power: In 1860, at the age of forty-nine, he looks forty-five years old. His hair is light and rather thick, forehead somewhat narrow, eyebrows thin, eyes between grey and blue, his expression calm and reserved. His nose would be fine, but is sharp, pointed, and bent a little to the left. His lips are "close like a New Englander's"; his teeth, especially those of the lower jaw, imperfect; cheeks fleshy; chin peaked. He is clean-shaven, except under the jaws, and his well-made hands are not disfigured by rings. His figure is large and broad-shouldered, but he stoops a little when standing. See *The City of the Saints and Across the Rocky Mountains to California*, by Richard F. Burton.

[3] Young is generally said to have had not a few wives whose relationship to him was publicly unknown. Among the women he married were:

1. *Mary Ann Angell Young*, who succeeded a wife that Young had married in his earlier Wesleyan days. Mary Ann Angell married Young on his first wife's death and followed him into Mormonism.

2. *Lucy Decker Seely Young*, the first of Young's "wives in polygamy."

3. *Clara Decker Young*, sister of the above.

4. *Harriet Cook Young*, said to have been at one time more than a match for her lord.

1877, leaving seventeen of the former and forty-five of the latter, sixteen sons and twenty-eight daughters,[1] to mourn with the 30,000 Saints that attended his funeral. That he was equally autocratic with his people, and with the United States Government, we already know. He would tolerate no murmurers in Zion, and held his followers in the bonds of an iron discipline that none but he could forge. He successfully led the Saints to Utah over a wintry country that, when the United States troops were sent against him, they could not successfully cross. He told his followers what to do, and they did it; when Federal judges were sent to interfere with the affairs of his territory, he made them

5. *Lucy Bigelow Young,* later sent to live in southern Utah.

6. *Twiss Young,* who, as is permitted to women in Zion, proposed herself to Young as his wife.

7. *Martha Bowker Young,* a somewhat neglected wife.

8. *Harriet Barney Seagers Young,* who left a Mormon husband, to whom she had borne three children, to marry Young.

9. *Eliza Burgess Young,* the only wife of Young born in England.

10. *Susan Snively Young,* a native of Germany.

11. *Margaret Price Young.*

12. *Emmeline Free Young.*

13. *Amelia Folsom Young,* for whom the Amelia Palace was built.

14. *Mary Van Cott Cobb Young.*

15. *Eliza-Ann Webb Dee Young.*

16. *Zina D. Huntington Jacobs Young,* one of the widows of Joseph Smith "taken over" by Young, who, at Joseph's death, told them that they might choose whom they would for husbands.

17. *Emily Partridge Young,* another relict of Joseph.

18. *Eliza R. Snow Young,* the Mormon "poetess," one more of Smith's widows.

19. *Augusta Cobb Young,* a Bostonian that fell in love with Young on hearing him preach, and left her husband to follow Young to Utah.

The chronological order of these wives has not been followed, the dates of their weddings not being obtainable, though of the fact of their weddings there seems no doubt. See Mrs Stenhouse's book.

[1] He is known to have been the father of fifty-six children.

the subjects of hidden attacks and open contempt; and yet he so frightened the Government that it made him the first territorial governor. He knew when to threaten, when to act, when to temporize, and even when to seem warmly to support his enemies.[1] That he had a supreme confidence in himself, as witness his call for "gulls" to end the locust-pest, seems likely; that he had personal magnetism, great resourcefulness, and large administrative skill is shown by the institution that, out of the ruins of Nauvoo, he established in Salt Lake City.

John Taylor, who followed Young as Prophet, was an Englishman by birth, but had come to the United States during the early struggles of the Saints, and had been in jail at Nauvoo. In Utah he was a superintendent of schools, a probate judge,[2] and finally for years Speaker of the Territorial House of Representatives, before he came to the leadership of Zion. He had a talent for organization, and a zeal for the letter of Mormonism, which he conscientiously developed along the lines laid down by his predecessor.

Of Wilford Woodruff enough has already been said.[3] He was a mild man, not without guile, who was unfortunate enough to have to reign at a time when the manifesto was necessary, and either he or the members of the First Presidency accordingly drew that manifesto and obtained statehood for Utah.

The next Prophet, Lorenzo Snow, who, as chief of

[1] Littell's *Living Age*, vol. xxx. p. 93.

[2] It was, it will be recalled, the probate judge's duty in Utah to turn over to the Church's immigration company all the property of deceased persons "when there is no legal claimant known *or sufficiently near to see to it in season*." See preceding chapter.

[3] Chapter X.

the Twelve Apostles, had moved the "acceptance" of the manifesto, was born at Mantua, Portage County, Ohio, 3rd April 1814. He went first to school at Ravenna, Ohio, and then entered Oberlin College, which he left in 1836, when he visited Kirtland and was converted to Mormonism by Joseph Smith himself. Both baptized and ordained an elder in 1837, he went enthusiastically into the mission-field, and by 1872 had travelled over 150,000 miles doing missionary work. In 1840 he came to England as counsellor to Parley P. Pratt,[1] president of the British Mission, and, on returning to Nauvoo, founded and captained a Mormon military company there, as well as taking charge of the Mormon schools.

In *The Mormons at Home* we have a picture of Snow's domestic *ménage* in early Utah. "He resides,"

[1] The Apostle Parley P. Pratt was one of the most prominent of early Mormon missionaries. He was born in New York State, at Burlington, on 12th April 1807, and murdered near Van Buren, Arkansas, 13th May 1857. He joined the Mormon Church in 1830; five years later became a member of the First Board of Twelve Apostles, and was one of the pioneers at Salt Lake—Parley's Peak and Parley's Cañon being named after him. He was in England in 1840, and again in 1846. He established and edited *The Millennial Star* in Manchester, England, and his writings were called by Joseph Smith the standard works of the Church.

Parley's brother, Orson Pratt, was almost equally well known. He pretended to, and perhaps had, some knowledge of "Hebrew and the higher mathematics," joined the Mormon Church in the same year that Parley joined it, became an Apostle five years later, again like his brother, and was also one of the Salt Lake pioneers. In 1852 he went to Washington, and in the capital of the United States edited and published a Mormon paper, *The Seer.* Later he became professor of mathematics in Deseret University, and in 1874 was appointed church historian. He was a defender of polygamy both in debate and in his writings, and was author of a series of lectures on astronomy and a treatise on the differential calculus.

writes the author of this book,[1] "... with six wives in two huts, and has twelve children. In the principal hut his real wife sits at the head of the table and pours out tea and coffee for the rest of the bevy. . . . Like all Mormon missionaries, he (Snow) was a beggar; and the story is that he has been so successful in his mendicity that the cottages are to give place to a large adobe mansion (*sic*), which will make a more convenient seraglio."

From 1852 until 1882 Snow "served continuously in the Utah legislature, part of the time in the Council, and part of the time in the House of Representatives. He founded and named Brigham City, Utah, in 1855, and organized there a successful co-operative system, which began with a general store. A tannery, a woollen factory, and several co-operative farms were afterwards added. He continued to take an active part in educational affairs in spite of the distraction occasioned by his numerous trips abroad. He went to Italy in 1849, to the Sandwich Islands in 1864, and in 1872 he travelled through Europe and Palestine. He crossed the Mississippi . . . in 1846, and three years later was ordained one of the Twelve Apostles."[2] In 1889 he became President of the Twelve, succeeding to the leadership of the Church upon the death of Woodruff, who, at the age of ninety-two, died in San Francisco in 1898. Snow was the author of several books on Mormonism.[3] He died in October 1901.

Joseph Fielding Smith, Snow's successor, the present

[1] *The Mormons at Home*, by Mrs B. G. Ferris.

[2] From an obituary of Snow published in *The New York Times*.

[3] Snow's writings included: *The Italian Mission* (London, 1851), and *The Only Way to be Saved* (published at the same time and place). The latter was translated into several languages. Snow also wrote

supreme ruler of Mormondom, thus writes himself down in *Who's Who in America?*[1]

"Smith, Joseph Fielding, president Ch. of Jesus Christ of Latter Day Saints; *b.* Far West, Mo., Nov. 13, 1838; *s.* Hyrum and Mary (Fielding) S. (nephew of Joseph Smith, 'Mormon' Prophet); drove an ox-team in the Exodus of 1846 to Winter Quarters on Missouri River; crossed plains and drove ox-team to Salt Lake Valley, 1848; worked as manual labourer, 1848–54; missionary to Sandwich Islands, 1854–58; sergeant-at-arms, territorial legislature, 1858–59; ordained a seventy, Mar. 20, 1858; high priest and mem. High Council, Oct. 16, 1858; missionary to Great Britain, 1860–63, 1874–75, and 1877, and missionary to European Continent and Sandwich Islands. Presided over European mission and edited *The Millennial Star*. Ordained Apostle, July 1, 1866; mem. council of 12, 1867; second councillor in First Presidency of Ch., 1880–1901; pres. of the Ch. since death of Lorenzo Snow, Oct. 1901. Several times mem. Utah legislature; several times mem. city council Salt Lake City; council (or senate) in Utah legislature, 1882; presided over Constl. Conv.[2] 1882, which framed constn. for State of Utah, and petitioned Congress for admission into the Union. Pres. of Zion's Co-operative Mercantile Instn., State Bank of Utah, Zion's Savings Bank and Trust Co., Utah Sugar Co., Consolidated Wagon and Machine Co., U.P.R.R. Co., and several other enterprises. Sr. editor *Juvenile Instructor* and

The Voice of Joseph (Liverpool, 1852), a sketch of the Mormons; a translation of *The Book of Mormon* into Italian, and *The Palestine Tourists*, a record of his European and Palestine travels.

[1] A. N. Marquis & Co., Chicago.

[2] *I.e.* Constitutional Convention.

The Improvement Era (monthly mag.), organ of the Young Men's Mutual Improvement Assns.[1] *Address:* Salt Lake City, Utah."[2]

And at the Smoot inquiry Prophet Smith testified:

"My principal business is being president of the Mormon Church. I am also engaged, however, in numerous other businesses. I am president of the Zion Co-operative Mercantile Institution, capital stock a little over a million; I am president of the Zion State Bank of Utah; of the Zion Savings Bank and Trust Company; of the Utah Sugar Company; of the Consolidated Wagon and Machine Company; of the Utah Light and Power Company; of the Salt Lake and Los Angeles Railway Company; of the Saltair Beach Company; of the Inland Crystal Salt Company; of the Salt Lake Dramatic Association; of the Salt Lake Knitting Company. As to the Union Pacific Railroad Company, I am a director; and I am also vice-president of the Bullion-Beck and

1 These are the Mormon equivalent of the Young Men's Christian Association, which has a large membership in other Christian denominations.

2 Joseph Fielding Smith should not be confused with Joseph Smith, head of what is called the "reformed" Mormon Church. The latter Smith, who lives at Independence, Missouri, was born at Kirtland, 6th November 1832, and is the son of Joseph Smith, the founder of Mormonism, and that founder's legal wife, Emma Hale. He was educated at Nauvoo, and has but one wife. After the removal of the larger portion of the Saints to Utah, he remained with his mother's family and repudiated the doctrine of polygamy, which Emma Hale Smith said her husband had never promulgated. This second Joseph kept a hotel, and was a farmer until he reached maturity, when, after some study of the law, he became (1860) President of the Reorganized Church of Latter Day Saints, which is opposed to polygamy and has no affiliation with the Salt Lake Mormons, being founded only on those principles of Mormonism which are unconnected with plural marriage.

Champion Mining Company.[1] Likewise I am editor of the Young Men's Mutual Improvement Association's *Improvement Era* and the *Juvenile Instructor.*"[2]

Here, then, is a man at the head of the Mormon Church with business connections that bring him into close touch with nation-wide financial interests, and having the tradition of the Mormon martyrs as a part of his family history. The nephew of Joseph and the son of Hyrum, Joseph F. Smith "vividly remembers the day when the dead bodies of his father and uncle were brought home."[3] Then he was but six years old. At the age of eight we see him starting from Nauvoo with his mother, and driving an ox-cart all the terrible way to Utah. His formal education, such as it was, he received on that journey, when his mother taught him to read by the glow of the camp-fire, and when his text-books were what have since been the practical limits of his literary knowledge: The Bible, *The Book of Mormon, The Pearl of Great Price,* and *The Doctrine and Covenants.* Small wonder that the man is a reactionary and fanatic! "From my youth to the present," he has said, "I have not believed that Joseph Smith was a Prophet, for *I have known that he was*: in other words, *my knowledge has superseded my belief.*"

Says Hendrick: "President Smith has spent all his days in the service of the Church; he went on his first mission to the Sandwich Islands when he was fifteen; and the succeeding years, until 1880, when he became first counsellor to President John Taylor, he spent

[1] In the early days of Zion the Saints were forbidden to mine, the hierarchy probably fearing the inrush of Gentiles that would be occasioned by the announcement of Utah's mineral wealth, and certainly desiring the faithful first to become firmly established as farmers.

[2] Lewis.

[3] Hendrick.

travelling over the world, without purse or script, frequently in rags, often hungry, preaching to every nation, kindred, tongue, and people the gospel of the last dispensation in the fulness of time. And to an unusual degree President Smith has participated in all the promised gifts of the Spirit. He has learned the languages of the strange peoples among whom he laboured, not so much as a result of study as it was a direct revelation from God. He has had the gift of healing and has performed many miracles. Once, in the Sandwich Islands, a woman was brought before him suffering from an evil spirit, visibly manifest in contortions of the face and insane cavortings.

"'In the name of the Lord Jesus Christ,' said Joseph, placing his hands on the maniac's head, 'I rebuke you.'

"And presently the devil fled."[1]

From the 17th of October 1901, when he succeeded Snow, Prophet Smith has officially asserted himself as a fanatical Mormon and a zealous believer in the legacy of divine power from the Church's founder not only to the office of the Prophet, but also to the family of Smith. He has helped every relative that he could help. The following Smiths have office under him in Zion:—

John Henry Smith, first cousin .	First Counsellor.
Hyrum Smith, son	Apostle.
Joseph F. Smith, junior, son . .	Apostle.
George A. Smith, son of John Henry	Apostle.
John Smith, brother . . .	Presiding Patriarch.
David S. Smith, grandson . .	Presiding Bishop of the Church.[2]

[1] *The Revival of Polygamy.*

[2] Hyrum was elected to the Apostleate because the Prophet received a direct revelation from God instructing him to instruct

The Prophet ardently believes in polygamy, and, in defiance of the law of the United States, openly practises his belief. He has four wives living, with whom he lives, and thirty-two children. When fined £60 for "living his religion,"[1] he gave out a statement in the course of which he said:

"So far as my own case is concerned, I, like others who had entered into solemn religious obligations, sought, to the best of my ability, to comply with all the requirements pertaining to the trying position in which I was placed. . . . Knowing the sacred covenants and obligations which I had assumed by reason of these marriages, I have conscientiously tried to discharge the responsibilities attending them without being offensive to anyone."[2]

In other words, as he explained before the Smoot committee:

"Each of my families has a home in Salt Lake City, and comparatively near each other. *I call the home of my first wife my 'Official Residence.' I 'visit' at the homes of the others.*"

In his manner, Smith appears to be a quiet man with a soft voice, meeting no challenge from the Gentile and showing no resentment to any insult offered by the profane; but among the Saints he is a Czar that will brook no questioning, a despot

the Apostles to elect this son. David is the son of Joseph F. Smith, junior. At the time of her death, Bathsheba W. Smith was president of the Church's Relief Societies.

[1] This was the occasion before mentioned, when he was first charged with polygamy and the charge later changed to that of unlawful cohabitation. Judge Ritchey's fine was the maximum, but the court omitted the jail sentence of from one day to six months that, under the law, might have been imposed.

[2] *Philadelphia Press*, 24th November 1906.

spiritual and temporal that will punish any offence or disobedience, however slight. Four or five years ago, he took five of his sons to a much-advertised prize-fight.[1] He has, of course, no sense of humour, and his only flow of language is that of the ready-made phrase, the preserved commonplace;[2] yet he is in receipt of an income like that which an absolute king draws from the treasury of his nation, affects the state of a monarch,[3] and pursues the policies of a tyrant. A man that has not scorned to invest in a theatre, a dancing pavilion, and a bathing beach, while he was conducting the operations with Sugar Trusts and transcontinental railways, the poverty that he brought to the post of Prophet has vanished and left a millionaire "trustee in trust" for all the Mormon millions. Finally, it must be remembered that he joined the militia called out by Brigham Young to resist the United States Government troops in 1857, and that, before the Smoot inquiry, he openly repudiated the assumed right of Congress to regulate his "private conduct":

"If the officers of the law have not done their duty toward me, I cannot blame them," he said; "I think they have some respect for me."

And to his own followers he declared in an address at Provo:

"He who says that I can rule him spiritually and not temporally, lies in the sight of God."[4]

Smith, in a word, governs as a man of his faith and

[1] Hendrick.

[2] Lewis.

[3] See United States Senator Thomas Kearns's speech in the Senate, 28th February 1905.

[4] Hendrick.

with his power must govern. He is the perfect product of his conditions.

For the Mormon Church, incredible as this may appear even to some citizens of the United States, began its territorial career by being, to all intents and purposes, the legally established Church of Utah. Indeed, so far as we know, it is the only Church that ever has been an established Church in the Republic.

The first section of an Act passed by the legislature of territorial Utah, a legislature deriving its authority from the Federal Government at Washington, on 8th February 1851, declares that "all that portion of the inhabitants of Utah who are or may become" Saints are by this Act constituted "a body corporate, with power to sue and be sued, defend and be defended, and to establish order and regulate worship, . . . and hold and occupy real and personal estate"; and the second section of that Act ordains that all such property so held "shall be free from taxation." Further, it provides for a "trustee in trust and assistants," and declares that "the trustees may receive property, real or personal, by gift, donation, bequest, or in any manner not incompatible with the principles of righteousness or rules of justice." Then follows section 3:

"Be it, etc.: That, as said Church holds the constitutional and original right in common with all civil and religious communities to worship God according to the dictates of conscience, to reverence communion agreeably with the principles of truth, and to solemnize marriage compatible with the revelations of Jesus Christ free to all; it is also declared that said Church does and shall possess and enjoy continually the power and authority in and of itself to originate, make, pass, and establish rules, regulations, ordinances, laws, customs, and criterions for the good order, safety, government, convenience, comfort, and control of said Church, and *for the punishment and forgiveness of all offences relative to fellowship according to Church covenants; that the pursuit of bliss, and the enjoyment of life in every capacity of public association and domestic happiness, temporal expansion or spiritual increase upon earth may not legally be questioned;* provided, however, that each and every act or practice so established or adopted for law or custom shall relate to solemnities, sacraments, ceremonies, consecrations, endowments, tithings, marriages, fellowship, or the religious duties of man to his Maker; inasmuch as the doctrines, principles, practices, or performances support virtue and increase morality, and are not inconsistent with or repugnant to the Constitution of the United States or of this State, *and are founded on the revelations of the Lord.*"

Indeed, "here," says Governor Eli H. Murray,[1] "is an Act of the legislature giving corporate powers to hold real and personal property free from taxation, 'not for purposes of worship only,' but for general business, and under this they held stores, farms, railway stock, banks, telegraphs, theatres, cattle, sheep, etc., such as are now held by the Church. This Act, adroitly drawn in several particulars, was intended to be a wall of defence about an established religion, so that 'it may not be legally questioned,' and to confer power upon courts, even to pains and penalties, in all matters relative to fellowship according to Church covenants." Both by its terminology and its effect, it recognized the Church of Jesus Christ of Latter Day Saints as the established Church of Utah.

[1] In *The North American Review* for January 1884, when Murray, a Gentile, was territorial governor of Utah.

Nor was the temporal power thus covertly implied contrary to the claims of the Mormon Church as made within that Church itself. "It is a fundamental doctrine of the Mormon Church that the president of the organization has the authority and right to control the business and politics of the people."[1] "When God," says Parley Pratt's *Millennial Star*,[2] "sets up a system of revelation, as he has done in these latter days, he sets up a system of government, (and) when I speak of government I mean what I say: *I mean a government that shall rule both temporal and spiritual affairs.*" Moreover, "this priesthood," says Parley Pratt, "*holds . . . the right . . . to appoint kings, priests, governors, and judges.*" That will be, when established, a nation of itself, the kingdom of God; and "the kingdom of God," says Orson Pratt, in developing his brother's thesis, "is an order of government established by divine authority. *It is only legal government that can exist in any part of the universe. All other governments are illegal and unauthorised.* God, having made all beings and worlds, has the supreme right to govern them by his own laws, and by officers of his own appointment. Any people attempting to govern themselves by laws of their own making, and by officers of their own appointment, are in direct rebellion against the kingdom of God."

As God, until his coming, is to rule the kingdom through revelation to his Prophet, the Prophet is an absolute monarch accountable to God alone. Brigham Young summed up the entire doctrine when he said:

"The first principle of our cause and work is to understand that there is a Prophet in the Church. He

[1] *Homiletic Review* for March 1903.

[2] *Millennial Star*, vol. xxiii. p. 214.

is at the head of the Church. Who called Joseph Smith to be a Prophet? God, and not the people. Had the people appointed a Prophet, he would have been accountable to the people. But, inasmuch as he was called by God, he is accountable to God only. We, the Twelve Apostles, are accountable to the Prophet and not to the Church for the courses we pursue, and we have learned to go and do as the Prophet tells us."[1]

[1] Quoted by Lewis.

XIV

THE POWER APPLIED

THE temporal power of the Mormons' patriarchal form of government has, wherever possible, been applied to every action in the life of the faithful. When Saints were fewer, when Gentiles had not encroached, and when life was simpler than the appearance of capitalism has made it, the application was a more easy matter than it is to-day, but even to-day the theory stands and the application is made as often as may be. Here was a kingdom in which, so Brigham Young preached, "kings were to be pages, thrones footstools, and none should prove so powerful or high but he would 'grovel before the First President of the Church of Jesus Christ of Latter Day Saints'";[1] and as the Mormon, when he is not "lying to the Gentiles' God," is a literal person, the Mormon Church has not scrupled not only to interfere in the private lives, business, and even thoughts of its members, but also to direct their thoughts, business, and private lives to its own uses. Instances are multitudinous, but a few, chosen from three stages of the Church's career, must suffice.

It will be remembered that when the first caravan of Saints reached the site of what is the Salt Lake City of to-day, their provisions were low and the out-

[1] Lewis.

look threatening. In those dreary days one of the pioneers, finding himself so poor that he feared he would be unable to survive the winter, went to Apostle Heber C. Kimball for assistance and advice. Kimball, who was by this time a member of the First Presidency, told him to marry a certain widow in their company.

"But how will that help me?" asked the hungry Saint. "I can't feed myself, and I certainly can't feed a wife."

"It is the will of the Lord," said the oracular Kimball: "if you have faith, He will provide."

The man had faith: he proposed to the widow and was accepted. Then, and only then, he discovered that she had a supply of provisions that would support them both until their next year's crops were harvested.[1]

When John Nicholson, Chief Recorder of the Mormon Temple, was subpœnaed to appear before the Congressional committee investigating the charges brought against Senator-Apostle Smoot, he was told to bring with him to Washington certain books, official Mormon records that, had they been produced at the hearing, would, it was supposed, reveal Mormon secrets that have never yet become known to the profane world. But Nicholson did not bring the books. Upon his confession of disobedience, when he came to the witness-stand, he was asked:

"If you were told by President Smith not to bring the books, you would refuse to bring them?"

"Yes, sir," said Nicholson.

"And if the Sergeant-at-Arms of the Senate should call on you with a warrant and demand the books, and arrest you, and put you in jail if you did not give them

[1] *Life of Heber C. Kimball.*

up, you would still refuse to give them up, wouldn't you?"

"Yes, sir."

When a syndicate of Gentiles, before the alliance of the Church with the trusts, formed a system to buy great portions of land in Mormondom and so strengthen the Gentiles' footing in Utah, some of the Saints, needing the proffered money, were tempted. At once Prophet Joseph F. Smith, learning of the plan, "advised" the faithful not to sell the Gentiles any land and not to aid them in any way, because the Gentile is "an enemy of God's people." The Saints refused to sell.

In Brigham City, Boxelder County, Utah, when there was a dispute between the city government and the company that held a franchise for the city's electric lighting, the Church interfered and arbitrarily settled the matter. When, in the same town, two Mormons thoughtlessly built a dancing pavilion that drew patronage away from a church-owned theatre, the hierarchy first "counselled" them, on pain of excommunication, to tear down the pavilion and sell its building material, and later agreed to allow the pavilion to open for business, provided that twenty-five per cent. of its net earnings was regularly paid into the Church treasury.

This is the way in which works the Mormon doctrine that imposes on Mormons "blind, implicit, unquestioning obedience." [1]

[1] When the effort was made to unseat Senator Smoot, there was evidence to show how the Church applies pressure even to Gentile business men: "Every financial institution, east or west, to which the Church could appeal," says Mr Cannon, "was solicited to demand a favourable hearing of the Smoot case from the senators of its state. Every political and business interest that could be reached was moved to protect the threatened people. The Sugar Trust magnates and

The public schools, that is, the free schools of the state, which are supported by taxation levied upon Gentile and Saint, and are supposed to be strictly non-sectarian, have not escaped from Mormon control. As long ago as 1883, Governor Murray said that these schools "are in every instance established on the same lot of ground and under the same roof (as), or in adjoining rooms to, the Church-ward meeting-houses. The entire system is taught (by) and under the control of the elders of the Church, and thousands who are taxed for their (the schools') support do not receive benefit in sending their children." Nor do conditions seem since to have mended. In the Smoot inquiry evidence

their senators were enlisted. The mercantile correspondents of the Church were urged to write letters to their Congressmen and to their Senators, and to use their power at home to check the anti-Mormon newspapers. The Utah representative of a powerful mercantile institution that had vital business relations with the Church confessed to me that he had been called east to consult with the head of his company, who had asked him to use his influence for Smoot.

"'I could not advise our president,' he said, 'to send the letter that was demanded of him. And yet I couldn't take the responsibility of injuring the company by advising him to refuse the Church request. You know, if we *had* refused it, point-blank, they would have destroyed every interest we had within the domain of their power. I should have been ruined financially. All our stockholders would have suffered. They would never have forgiven me.'

"The president of the company failed to send the letter. His failure became known, through the Church's espionage and the report of the Church's friends in the Senate. Pressure was brought to bear upon him; and, with the aid of his Utah representative, he compromised on a letter that did partial violence to his conscience and partially endangered his business relations with the Church.

"Both these men were aware that the Church had broken its covenants to the country, and that Apostle Smoot could not be either a loyal citizen of the nation or a free representative of the people of his state." (*Everybody's Magazine*, May 1911.)

was offered to show that a minor Church official of some independence of mind had been deposed "for distributing, at a school election, a ticket different from that prescribed by the Church authorities." On the same occasion, Arthur Morning, a teacher in the public schools of Utah, testified that he had been called upon by the Mormon Church to conduct religious classes in his school, and he read letters from the hierarchy instructing him so to do. There were offered in evidence "passages from the books in Mormonism sent to all grades of the schools and largely composed of biographies of prominent Mormons."[1] Shortly afterwards a United States Senator told the Senate that the Mormon Prophet "dips into the sacred public-school fund and extracts from every Mormon school-teacher one-tenth of his or her earnings and uses it for his unaccounted purposes."[2] The Church's educational institutions often have teachers that are polygamists: Josiah Hickman, head of the Murdock Academy at Beaver, and George M. Brimhall, president of the co-educational Brigham Young University; and in 1903, as Utah's representative to the first International Congress for School Hygiene at Nuremberg, Governor Heber M. Wells, a Mormon who had been one of the framers of the Utah "anti-polygamy" constitution, appointed Apostle Heber J. Grant, Mormon polygamist and, at that time, a fugitive from justice.[3]

Since territorial days, when Brigham Young and his

[1] *New York Times*, 14th December 1904. After the exposure, these orders were said to have been withdrawn.

[2] Senator Thomas Kearns, 28th February 1905. See *Congressional Record*. The Senator referred, of course, to the tithing system.

[3] A warrant had been issued for Heber J. Grant's arrest on the charge of "unlawful cohabitation."

associates flouted the Federal judges, the temporal power of the Church has, as we have seen, influenced the people to a scorn of many of the laws. Mormon governors appoint polygamous Mormons to high state offices, and Mormon voters elect Mormon polygamists to the Utah legislature.[1] Even in the administration of the laws the same power is felt. Save "for the good of the Church," the average Mormon, who is also, remember, a total abstainer from alcoholic liquor, would not be likely to commit petty crimes, for upon this point his faith is rigid; yet the police, who have a "respect" for the person of the Prophet, seem to feel some measure of respect for the persons of his followers, and it is at anyrate remarkable that, excepting when the Federal Government was conducting its anti-polygamy crusade, the Mormons, although they comprise a vast majority of the population, have contributed no more than one-eighth to the number of arrests in Utah.[2] Certainly the legal authorities are scorned. Even during the anti-polygamy agitation of 1899, when many prosecutions were attempted, the prosecuting attorneys would often refuse to bring cases to trial, however strong the information; when there was a prosecution and conviction, the fines imposed were generally nominal, were in some cases never paid, were in others paid by popular subscription, the released prisoner being received in his home-town with public enthusiasm and demonstration, and the greater number of prosecutions at last abandoned.[3]

[1] Hendrick.

[2] It must, however, in fairness be borne in mind that, so long as the commands of the hierarchy and the good of the faith are not involved, the Mormon is far more law-abiding than those representatives of other sects by whom he is surrounded.

[3] Thus Cannon, himself a Democrat, writing of the case of the "Democrat" Mormon Congressman, Brigham H. Roberts.

The Church has, of course, its own courts. Of these Prophet Taylor once wrote:[1] "Our Church courts are simply courts of reconciliation or arbitration between Church members, and for determining charges of transgression, and in no way affect the civil powers or the duties and rights of the various courts of law, Federal or local." But how, in fact, do these courts operate? In 1901 a Mormon woman, Cora Birdsall, of Monroe Ward, Sevier County, Utah, had a dispute concerning a land-title with a fellow-Mormon, James E. Leavitt, who took the matter to the Mormon bishop's court and secured a decision in his own favour. Birdsall wrote to Prophet Smith and asked his permission to appeal the case to him or else to go to the civil courts, and the Prophet's reply was a virtual command that she "follow the order provided of the Lord to govern in your case"—in other words, that she should abide by the decision of the bishop's court. When Birdsall disobeyed these instructions and would not comply with the bishop's order that she deed the disputed land to Leavitt, she was officially excommunicated by the High Council of the Sevier stake of Zion. This excommunication preyed on the woman's mind. She went mad, and her mother begged the Church stake president to mitigate the sentence of the council. The stake president replied:

"Her only relief will be in complying with President Smith's wishes. You say she has never broken a rule of the Church. You forget that she has done so by failing to abide by the decision of the mouthpiece of God."

Birdsall had to capitulate. She deeded away the land that had been in dispute, and was then re-baptized.[2]

[1] In *The North American Review* for January 1884.

[2] Cannon, in *Everybody's Magazine* for May 1911. There is some evidence to show, however, that the Birdsall-Leavitt case was

Since the Mormon Church believes that it has been divinely established to regulate the affairs of its people, there is no matter for wonder at its endeavour to carry out its mission in the legal as well as in the business and spiritual fields. In a letter published in the Salt Lake City newspapers in the course of a controversy, and written by President Taylor to Dr Henry Randall Waite, Statistician of the Tenth Census of the United States, Taylor clearly assumes the right "to administer the judicial laws upon the statute-book," and this "right," according to Dr Waite's testimony, is so employed that it substitutes for civil courts "religious tribunals which, if not secret, are open only to the audience of the faithful."[1] Indeed, the Mormon *Journal of Discourses* explicitly teaches that, as is declared by the ruling priesthood of the Church, the priests of Zion form "the best legislative body there is upon the face of the earth, because they hold the priesthood";[2] and in the Smoot inquiry testimony was produced to show that the Mormon hierarchy, in 1896, established a committee of six elders of the Church to study all bills introduced into the Utah legislature to decide which bills were "proper" to be passed.[3] The taint even spread to the neighbour state of Idaho, where, in 1904, the legislature "unanimously and without discussion passed a motion for a new constitution that should omit the anti-polygamy test oath, because it was objectionable to the Mormons."

exceptional in one respect. The Church courts did not generally, especially in Prophet Woodruff's reign, interfere in disputes over land-titles. In other disputes and offences they were and are inclined to assume jurisdiction.

[1] *Illiteracy and Mormonism*, p. 38.

[2] *Journal of Discourses*, vol. vi. p. 129.

[3] Cannon.

The Utah elections are now, of course, in control of the Mormon authorities. The Mormons are in a large majority, and the Mormon that wants office must first secure permission from the Church hierarchy to become a candidate. Prophet Smith, asked by the Congressional committee on the Smoot case whether it was necessary for Apostle Smoot to secure such permission for his candidacy to the United States Senate, answered: "He had to get the consent of his associate Apostles in the First Presidency. . . . He obtained that consent."[1]

One Mormon that neglected to apply for ecclesiastical permission, Moses Thatcher,[2] was degraded from his rank in the Church, and his case is said to have made permanent the present rule requiring formal permission.[3] Following the same principle, the Republican that was a candidate for Congress against the polygamous and Democratic Brigham H. Roberts and the Republican that was at the same time a candidate for Justice of the Supreme Court of Utah[4] were both told by the Church hierarchy not to mention Roberts's polygamy in their campaign-speeches against Roberts, and both agreed.

Of course, Mormon political control in Utah is not a simple process; like everything that must be secret, it is complex. It is exercised solely to further the financial operations of the Church, and so, when Zion executed its political master-stroke and, dissolving the Church party, divided its forces between the Republican and Democratic parties in such a manner as to control

[1] Alfred Henry Lewis.

[2] Died in 1909.

[3] *Homiletic Review,* March 1903.

[4] This office is elective in Utah.

both these parties within the boundaries of Utah, it proceeded to make political use of the "machine" that was ready to hand in its carefully devised ecclesiastical establishment and its rule demanding implicit obedience.

Of this "machine" it has made good use. "The ward-teachers who visit from house to house," says Schick,[1] "are the eyes, ears, and tongues of the central authorities. Through them *counsel*[2] is given to the lay members. They are the most important cogs in the political machine. On occasion they sound the voters as to their political views and advise all who can be influenced as to the wishes of the leaders. The teachers do not say:

"'President Smith commands you to vote the Republican ticket.'

"That would be dictation. They put it in this way:

"'The Church has important interests at stake. You are the Church, so these interests are your interests. The authorities have looked into the matter very closely, and they believe that the election of the Republican ticket is necessary for your prosperity.'

"The strength of the argument lies in its partial truth. If we concede that the success of the Church in business benefits the mass of its people, the argument is unanswerable. It is of the same piece as the plea of the railroad companies for the votes of the railroad men.

"The Mormon who refuses to heed such an appeal is regarded as lukewarm in the faith, and open opposition is looked upon as opposition to the welfare of the Church. There is no prescribed penalty for the offence, but the offender is likely to suffer in his social relations,

[1] "Mormon and Mammon."

[2] Our italics.

his business, and his chance of ecclesiastical advancement." If the Church can make him lose his job or his money, it will do so. In other words, he is treated by the capitalistic Church just as the employé that "votes wrong" is apt to be treated by the employer under capitalism.

That is the way that the "machine" works, and it works thoroughly. It is generally Republican because the Republican party protects the trusts in which the Church has a financial interest; but if the Democratic party came into national power, it would of course—because it is a capitalistic party, too, and has no declaration of principles essentially different from that of the Republican—be of equal service, as it has been in the past, to the trusts; and the Mormon Church would then be Democratic. The trusts have no politics; they want to be protected and enriched. The Mormon Church has no politics; it wants to be enriched and protected. The trusts contribute to the "campaign funds" of both the capitalistic parties; the Mormon Church contributes, in every national campaign, $100,000 to whichever capitalistic party happens to be dominant.[1] Both the trusts and the Mormon Church have representatives among the leaders of both the capitalistic parties, and in many cases one man represents both the trusts and the Mormon Church.

Once only has it been necessary for the Church to teach one of the capitalistic parties a severe lesson. That was in the days when the late Senator Mark Hanna was national "boss" of the Republican party. At that time the Mormon vote had long made Utah overwhelmingly Republican, because the Republican party had long served the Church. Hanna had come

[1] Alfred Henry Lewis.

to think that the Church was "safe." Three days before an election he offended Prophet Smith, and at the election "Republican Utah" was carried by a 51,000 Democratic majority.

This sort of thing, as has already been evidenced, does not obtain in Utah alone. At the Smoot inquiry it was testified that it is "impossible for any man or party to go against the Mormon Church in Idaho." A little later it was sworn that, before an election, the State Chairmen of both the Democratic and Republican parties in Idaho, ostensibly bitter rivals, always go to Salt Lake City, the capital of another state, there to receive election orders[1] from the Mormon hierarchy; that the Idaho political leaders always do whatever the hierarchy wants them to do; and that six of the twenty-one counties into which Idaho is divided are absolutely controlled by the Mormons, who hold the balance of power in six counties more. Apostle John Henry Smith, First Counsellor of the Prophet, and his first cousin, admitted that one-third of the population of Idaho is Mormon; that one-quarter of the population of Wyoming is Mormon; and that there are "large Mormon settlements" in Arizona, Nevada, Colorado, and California. Other politicians say that the Mormons directly control election in the seven states nearest Utah, not to mention their influence, through the trusts, on the politics of all states. It is generally granted that Senator Dubois, of Idaho, lost in his attempt to return to the United States Senate largely because of his opposition to Mormon interests in the Smoot case. It is common gossip in Washington that the Mormons already master twelve seats in the Senate, and that, as other territories become states, they will

[1] The testimony used the softer word "consult."

master at least sixteen, or one-sixth of the total, and that even now, through their financial relations, they can prevent any constitutional amendment giving the Federal courts power to punish polygamy or otherwise injure the interests or shorten the power of Zion.

Is that all that the Mormon Church wants? Its constant complaint has been that all it wants is to be let alone. But is that true? Does the hierarchy desire power and wealth only to preserve Utah for itself? There are critics who set Zion's ambition a good deal higher and point to the Mormon doctrine and ritual as evidence.

It is, of course, a fundamental belief of the Mormon that the Latter Day Saints are the chosen people of God, and that Salt Lake City, their city, is to be the capital from which God, for the thousand years following the Second Coming, will rule over all other rulers. When the faithful reply that this is to be conquest effected by God and not effected before His coming, they produce that article of their creed which expresses their belief in submission to established authority. This article, you will recall, runs thus:

"*We believe in being subject to kings, presidents, rulers, and magistrates, in obeying, honouring, and sustaining the law.*"

The article was, however, drafted before Utah was so much as dreamed of. It was retained when the plan of the Saints was, undoubtedly, to found a theocracy independent of the United States, on what was at that time Mexican soil, and in numbers soon to be strong enough to separate their land from Mexico. It was published when, Mexico having ceded Utah to the United States, the wilderness still kept Utah at a vast distance from Washington, and when there was excellent reason to believe that, at such a distance, the Saints could remain in merely nominal submission to Washington, all the while actually their own law-makers and all the while—in an era when secession was considered a right by the Southern States—preparing for the day when they would be able to gain statehood and then secede. The Saints, in brief, believed in being subject to *their own* kings, presidents, rulers, and magistrates, and in obeying *their own* laws. When the War of the Rebellion ended the dream of secession, when the gold-rush to California and the following opening of the west brought Utah so much closer to Washington, the Mormons wrote for themselves a history that gave the lie to any other interpretation of the article but this which we have offered. And now, say the severer critics, when craft has succeeded to revolt in Zion's policy, the article is allowed to stand as an excellent mask of the truth.

In the early days of Utah, the clergy of the Mormon Church preached that Mormondom was to "go as an empire from east to west"; it was to "spread until it touched every ocean"; it would "cross the Atlantic, cross the Pacific, and rule the nations of the earth";[1] and the men that preached this took pains to have their hearers interpret them, in this respect, literally. They taught that "there is a government, founded since that of the United States, which is perfect in its nature, having emanated from a being which is perfect."[2] And if one of the faithful suffered twinges of loyalty to the Federal Government, he had but to read Orson Pratt: "Is it lawful for another government to be organized within the United States, of a theological character?

[1] Lewis.

[2] *Journal of Discourses,* vol. iii. p. 72.

Yes, perfectly. The kingdom of God . . . is the only legal government that can exist in any part of the universe. *All other governments are illegal and unauthorized.*"[1] That this theory has been kept alive and that it translates itself into active hatred of the United States is the frequent declaration of the enemies of Mormonism, who find their proofs in the doctrine of Blood Atonement and the ceremonies of the Endowment House.

The doctrine of Blood Atonement is thus explained by Brigham Young:

"There are sins which men commit for which they cannot receive forgiveness in this world or in the world to come, and if they had their eyes open to their true condition they would be perfectly willing to have their blood spilt upon the ground that the smoke thereof might ascend to heaven as an offering for their sins, and the smoking incense would atone for their sins. . . .

"I could refer you to plenty of instances where men have been righteously slain in order to atone for their sins. This is but loving our neighbour as ourselves. If he needs help, help him. *If he wants salvation, and it is necessary to spill his blood upon the ground in order that he may be saved, spill it. This is the way to love mankind.* The wickedness and ignorance of the nations forbid this principle being in full force, but the time will come when the law of God will be in full force. *Will you love man or woman well enough to shed their blood? That is what Jesus Christ meant.* He never told a man to love his enemies in their wickedness. He never intended any such thing. I have known scores and hundreds of people for whom there would

[1] Orson Pratt, *The Kingdom of God* (1855).

have been a chance in the last resurrection if their lives had been taken and their blood spilled upon the ground as a smoking incense to the Almighty."[1]

It was on this simple food that the souls of the Saints were fed, and their lowly living and high thinking resulted in those Destroying Angels, Porter Rockwell, Bill Hickman, John Doyle Lee and other Danites, unofficial as well as official, authorised as well as self-appointed, who conducted the Mountain Meadows Massacre, who planned and executed many an assassination, and who, at least pretending to believe in killing as a "means of grace," murdered for "the soul's sake."

That was in the days when the Mormon hated the Gentile because he feared him. All hatred has its origin in fear, and the Mormon of early Utah feared that the Gentile, free from tithing, would hurt the Mormon economically. But he also hated and feared the Gentile because the Gentile and the Gentile's Government had murdered Joseph and Hyrum Smith and had oppressed and persecuted the Saints. It was the Gentile that sinned against God by refusing to receive and believe the gospel of Mormonism; it was the apostate that turned his back upon the faith; it was the United States Government, which aided and sheltered these sinners, that could be saved only through Blood Atonement. Has the passage of time erased the memory of the early martyrs? Has it changed the letter or the spirit of the doctrine? As late as 1884, Charles W. Penrose, an accredited mouthpiece of the Mormon hierarchy, said:

"There are some sins that cannot be atoned for

[1] As all men are to have eternal life of sorts, it is to be supposed that Young meant "exaltation" when he implied "salvation."

through the blood of Christ. They can only be atoned for by the sinner's blood."[1]

It has been charged that this doctrine took concrete form from the ceremonies of the Endowment House. These ceremonies are to the Mormon religion very much what the "degrees" are to most secret fraternities, and the "endowments" used to be "given" in the manner in which "degrees" are "taken" or "conferred"; and many Mormons renew them by going through the ceremony every year. This may be done in any Mormon temple. In Salt Lake City it used to be done in a specially designed building known as the Endowment House, but that house was razed on the completion of the new Salt Lake Temple, in which quarters, resembling "lodge-rooms," were provided for the "work." About the ritual and meaning of the performance a tremendous secrecy was long maintained and is still maintained in Mormondom, but on various occasions, before Federal courts and Congressional investigating committees,[2] apostates have made revelations from which, allowing for the prejudices of the witnesses, something close to the truth can probably be deduced. The only important question concerning the endowments is not with what absurdities they are invested, but whether, as the enemies of the Mormons declare, they are of a character dangerous to the governments that oppose Mormonism, or whether, as the Mormons publicly assert, they are entirely innocent of any threat.

In 1899, when certain alien-born Mormons were seeking naturalization as United States citizens, their application, you will recall, was resisted by Gentiles

[1] In a sermon preached 12th October 1884.

[2] See also the account given by Mrs Stenhouse, already quoted.

on the ground that, especially in the matter of the Endowment House ceremonies, the Mormon Church was a "treasonable organization in its teachings and in its practices."[1] The protest was based on a statute that reads: "It shall be made to appear to the satisfaction of the court admitting such alien that he has resided in the United States five years at least, and within the state or territory where such court is at the time held, one year at least, and that during that time he has behaved as a man of good moral character, attached to the principles of the Constitution of the United States, and well disposed to the good order and happiness of the same."[2] Many witnesses were called for both sides, the Mormon Church officially fighting for the applicants. From the testimony thus given the following excerpts are made, beginning with the witnesses for Zion:—

"*Apostle John Henry Smith, examined and*
"*cross-examined.*

"Q. I will ask you, Mr Smith, if, in the course of the administration of the ceremonies there in the Endowment House, there is any covenant or oath or affirmation made by, or required of, those passing through there, that they will avenge the blood of the prophets on this nation or its people, or against the Government of the United States? Has there ever been since you first went through there?

"A. I absolutely declare that there was no such

[1] Opinion of Judge Anderson, rendered in the Third Judicial Court at Salt Lake City, Utah, 30th November 1889, in which naturalization was denied to John Moore *et al.*

[2] Third subdivision, section 2165, Revised Statutes of the United States.

oath, or such covenant, no such bond entered into by me, nor did I ever administer such an oath, covenant, or bond to any man, that could be construed, by any reasonable construction of language, any way upon the earth, to mean a thing of that kind; and will say here for myself, that had any man presented to me an oath that bound me to become a deliberate enemy of my country that I love and respect, I would have repudiated it upon the spot. . . .

"Q. Are you a polygamist?

"A. Yes, sir.

"Q. When did you enter into polygamy?

"A. I entered into polygamy twelve years ago.

"Q. Didn't you know that that was against the law of your country?

"A. I knew there was a contest as to the constitutionality of a law that had been passed by Congress.

"Q. Didn't you know that that was against the law of your country, and that the law had been declared, prior to that, to be a constitutional and valid law?

"A. No, sir.

"Q. Did you continue, after the passage of the law in 1882, to live in violation of it?

"A. I decline to answer that question, sir.

"Q. If you did continue to live in violation of that law after you knew that its constitutionality had been upheld by the Supreme Court of the United States, would you still maintain that you had a deep affection for the laws of your country?

"A. Yes, sir—the law of Congress was directed against the principle of my faith, and that principle of my faith was introduced, acknowledged, and had been taught and established for nearly forty years.

"Q. Didn't you know that the Congress of the United

States had, as early as 1862, prohibited the practice of polygamy in the territory of Utah?

"A. No, sir; it prohibited the practice of bigamy in the territory of Utah.

"Q. Well, what distinction do you make between bigamy and polygamy?

"A. I make this distinction: *that a bigamist is a man that marries a wife, and then marries another, deceiving the first by not permitting her to know that he had married a second, or the second to know that he had married the first.* . . .

"Q. Weren't the people instructed to pray the Lord to avenge the blood of the prophets, and to teach that to their children and their children's children?

"A. I have no remembrance of any such instructions of that positive kind.

"Q. Well, that they were instructed to pray to the Lord to avenge the blood of the prophets—wasn't that it?

"A. I decline to answer any further questions with regard to that.

"Q. What penalties were attached to a violation of the covenants that you took in the Endowment House?

"A. I decline to make any statement.

"Q. Wasn't one of the penalties that you would have your throat cut?

"A. I decline to make any answer. I would like to make one statement right here: that Oliver Cowdrey, the immediate friend and associate of Joseph Smith, apostatized from the Mormon Church; he was never killed; he knew all that Joseph Smith knew. David Whitmer and Martin Harris, who were his immediate associates, apostatized from the Church; they were never harmed or hurt in any degree—every one of them died out of the Church. . . ."

"*Dr Heber John Richards, examined and*
"*cross-examined.*

"Q. In the endowment ceremony, what was said about avenging the blood of the prophets?

"A. In the first part of the ceremony, in the anointing they anointed my right arm that it might be strong to avenge the blood of the prophets, but that was all that was said. . . .

"Q. Well, Doctor, it has been stated upon the witness-stand that those covenants were taken, and the penalty understood to be, that if a man apostatized from the Church, the duty of those who had been through the Endowment House was to go and murder him, or kill him; did you ever hear anything of that sort?

"A. No, sir; I can explain to you what I understood by that was simply this: that after I had become a member of the Church, if I then fell away, I could get remission if I went voluntarily and asked for the atonement of my blood, but not without it; it must come by my desire, the same as baptism does; if I was taken out and baptized against my will, it would do me no good, and if I was killed against my will, it would do me no good.

"Q. And it would be appropriate, when they made the request, for some brother to shed his blood?

"A. Yes, some person who was authorized to do so.

"Q. And it wouldn't be murder?

"A. It wouldn't be murder—it would be murder probably in the eyes of the law, but not in the eyes of the Church.

"Q. And that was taught?

"A. That was taught."

One of the lawyers for Zion was a Mr Moyle, himself a Mormon. Mr Moyle, in the heat of his zeal, had himself sworn and testified that he had twice "been through the Endowment House."

"Q. Did you take your endowments at that time?
"A. I took my endowments both times.
"Q. Did you take any oath at that time?
"A. No, sir.
"Q. Or covenant?
"A. No, sir.
"Q. What?
"A. Well, covenant—excuse me; certainly, I took a number of covenants.
"Q. Did you take any obligation upon yourself?
"A. Yes, sir.
"Q. With reference to the priesthood?
"A. In what respect?
"Q. Obedience to the priesthood?
"A. No, sir.
"Q. Nothing of the kind?
"A. No, sir.
"Q. Not even by implication?
"A. No, sir; not even by implication.
"Q. Are you testifying without any mental reservation about it?
"A. I am, positively, without any mental reservation whatever.
"Q. Was there any penalty explained to you, or spoken of, as a consequence of a violation of your covenants?
"A. That I decline to answer.
"Q. Why?
"A. Simply because it is a matter which I regard

as sacred; I say there was no covenant, or nothing that was there done, in which I in any way——

"Q. Just answer my question, sir.

"A. I decline to answer.

"Q. Then stop when you decline to answer.

"A. Yes, sir, I decline to answer.

"Q. That is all.

"A. And in behalf of my declaration to the court, I want to say this, that my reason for it is this, that there was nothing—there was no covenant taken, no promise made, but for the chastity, and for honour, and for good conduct; there was nothing said by which I bound myself in any way against the Government, or made, or vowed that I would in any way act in antagonism to the Government, or anything that has any bearing or relevancy to this issue."

"Q. Now, are you through?

"A. As to those matters that I regard as secret and sacred, I decline to answer.

"Q. Are you through now?

"A. Because it has nothing to do with this case.

"Q. Have you finished?

"A. I don't know whether I have or not; if you have anything to ask I am ready to hear it.

"Q. I don't want to interrupt you. Are you through with your explanation?

"A. I am prepared to hear you.

"Q. Was there anything said by any person in your hearing about avenging the death of the prophets?

"A. Yes, sir.

"Q. What was it?

"A. It would be a matter of impossibility for me to relate exactly what it is.

"Q. I mean the prophets, Joseph and Hyrum?

"A. Nothing whatever.

"Q. The martyred prophets?

"A. The martyred prophets; yes, sir.

"Q. What was it?

"A. It was nothing more or less than this: the passage of Scripture—I can't recall it. If I had the Bible here I could find it. It is in the Book of Revelations (*sic*); it runs something like this: Oh, Lord, holy and true, how long shall our blood remain unavenged? It was something of that kind, and I am not certain but what—my recollection is that there was something said in connection with that, as a matter of instruction. I will state this much in order that the matter may be fully explained, that in the process of receiving endowments there are addresses delivered by elders who are officiating, and in one address instruction is given that we should pray that God would avenge the blood of His martyred prophets, and that is all.

"Q. That is all?

"A. That is all.

"Q. Wasn't there a penalty of death pronounced there—wasn't it explained to you that the penalty of a violation of any of your covenants would be death?

"A. I decline to answer. . . .

"Q. Wasn't one of those penalties that your throat should be cut across?

"A. With reference to what covenant?

"Q. Well, with reference to the covenants you took there?

"A. I decline to answer.

"Q. Wasn't that penalty that your bowels should be torn out?

"A. I decline to answer that. . . .

"Q. And that your heart should be torn out?"
(No response.)

One of the first witnesses for the Gentiles was John Bond. Concerning the endowment oath, he said:

"In its administration, the one going through takes the right hand of the party that officiates there; presses the knuckle of the index finger: that was a token of the lesser priesthood, as I remember, that was binding upon me. . . .

"As far as I remember I took the obligation; pressed their thumb with the index finger: that is the Aaronic or lesser priesthood; this confined me to believe every doctrine that was taught by the Mormon Church, especially against the Government of the United States, as I understood it. The penalty of divulging that, I was to have my throat cut from ear to ear, and my tongue torn out. I was required to hold my hands to high heaven in the presence of those there, that they might see that I granted this act to be done. This is the first as far as I remember.

"The second one I was put under was to avenge the blood of the prophets against the Government of the United States, teach that to my children and my children's children from generation to generation, and everlastingly keep after them. The penalty, I believe, was that the heart, or the bowels, would be torn out—something to that effect, so far as my memory will carry me. . . .

"I should judge there were about fifty men and women with me that day. The oath was administered by Wilford Woodruff. . . ."

The attorneys for the Church fought hard to have the court suppress all questions regarding the secret ceremonies of the Endowment House, but to no purpose, so that Martin D. Wardell, an Englishman born, was permitted to corroborate Bond's testimony. Wardell, speaking of the Endowment House ritual, said:

"After we were taught a good many things that had transpired and passed up to the present, the oath was taken that we should avenge the blood of Joseph Smith on this nation, down from the President to the last man; and after we had done that we were talked to a little bit more in another room, and we took another oath, that if we divulged any of the secrets we should have our throats cut, and our bowels ripped out; that is to be teached to the children and the children's children down to the third and fourth generations.

"Q. I will ask you, Mr Wardell, if you ever saw the penalty inflicted?

"A. Yes, sir, in the latter part of 1862, about twenty miles this side of Green River, upon a man by the name of Green. They were coming to Salt Lake City, returning from the States; they had been here once. It was the last of the Church train. W. H. Dane was captain of the train. Billy Williams, who used to be in Walker's store, was the chaplain of the train. . . . Green had an outfit of two teams—three yoke of oxen to each wagon. Well, when we got about twenty miles this side of Green River, Captain Dane came and took me by the shoulder and he says: 'We didn't do much last night; the brethren hasn't got cleaned up; we will take an early sit to-night, and let them have time to finish up'—took me by the shoulder and led me outside of the train and pointed over, and I saw eleven men dressed in buckskin clothes, in a circle, and the horses outside. 'Now,' he says, 'these are mountaineers.' And finally, about nine o'clock, three men comes up and they call on this man Green; he was in his wagon and didn't come out. He was a little afeard. They called him once or twice. I got up. I was in the wagon with my family, and just as I got out, they took the man, and there was two or three around—these men that I mention now—and they pulled the man out of the wagon by the coat, and he stood on his feet, and he hadn't stood there more than about three minutes—maybe three minutes—until a man took him by the hair of the head, and the other cut his throat; and when he laid down they opened his clothes and took a belt off from him with $5000. When we commenced to make trouble about it, John W. Young told us if we didn't shut our mouths they would serve us the same and leave us for the wolves to eat. The man that was with Green was inquiring where he was, and he looked all around for him: he was away herding cattle when the thing happened, and didn't know anything about it, only what he was told; and Captain Dane said that he had apostatized from the Church once, and he had apostatized again and gone to hell now.

"Q. Was there anything in that oath of obligation which you took about apostasy from the Church?

"A. Yes: you should have your throat cut and your bowels ripped out."

"*Former Bishop Andrew Cahoon, examined and*
"*cross-examined.*

"Q. Was there anything said in that obligation about tearing out the heart, or tongue, or disembowelment?

"A. They forfeited their lives if they apostatized; I

think the right hand was forfeited for some offence—quite difficult for me to mind how these oaths were administered and what for, but I know there were fearful penalties, one for divulging anything received, another for disobeying the priesthood; they were to yield implicit obedience to the priesthood. . . . It was considered no crime to take from those who opposed the Church, because they were the enemies of the kingdom of God. . . . All those that pretended to lead and guide and govern the Church taught that it was lawful to take anything from our foes, from those that were enemies to the kingdom. . . .

"Q. Did they ever teach you anything in regard to overthrowing the Constitution of the United States—did you ever hear that at all?

"A. The Constitution of the United States would be, perhaps, an after-consideration; after the Government was overthrown the leaders of the Mormon Church would reform that document to suit themselves.

"Q. Did you ever hear them say that the document needed reforming?

"A. Oh yes.

"Q. You never heard it taught that that was a Divine document?

"A. Oh yes, they taught that it was an inspired document, but that it would be better—eventually it would be better.

"Q. Who was going to better it?

"A. The priesthood of the Mormon Church.

"Q. When?

"A. Well, when they got it in their hands.

"Q. When was that going to be?

"A. Well, directly, it has been put off from time to time. They say it is pretty near now.

"Q. State when and where you heard it?

"A. Heard it all the while, ever since I was in the Church. . . .

"Q. Explain what you mean by that?

"A. Why, if they violated any of their oaths, the penalties, if inflicted upon them, would save them; they would be saved if they were killed, that is, the penalties were inflicted. . . .

"Q. Had you ever heard that the obligation that was administered in the Endowment House when you went through had ever been changed at all?

"A. I have never heard that it was. . . . The teachings of the leaders of the people was that the kingdom of God was set up on earth and that they were bound and pledged to sustain and build it up in conflict with all other powers and governments. The kings of that kingdom that was set up on the earth was the head of the Church. Brigham Young proclaimed himself king here in Salt Lake Valley before there was a house built, in 1847. . . .

"Q. Would you regard it as treasonable for a God, if there is a God, or the Saviour, if there is a Saviour, to come and take charge of this earth?

"A. When a man prays for the overthrow of the Government of the United States I consider that treasonable. I have heard that prayer many times; yes, sir, hundreds of times. I have never heard a leader of the Mormon Church pray for the President of the United States, or for the Government.

"Q. Have you ever heard the leaders of the Mormon Church pray for the overthrow of the Government?

"A. I have, many times.

"Q. Mention an instance where that was done?

"A. Why, it is so common, every child is familiar with it. I have heard it almost universally in public.

"Q. Can you remember a living man who has ever made that prayer in your hearing?

"A. Wilford Woodruff, the present President of the Mormon Church; it is a common thing for him to pray for the overthrow of the Government; yes, and Heber C. Kimball."

"*Joseph Silver, a native of England, examined and*
"*cross-examined.*

"Q. Were you enclothed with what is known as endowment garments in that ceremony, with signs and slits upon them?

"A. Yes, sir. . . .

"Q. What was there about your heart on the endowment garment?

"A. A slit right here, opposite the heart. It signified that if the covenant or the oath was revealed or broken by the recipient, that, of course, the heart would be taken out.

"Q. How was it with relation to the throat?

"A. I don't remember that there was any special sign on the throat; but there was a sign on the navel here, yes, and on the knee as well. . . .

"Q. . . . What was enjoined upon you in relation to your wearing those garments, and the purpose for which you were to wear them?

"A. The impression that I obtained was simply this: that if I was unfaithful in disrobing myself of the garments, that there would be every possibility and probability of my—of course being sick and dying, and so on; in fact, the instructions were to the effect, in substance, that it was unsafe to leave the garments off, and Heber C. Kimball went so far as to instruct us to be sure, in putting on a clean garment, to put one leg in at a time. . . .

"Q. About the penalty of disobedience?

"A. The penalty of disobedience to the priesthood was that my throat was to be cut; I was to be disembowelled, my heart taken out.

"Q. Who was to do that?

"A. That is the question; perhaps some Danite.

"Q. Do you know anything about it?

"A. Some Danite, or Destroying Angel, especially appointed—especially appointed. . . ."

Henry W. Lawrence, who had himself officiated in Endowment House, gave this as the substance of the Endowment House oath:

"In substance it is: 'You, each and all of you, covenant and agree to avenge the blood of the prophets, Joseph and Hyrum, who have sealed their testimony with their blood, This you will teach to your children and their children's children unto the third and fourth generations'—with some other things that are added to it. In different apartments there are different degrees, and sometimes these ceremonies are administered, a number of them together, 'This you do in the presence of God, angels, and these witnesses.'"

That forms have not altered in the Endowment House since 1889 was shown in the Smoot investigation, when witnesses disagreed as much as they had done in the earlier testimony. Senator Smoot, the Apostle, himself declared:

"There does not exist in the Endowment ceremonies of the Mormon Church the remotest suggestion of hostility or antagonism to the United States or any other nation. They are of a purely religious nature, wholly between the person taking them and his God, and, as with the ritual of various fraternal organizations, regarded as sacred and secret."

J. H. Wallis, senior, testified that he joined the Mormon Church in London, "and came to this country (the United States) in 1890, settling in Utah." He said he had a distinct recollection of the ceremonies within the Temple. He recited the oaths taken by those who participated, and gave a description of the secret signs executed by each person. Nearly all the obligations were requirements that those who took part would not reveal anything they saw or heard, on penalties of mutilation of the person. Everyone who passed through the temple, said the witness, was compelled to agree to the conditions laid down by the priests.

"The penalties agreed to were given by Mr Wallis as follows: That the throat be cut from ear to ear and the tongue be torn out. That the breast be cut asunder and the heart and vitals be torn from the body. That the body be cut asunder at the middle and the bowels be cut out. That, if demanded, we will give all we possess to the Church.

"Another obligation was that 'We will never cease to importune high Heaven to avenge the blood of the prophets upon the nations of the earth,' or 'the inhabitants of the earth.'

"'I don't just remember which,' said the witness. 'This was followed by a quotation from the Scriptures, I think Revelations (*sic*) vi. 9: "The souls of those slain cried aloud on the altars for vengeance."'"[1]

In short, the testimony in both cases was about the

[1] *Philadelphia Ledger*, 14th December 1904.

same. In both cases the loyal Saints contradicted one another in their defence of their faith. In both cases their opponents were apostates. Yet, in 1889, when Gentile business interests were opposed to Mormon business interests, the court decided that the Mormon Church was a treasonable organization; and in 1907, when Gentile trusts were in partnership with the Mormon hierarchy, the Senate decided that the Mormon Church was not treasonable at all.

XV

THE FUTURE OF MORMONISM

THE history of Joseph Smith has been repeated in the history of the religion that he fathered. That history is the history of all religions, and its end will be the end common to all.

In a time when economic unrest was producing pioneers material and spiritual, Smith went through the age of puberty in a poverty-stricken home presided over by a shiftless and roguish mystic, who was his father, and a neurotic and superstitious seeress, who was his mother, and scorned by all the neighbouring families of a rustic community in which emotional evangelicism was rampant and its preachers the only persons of power. Physically weak, Smith was bullied and laughed at, and, like all weak victims of tyranny and jeers, he was forced to retaliation by craft. He wanted, as we all do, the things that he did not have: he wanted prosperity and respect. The line of least resistance towards these, the line of craft, led him by way of the roguery of his father, the superstition of his mother, and the evangelicism of his community. A sort of auto-hypnosis did the rest, and produced in Smith the compelling enthusiasm that is found in every great religious teacher from Buddha to Wesley.[1]

[1] See Greig's *United States*, pp. 160–161.

With not a few of these Smith frankly invited comparison. Not only did he proclaim himself the appointed prophet of God; he chose, now and again, to represent himself as the reincarnation of certain other appointees, with an especial leaning toward Moses and Mahomet. Nor is comparison wholly absurd.

The orthodox Christian, and we venture to think Jewish, conception of Moses is about that expressed in an early volume of *The Christian Observer.*[1] Moses was "the man who, as the instrument of the Almighty, reared out of ruins and ashes a stupendous and enduring fabric, and moulded a great nation and a glorious Church out of a horde of ignorant and broken-spirited slaves"; a man who was "the minister of a new dispensation"; a man who began his career of deliverance by bidding his followers, "Put every man his sword by his side, and slay every man his brother, and every man his companion, and every man his neighbour." These, according to *The Christian Observer*, are the words and actions "of a warm and vehement spirit accustomed to feel strongly, and to express its feelings with *irresistible energy.*"

But there is another side to the character of Moses, which the more naïve of us sometimes overlook. It is the side seen by the scarcely naïve Voltaire:

"Le maître de la nature donne seul la force au bas qu'il daigne choisir. Tout est surnaturel dans Moïse. Plus d'un savant l'a regardé comme un politique très-habile: d'autres ne voient en lui qu'un roseau faible dont la main divine daigne se servir pour le destin des empires. Qu'est en effet qu'un vieillard de quatre-vingt ans pour entreprendre de conduire par lui-même tout un peuple, sur lequel il n'a aucun droit? Son bras ne

[1] *The Christian Observer*, 1852.

peut combattre, et sa langue ne peut articuler. Il est peint décrépit et bègue. Il ne conduit ses suivans que dans des solitudes affreuses pendant quarante années: il veut leur donner un établissement, et il ne leur en donne aucun. . . . Un législateur, selon nos notions communes, doit se faire aimer et craindre; mais il ne doit pousser la sévérité jusqu'à la barbarie; il ne doit pas, au lieu d'infliger par les ministres de la loi quelques supplices aux coupables, faire égorger au hasard une grande partie de sa nation par l'autre. . . . Moïse avait épousé une Madianite, fille de Jéthro, grand-prêtre de Madian dans l'Arabie pétrée. Jéthro l'avait comblé de bienfaits; il lui avait donné son fils pour lui servir de guide dans les deserts: par quelle cruauté opposé à la politique (à ne juger que par nos faibles notions) Moïse aurait-il pu immoler vingt-quatre mille hommes de sa nation, sur prétexte qu'on a trouvé un Juif couché avec une Madianite? Et comment peut-on dire, après ces étonnantes boucheries, que 'Moïse était le plus doux de tous les hommes'?"[1]

Between Smith and Mahomet, moreover, points of resemblance are by no means lacking. Though the latter worked on a larger canvas and with a freer hand, each occupied a confidential position with a favourable God, each taught polygamy, and each received revelations when revelation was convenient to his material comfort. In the same essay in which he speaks, as we have seen, of Moses, the hero of Lord Morley before Lord Morley accepted a title says of Mahomet:

"After becoming well acquainted with the character of his fellow-citizens, their ignorance, their credulity, . . . he saw that he could raise himself to a prophet. . . . It is to be believed that, like all enthusiasts,

[1] *Essai sur les Mœurs.*

Mahomet was violently impressed by his own ideas, uttered them in good faith, strengthened them by dreams, deceived himself while deceiving others, and, by the necessary impostures, finally supported a doctrine that he believed good. . . . His fellow-citizens rose against him, . . . his reply to the menaces of Coracites marks the faith of his character and the manner of self-expression common to his nation:

"'If you should come to me,' he said, 'with the sun at your right and the moon at your left, I should not draw back in my career.'"

It is granted of Mahomet that "il était poète: la plupart des derniers versets de ses chapitres sont rimés; la reste est prose cadencée: la poésie ne servait pas peu à rendre son Alcoran respectable"—whereas there is no lyric quality, although there is a certain epic force, about the turgid sweep and questionable grammar of *The Book of Mormon.* Nevertheless, if, as Voltaire more than hints, it may be said of the Oriental that there was nothing new in his message unless it was that he was the prophet of God, so it may be said of Joseph Smith that, however supernaturally appointed, he had no new message for the world.

In any case, the followers of Smith, at least during the earlier days of Mormonism, received through their illiterate preachers[1] much that was inherited from the Puritans, and their preference for the Old Testament as against the New; some things that were borrowed from the Baptists and Primitive Methodists, and others that were derived from a half-dozen minor and peculiar sects. That amusing system of fraud which passes under the name of "Spiritualism," and which interferes with the personal rights of the defenceless dead by

[1] Greig's *United States,* p. 161.

making what is dignified ridiculous and what was intelligent idiotic, contributed its "trances" to the Prophet and claimed him as a "medium" that was inspired by "spirits";[1] and the first Mormons, moved by a madness for combination and a craze for "taking their own where they found it," went to Pythagoras for their theory of "exaltation," to Leucippus and Democritus for their atomic materialism, to Epicurus for their ideal of ultimate good, and to Plato and the Gnostics for their "moving principles in element."[2]

To compare their religion with pure Buddhism, as it has been compared, is, however, absurd. Genuine Buddhism is the one faith that Mormon scissors and paste seem quite to have overlooked. Gautama Buddha, far from recognizing many gods, recognized no Supreme Intelligence at all. He discarded revelation for discovery. He founded no kingdom on earth, because existence, the consequence of a natural law (*upádána*, or attachment to life) is unhappiness. Man was not divine to Buddha; he was earth-bound and evil, and his one chance of enfranchisement was not a chance of happiness and power, but of rest and impotence through conquering the *upádána*, and, if not ceasing to be, at least, by attaining *nirwan*, ceasing to be conscious of being. The only things that Mormonism has in common with the original Buddhism it has in common with the original Christianity: a faulty astronomy and a frank materialism.[3]

[1] Greig.

[2] See Burton's *City of the Saints*.

[3] Buddhism makes no endeavour to account for the origin of the cosmos. The fact of the world and conscious life in the world suffices. Life and the world are in a constant state of flux, and the only law is the law of cause and effect. Countless worlds in sets of three surround the great mountain *Màha Meru,* above which lie

Wonderful as is what the Mormons believe, what the Mormons have done is, though in a different sense, far more wonderful. Their early patriarchs had many of the virtues as well as most of the vices of the Biblical patriarchs whom they reverenced and imitated, and their early congregation of Saints practised an industry and thrift that have few equals in modern times. The dreary wastes of sage-brush and alkali have become gardens and granaries; the desert has been made to blossom.[1] A system of combination was evolved that withstood the competition of the Gentile, and, when Mormon combination was not enough, a system of capitalism was evolved that, by joining hands with the capitalism which rules the United States, secured immunity, wealth, and power for Zion. These are evidences that confute derision.

The riches and influence of Mormonism may be overestimated by its enemies. Even under the Prophet there are Saints that "cheat the Lord" and tithe-payers that default.[2] But these things have not always

twenty-four heavens, and below which, and below the earth, are eight hells. Fire, wind, or water periodically destroy the earth, which is periodically renewed by the *upádána* of its creatures, the population of the renewed earth being lessened only by the number of those beings who have attained *nirwan*. There is no sentient soul divisible from the body, and when a man gains *nirwan* through the eight merits—right views, thought, speech, actions, living, exertion, recollection, and meditation—he loses the power of hoping, fearing, thinking, and feeling. Demerits lead in the other direction; but, strictly speaking, there is no such thing as sin under the *abhidharma*, or philosophy, of Buddhism; the idea is unknown; there are simply cause and effect.

[1] See *Utah and its People*, by "An ex-United States Official."

[2] "Alfred Henry Lewis's vision of a world-wide Mormon empire based on tithes is on a par with the amateur poultry-raiser's estimate of a world overrun with chickens, based on a geometrical ratio of

been; and before they began to be, the tithes of the faithful had placed in the hands of their capitalistic exploiters a huge fortune that has been wisely invested. The severer critics produce evidence to show that politically the will of the Mormon hierarchy is the law in Utah; that it determines the balance of power in Idaho, Colorado, Nevada, Montana, Wyoming, Arizona, and New Mexico; and that it is felt in the three states that front the Pacific Coast.[1] But even if this is too broad an assertion, the fact remains that so long as Mormon capital can remain a partner of eastern capital and not be swallowed by its working-mate, it will be able to protect itself in the Congress of the United States, and at least maintain Zion in all its power for the converts of those zealous Mormon missionaries who are daily winning women and men in Denmark, Sweden, Norway, and England.

This being the case, it is scarcely likely that the United States Government will seriously undertake any measures, in the near future, to suppress Mormonism. What it did in the past was precisely what his rustic neighbours did to young Joseph Smith, with precisely the same result. It began by disregarding Mormonism; then it regarded Mormonism as a joke; and finally it tried, by crude and therefore abortive methods, to

increase. His 'one tithe-payer who pays $10,000 a month' is recognizable as Jesse Knight, a rich mine-owner. Mr Knight probably did pay the amount designated during a few months of unusual prosperity, but his case is exceptional, if not unique. The Church is reputed to have invested $100,000 in the Knight smelter, which is practically lost. Thousands of nominal Mormons pay no tithing at all. Thousands more 'cheat the Lord' by paying less than the specified ten per cent."—Murray Schick in "Mormon and Mammon."

[1] The states of Washington, Oregon, and California.

annihilate Mormonism. Given the favourable economic conditions—and we have seen that the economic conditions were favourable to Mormonism—the growth of any cult or sect is largely dependent upon opposition to it during the period in which it is, so to speak, coming of age. Right or wrong, a sect requires, to become established, the advertisement of antagonism sufficient to produce martyrs, and enough antagonism has an almost unlimited capacity to establish religions. The sect will grow in inverse ratio, and Mormonism, under economic determinism, has grown accordingly.

As the neurasthenic lad, Joseph Smith, was overlooked by his associates, so was Mormonism overlooked. As the boy was smeared with ink by the boors of the village printing-shop, so was the religion attacked by the bitter, if powerless, Federal judges and the sometimes murderous, if generally futile, soldiery sent against it.

The clowns of an Ohio countryside mocked at the early Saints. The militia of Illinois murdered Joseph and Hyrum. The Federal troops were held at bay by no enemy save their own cowardice. Making all allowance for the circumstances, the proceedings of some of the Federal civil authorities was worse. One of the first acts of the commissioners appointed under the Edmunds Act was the framing of a test oath whereby no citizen of Utah could exercise the privilege of the ballot, and Jew, Gentile, and Mormon were disenfranchised "without indictment and without trial," not unless he would swear that he had never lived simultaneously with more than one woman, but unless he would swear that he had never lived simultaneously with more than one woman "*in the marriage relation.*" Distinction was made against polygamy and in favour of what the law chooses to consider a misdemeanour under the name of adultery. The action was *ex post facto*, and it amounted to a bill of attainder.[1]

Now, of course, Utah is, and for years has been, a state. The Mormon Church became a capitalistic institution; as such it joined hands with the ruling capitalistic institutions of the country, and there was no longer an economic need of opposition. The Mormons, being in the majority in their autonomous commonwealth, legislate to suit themselves. Yet what the Federal Government could do if it wished is plain enough.

When, in 1888, Zion appealed to be relieved of the burden of government by Federal governors as a

[1] "The first anti-polygamy law of Congress was passed in 1862, and all those who had, previous to that time, from deep religious conviction, received and entered into that order of marriage, but had never broken a law of the United States by so doing, for the simple reason that there was no such law, were, by the commissioners' rulings, equally debarred from voting with those who had married in plurality subsequent to that date. . . . The remarkable interpolation in the commissioners' test oath of the words 'in the marriage relation,' *which do not appear in the law*, has led to many curious incidents, some of which would be ludicrous if they were not so humiliating. Here is a case in point: A former mayor of Salt Lake City, Mr Feramorz Little, a very honourable gentleman, and highly respected, came to this territory many years ago, before there was any law of Congress against plural marriage, and espoused two wives. Subsequently, one of those wives died, then the other, and at the time that this incident occurred he had been for years without a wife. He had a son who was appointed registrar for a certain district in this city, and this son had the mortification of being compelled, under the ruling of the commission, to refuse his father permission to register, and consequently deprived him of the right to vote—a privilege which he had a perfect right to exercise, both because of the provision in the Constitution that no *ex post facto* law shall be made, and again by reason of the Statute of Limitations, which bars all action in such cases after the expiration of three years."—Prophet John Taylor, in *The North American Review* for January 1884.

territory, and to be given statehood, Jeremiah M. Wilson was a lawyer employed by the Mormons to plead their cause. Speaking before a Congressional committee, and referring to the Mormons' pledge to abandon polygamy if statehood was granted, this advocate of the Latter Day Saints said:

"It is idle to say that such a compact may be made, and then, when considerations have been mutually received—statehood on the one side and the pledge not to do a particular thing on the other—either party can violate it without remedy to the other. But you ask me what is the remedy, and I answer that there are plenty of remedies in your own hands.

"Suppose they violate this compact; suppose that after they put this into the Constitution, and thereby induce you to grant them the high privilege and political right of statehood, they should turn right around and exercise the bad faith which is attributed to them here—what would you do? You could shut the doors of the Senate and House of Representatives against them; you could deny them a voice in the councils of this nation, because they have acted in bad faith and violated their solemn agreement by which they succeeded in getting themselves into the condition of statehood. You could deny them the Federal judiciary; you could deny them the right to use the mails—that indispensable thing in the matter of trade and commerce in this country."[1]

All this the United States Government could do, and perhaps more. It might even be possible to recall the gift of statehood: it would certainly be legal, by an amendment to the Constitution, to make polygamy an offence punishable by the Federal courts.

[1] See "Under the Prophet in Utah."

But none of these things has been done. In the past, butchery has been tried, and the Mormons have retaliated with more butchery; laws have been tried, and the Mormons have found lawyers clever enough to nullify the laws; business has been tried, and the Mormons have entered into partnership with the conquering business interests of the country; politics has been tried, and the Mormons have proved themselves masters in politics; favours have been tried, and the Mormons have accepted the little that was offered and seized the much that the offerers would have withheld. Oppression could not end Mormonism, and so the oppressors, far from following the suggestions made by Mr Wilson in 1888, have admitted Mormons to the Senate and the House of Representatives, have made the Federal judiciary in Utah subservient to the Mormon hierarchy, and have appointed Mormons to the conduct of those very postal facilities the use of which Mr Wilson, the lawyer for the Mormons, himself declared could be taken from Mormondom. In brief, Mormonism has become a part, however small, of the capitalistic system in the United States.

This is not by way of being a defence of Mormonism. We recognize the absurdity of the religion, though it seems to us not more absurd—only more recent—than certain other and widely accepted religions, and we especially oppose a system of marriage under which a man is permitted to take plural wives against the free consent of the wife or wives that he already has,[1] while a woman is refused plural husbands. Such a one-sided system is indeed what Mr Lewis says

[1] The "consent" to plural marriage given in Mormondom by wives whose husband is about to add to the number of his spouses is, of course, as often as not a mere farce.

of polygamy in general: "a moral menace and a threat to the whiteness of womanhood."[1] The question just here involved is not one of polygamy as against monogamy, but one of common justice. Women are slaves under Mormonism, but there are many more women-slaves under Gentile capitalism, which refuses women the ballot and produces prostitutes by the wage-system. A man may have more than one wife in Mormonism, but the Mormon must at least support his wives and children, whereas, outside of Mormonism, a man may have as many unpaid mistresses as he can manage to cajole.

Yet will the present revival of that polygamy which obtained before the publication of the Woodruff manifesto[2] long continue? Some of the best-informed

1 "The Viper's Trail."

2 "There is a great deal of misapprehension existing in the minds of the people with regard to our marriage institution. None but the very best of our community—the virtuous, the honest, and upright—are permitted to take more than one wife. They must be recommended as worthy by their bishop, and by the president of the stake in which they reside. We are, of all people, the most strict in our ideas with regard to morality and virtue. If a man who is a member of our Church commit adultery, fornication, or bigamy, he is at once cut off from the communion of the Saints, and all fellowship in the Church is withdrawn from him; for we regard those sins as among the most abominable of evils, the most hideous next to the shedding of innocent blood. There is not to-day a more virtuous community in the world, or one where female chastity is more highly regarded or more vigorously protected." Thus naïvely Prophet Taylor in *The North American Review*, article previously quoted. Mr Taylor continues: "In plural marriage a man is expected to provide for all his wives and their (*sic*) children. We have no waifs and strays such as are found in the large cities of Christendom—the result of men breaking the laws of social purity. The children of our families do not gravitate to the poorhouse, for we have no such establishments, . . . and our poor are cared for by the bishops and by the members of our ladies' relief societies."

authorities think not, and one of them, Mr Utter, thus states his reasons:[1]

"First, . . . testimony may be had from women who lived in polygamy for years, and who are Mormons yet, that they never were reconciled to it; and that, though they tried to think the fault lay in themselves, the practice was always a sore cross. . . .

"Second, the opinion of the world is more felt in Utah than formerly, and this is, and will be, an increasing influence against the doctrine. . . . A child (born of polygamy) arrived at man's estate, having gone east to be educated or to engage in business, soon hears slurs and contemptuous remarks about Utah and the Mormons that he cannot attribute wholly to religious prejudice. He perhaps feels that he would like to fight for the honour of his father and mother, who were only mistaken at the worst, but after a while he comes to think of that mistake as far more serious than he once regarded it, and as one not to be repeated in his own life. As more and more of the young people go away to complete their studies, or even as they give more time and thought to self-culture at home, and become acquainted with the world's literature and thought through the medium of books and magazines and with works of art, the more they will be made to feel that the polygamous lapse in Utah is a stain upon the history of the State. Many will feel this who will never put it into words, nor acknowledge it when charged by others. The influence of all such will be against . . . repeating the sad experiences of the past.

"Third, the conditions are now unfavourable to polygamous life, even if there were no opposition to it. There is less room here than formerly, even for those

[1] "Mormonism To-Day."

who were content to live on farms, all doing work. For those who have felt the many desires of modern civilized life, the difficulty of supporting even one wife is more than the young man can overcome. And if the young man cannot afford to marry at all, he will not stand by and see the elderly men making plural marriages!"

This third reason, though not fully elaborated, seems to us to be the strongest, and seems to us strong enough eventually to end polygamy. Since Utah has become but a province of the capitalistic system, it has felt, and will more and more feel, those influences which have made polygamy unprofitable, and so at last wicked, elsewhere. The economic value of half-grown children has declined because labour has become cheaper and more plentiful, and so wives have become "liabilities rather than assets."[1] Consequently, the practice of polygamy, always the privilege of the man that could support his wives and their children, has now become, even in its revived state, the perquisite of the capitalist class, just as concubinage is the perquisite of the capitalistic class elsewhere.[2] Eventually, as polygamy thus decreases until the few that practise it are only the very rich, since the present structure of the Mormon

[1] Murray Schick, "Mormon and Mammon."

[2] "Restrictive legislation by the United States Government," says Schick, "may have had some effect in discouraging polygamy, but it also united the Mormons more firmly in defence of the doctrine, and halted the disintegrating process at work within the Church itself. Its principal effect was to draw a veil of secrecy over the practice, and put the plural wife practically in the position of a mistress. The main difference in late years between Mormon polygamy and Gentile concubinage has been psychological; a majority of those entering into it (polygamy) doing so with no consciousness of moral guilt and with a high sense of religious exaltation."

faith rests on the institution, these few, which of course will be the hierarchy, will be confronted with a situation in which they preach a salvation—the salvation, or at least exaltation, by plural marriage—for which their followers have not the wealth to qualify. That is a paradox on which no religion can continue. There will result a reformation, such as the earlier Christian Church saw, and a new creed will be constructed out of selected stones from the ruin of the old, a new creed with the old name, which will go, with the spread of education and the social progress of the nation, the way that, when capitalism ends, all faiths not founded upon truth must go.

For Mormonism stands squarely upon revelation. Either Joseph Smith was inspired by God or else he was a fraud and a cheat. There is no avoiding the issue, and when the new generations of Mormons, profiting by the advance of education, meet this issue, how will they decide it? How can they accept the faulty story of *The Golden Book*, with its translation by a miracle, with its bad grammar, its bad astronomy, its bad ethnology? How can they accept *The Book of Abraham*, which professes to be a "translation from some Ancient Records that have fallen into our hands from the Catacombs of Egypt, the Writings of Abraham while he was in Egypt, . . . written by his own hand upon papyrus"? How can they accept the sample "hieroglyphics" given in the "translation" when, by comparing them with other hieroglyphics, they discover arrant mistranslations and sublimely mistaken guesswork? How can they accept the similar errors that they will find throughout the entire body of inspirational Mormonism? They cannot accept them, and they will not.

In the meantime, would the United States Government be wise to interfere with Mormonism, apart from polygamy, even were it inclined and were it permitted to do so? Prophet Taylor, speaking of the plural marriages of his people, praised the Government of Great Britain because, although it suppressed the suttee, "it has not only tolerated but legislated to protect in their institutions upwards of 240,000,000 of its polygamic subjects in India";[1] and the Prophet was plainly of the opinion that the United States Government should do as much for polygamy under Mormonism. Yet, polygamy aside — or, rather, if polygamy dies, as die it must — and political and financial influence aside—or, rather, if those influences were withdrawn, as withdrawn they will not be under capitalism—what would be the position of the United States Government in regard to Mormonism?

At this late date, it is rather idle to suppose that the Mormon Church is really a "treasonable organization," at least in the spirit of that term. There can be no doubt but that it was at one time actively "treasonable," and that the oaths of the Endowment House pledging vengeance upon the slayers of the prophets struck close to the heart of the nation. But, as in the case of the treasonable Ku Klux Klan in the unreconstructed Southern States, "an oath must have its day," and all oaths, like all profanity, lose their force by repetition. The tendency of ritual is toward empty form. Few Mormons must now take those "obligations" literally, and the Mormon hierarchy has financial interests at stake that make it more than satisfied with things as they are. The only interesting facts about the Endowment House ceremonies are the manner in

[1] *North American Review* for January 1884.

which the telling of them served to prevent alien-born Mormons from naturalization when economic forces were against Mormonism, and the manner in which that telling failed to bar Apostle Smoot from the Senate of the United States when economic forces were with his Church.

It is true that the Mormon Prophet considers himself a business-agent of the Almighty; but only a few years ago George F. Baer, a member of an accepted Protestant sect and the mask for Mr Morgan in command of the United States Anthracite-coal Trust, publicly declared himself as, in his mine-owning capacity, the delegate of God.[1] It is true that Utah's industries are largely under the control of the Mormon hierarchy; but it is also true that all the nation's industries are under the control of a capitalistic oligarchy which is the hierarchy's superior partner. It is true that the Utah courts are the puppets of the hierarchy; but it is also true that practically all the nation's courts are the puppets of the oligarchy. It is true that the hierarchy controls the politics of Utah; but it is also true that the oligarchy, its partner, controls the politics of the nation.

Belief in God or gods has little to do with the form or practice of any religion. Religious forms are the spiritual results of the economic conditions prevailing at the time of the religion's beginning, and religious practices are modified by the modifications of the economic conditions that prevail during the time of the religion's existence. The civilization of one period of

[1] Baer was then, and probably still is, simultaneously president of coal-mining companies and coal-carrying railways. Although this combination was contrary to the law, Baer calmly admitted it on the witness-stand and remained scot-free.

the world produced a ruling class that, fearing the encroachments of the classes below it, brought forth Brahminism to prevent such encroachments. The civilization of a later period produced a prosperous bourgeoisie that, developing the nervous ailments attendant upon prosperity rapidly acquired, brought forth Christian "Science" to cure such ailments. The civilization of the early part of the nineteenth century produced an economic oppression in crowded centres of population that needed free land in a new country and brought forth Mormonism. When social evolution or revolution ends caste in India, Brahminism will cease. When capitalism, reaching its expiring state of perfect development in the United States, raises a few more of the bourgeoisie to the capitalistic class and forces the many back into the ranks of the proletariat, Christian "Science" will end. When the same stage of development in the same way results in the completed division of Zion, Mormonism, in which the hierarchy is already exploiting instead of benefiting the laity, will pass away. Until that time it will, in one form or another, remain.

BIBLIOGRAPHY

Anti-Mormon Almanac for 1842.

Articles of Faith, The: A Text-book for Mormon Schools, by James E. Talmage.

Atlantic Monthly for April 1864 and December 1869.

Blood Atonement as understood by the Saints, by C. W. Penrose.

Book of Mormon, The.

Bradstreet's Review for 3rd November 1894.

Brief History of the Church of Jesus Christ of Latter Day Saints, A, by John Corrill.

Christian Observer, The, for 1852.

City of the Saints and Across the Rocky Mountains to California, The, by Richard F. Burton.

Congressional Record, The.

Corianton, a Nephite Story, by Elder B. H. Roberts.

Danites in the Sierras, by Joaquin Miller.

Death of a False Prophet, The, by Samuel Wright.

Debates of Congress, Benton's Abridgments of.

Deseret News, files of.

Dialogue between Joseph Smith and the Devil, Anon. (New York, 1844.)

Dictionary of the Book of Mormon.

Doctrines and Covenants of the Church of Jesus Christ of Latter Day Saints, The Book of.

Does the Bible sanction Polygamy? by Elder Orson Pratt and Dr J. P. Newman, with additions by George A. Smith and George Q. Cannon.

Early Days of Mormonism, by J. H. Kennedy.

Economic Influences upon Educational Progress in the United States, by Frank T. Carlton.

Exposé of Mormonism, by John C. Bennett.

False Star, The, by A. D. Nash.

Fifteen Years among the Mormons, being the narrative of Mrs Ettie V. Smith, a sister of a Mormon High Priest.

Golden Bible, or the Book of Book of Mormon, The: Is it from God? Anon.

Great Salt Lake Trail, The, by Col. Henry Inman and Col. William F. Cody ("Buffalo Bill").

Hampton's Magazine for January 1911.

Harp of Zion, The (Mormon verse).

History of all the Religious Denominations in the United States, edited by John Winebrenner.

History of the Bible Christians, by Rev. William Metcalfe.

History of Education in the United States, by Frank T. Carlton.

"History and Idea of the Mormons," from *The Westminster Review* for January 1853.

History of Joseph Smith, junior, by Mrs Lucy Smith.

History of the Latter Day Saints, by Joseph Smith.

History of Philip and Gorham's Purchase.

History of the Saints, by John C. Bennett.

History of Utah (1840–1887), by H. H. Bancroft.

Homiletic Review (Rev. Dr S. E. Wishard) for March 1903.

Illiteracy and Mormonism, by Henry Randall Waite, Ph.D.

Industrial Evolution in the United States, by C. D. Wright.

Italian Mission, The, by Lorenzo Snow.

Journal of Discourses, The.

Kimball, Life of Heber C.

Kingdom of God, The, by Orson Pratt.

Letters of Orson Spencer, The.

Life and Confession of John D. Lee, The, Anon.

Life in Utah, by J. H. Beadle.

Littell's *Living Age*, vol. xxx.

M'Clure's Magazine for 1911 (Hendrick's articles on "The Revival of Polygamy in Utah").

Maxwell v. *Cannon* (Papers in the case of George R. Maxwell *v.* George Q. Cannon for a seat as Delegate from Utah Territory in the Forty-third Congress).

Millennial Star, The, files of.

Missouri Persecutions, The, by Elder B. H. Roberts.

"Mormon and Mammon," by Murray Schick (*The Coming Nation*, 1911).

Mormon, The Book of.

Mormon Country, The, by John Codman.

Mormon Doctrine of Deity, by Elder Brigham H. Roberts.

"Mormon Episode, A (The War of 1857)," from *The Magazine of Western History.*

Mormon Hymn-Book, The.

Mormon Monster, The, by Rev. Dr Edgar E. Folk.

Mormon Portraits; or, The Truth about the Mormon Leaders from 1830 to 1886, by Dr W. Wyl.

"Mormon Prophet's Tragedy, The," by John Hay (*Atlantic Monthly* for December 1869).

Mormon Puzzle and How to Solve It, by R. W. Beers.

Mormon Wives, by Metta V. Fuller.

Mormoniad, The (verse, Anon., Boston, 1858).

Mormonism, by Judge John Cradlebaugh.

Mormonism Explained, by Rev. D. Burns.

Mormonism, The Inside of: A Judicial Examination, etc., reported from proceedings in the United States District Court by Frank E. M'Gurrin, court stenographer.

"Mormonism To-Day," by David Utter (*The Arena*).

Mormonism Triumphant, by J. H. Flanigan.

Mormonism Unveiled, by John E. Davis.

Mormons at Home, The, by Mrs B. G. Ferris.

Mormons Unmasked, The, by C. Sheridan Jones.

Morning Chronicle (London), files of.

Mountain Meadows Massacre, The, by C. W. Penrose.

New York Herald, files of.

New York Times, files of.

New York World, files of.

North American Review for January 1884.

Omaha Bee for 2nd April 1893.

Only Way to be Saved, The, by Lorenzo Snow.

Palestine Tourists, The, by Lorenzo Snow.

Parley Pratt, The Works of.

Passing of the Mormon, The, by A. L. Mearkle.

Pearl of Great Price, The.

Philadelphia Bulletin, files of.

Philadelphia North American, files of.

Philadelphia Press, files of.

Report No. 1351, Forty-eighth Congress, First Session, House of Representatives of the United States.

Report of the Secretary of War (of the United States) *in Messages and Documents*, vol. ii., 1858–1859.

Revised Statutes of the United States.

Revised Statutes of Utah.

"Revival of Polygamy in Utah, The," by Burton Hendrick in *M'Clure's Magazine* for 1911.

Salt Lake Fruit, by "An American."

Salt Lake Tribune, files of.

Social Forces in American History, by A. M. Simons.

Spiritual Wife System Proven False, The, by G. Hedrick.

Story of the Mormons, The, by William Alexander Linn.

Tyranny of Mormonism, The, by Mrs Fanny Stenhouse.

"Under the Prophet in Utah," by Frank J. Cannon (*Everybody's Magazine*, 1911).

Utah and its People, by "A Gentile, an ex-United States Official."

"Viper's Trail, The," by A. H. Lewis (*Cosmopolitan Magazine*, 1911).

Visit to Salt Lake City, A, William Chandless (1857).

Voice of Joseph, The, by Lorenzo Snow.

Voice of Warning, A ; or, Introduction to the Faith and Doctrine of Mormonism.

Voltaire's *Essai sur les Mœurs.*

Who's Who in America (for 1910–1911).

Women of Mormonism, The ; or, The Story of Polygamy as Told by the Victims Themselves, by Jennie Anderson Froiseth.

Writings from *The Western Standard*, by George Quayle Cannon.

INDEX

THE LATTER DAY SAINTS